VOYAGE IN THE BEAGLE

VOYAGE IN THE BEAGLE

JOHN GOLDSMITH

1978
CHATTO & WINDUS
LONDON

Published by
Chatto & Windus Ltd
40 William IV Street
London WC2N 4DF

*

Clarke, Irwin & Co. Ltd.
Toronto

British Library Cataloguing in Publication Data
Goldsmith, John, b.1947
Voyage in the 'Beagle'.
1. Beagle (*Ship*)   2. South America –
Description and travel – 1951 –
I. Title
918'.04'3   F2224
ISBN 0-7011-2394-X

Printed and bound in Great Britain by
REDWOOD BURN LIMITED
Trowbridge & Esher

To the crew of the *Beagle*

ACKNOWLEDGEMENTS

The author would like to thank Robin Cecil-Wright and Mark Litchfield who provided the diagrams and line drawings for this book; who helped in the preparation of maps, which were drawn by Neil Hyslop, and provided photographs. He would like to thank another shipmate, David Langley, who also provided photographs. His gratitude is also due to David Jones, Christopher Ralling and Ned Kelly of the BBC for their help and advice; to his editors, Norah Smallwood and John Charlton, and his unofficial editor, Robin Cecil-Wright; and to Mary Bennett who prepared the index.

CONTENTS

ILLUSTRATIONS

PRELUDE

SOMEWHERE in this book I express the opinion that very few people bother to read Prefaces and Introductions and I am sure the same applies to Preludes. For this reason I originally included much of what follows in the first chapter where it sat in the narrative like a ton of blotting paper dumped in a stream.

With reluctance I decided it would have to be removed even though it seemed to me important to establish briefly, and at an early stage, the historical background and consequence of the original voyage of the *Beagle* for those who might not know much about it. It also seemed logical to say something about the BBC television film which made the second voyage of the *Beagle* possible, and the history of the ship which re-enacted it. If this could not be done in the first chapter, we would have to have a Prelude.

If you do not read it you may find the narrative itself confusing in parts ; if you do read it there is a faint possibility that things will be clearer.

One hundred and forty-six years ago, on December 27th 1831, H.M.S. *Beagle* set sail from Devonport on the first leg of her voyage across the Atlantic to Salvador, Brazil. Her commander was Captain Robert Fitzroy, an aristocrat and an illegitimate descendant of King Charles II via his mistress Barbara Villiers, Duchess of Cleveland. Fitzroy was one of the finest seamen ever produced by the Royal Navy. His mission in the *Beagle* was to complete the survey and charting of the coasts of Patagonia and Tierra del Fuego, and to carry out a series of time-measurements round the world while generally showing the flag and making the British presence felt in an unstable, half-explored, revolution-prone part of the New World which was nonetheless beginning to interest the commercially-minded gentlemen who were busy putting together the British Empire.

The original purpose of the *Beagle*'s voyage has been largely forgotten because Fitzroy invited a young naturalist called Charles Darwin to accompany him.

Darwin was 22 at the time and had just come down from
Cambridge. Apart from natural history, the main passion of his
life was hunting and shooting. His family was upper middle
class, affluent and distinguished. His grandfather was Erasmus
Darwin, poet, scientist and philosopher, his father was Dr. Robert
Darwin, one of the prominent medical men of his day. On his
mother's side he was related to the Wedgwoods and it was due
to the intervention of his uncle, Josiah Wedgwood II, that his
father was persuaded to allow him to join the *Beagle* expedition.
Dr. Darwin regarded the whole idea as likely to be a fruitless
waste of time and money.

Fitzroy and Darwin took to each other almost from the start,
'almost' because initially Fitzroy, who was a convinced phren-
ologist and tended to judge a man by the cut of his jib, objected
to the shape of Darwin's nose. It was not, he considered, the
nose of a man likely to withstand the hardships of life at sea.
This olfactory objection was soon overcome, however, and the
two young men — Fitzroy himself was only 26 — became friends.
It must surely have been the attraction of opposites. Fitzroy was
aristocratic, arrogant, Tory ; Darwin was liberal-minded, Whig
and cheerfully open-natured. Fitzroy was moody and given to
black depressions, Darwin was perpetually cheerful and glad to
be alive. Fitzroy was a fundamentalist Christian, Darwin had
an open mind. The truth is that each recognised extraordinary
qualities in the other.

Darwin spent five years in the *Beagle*. In Brazil, in Patagonia,
in Tierra del Fuego, in the Andes, in the Galapagos Islands he
explored, observed, speculated on and immersed himself in the
world of nature with a freshness and broadness of vision, with a
meticulous attention to detail and at the same time a unique
awareness of fundamental patterns and balances that, even today,
commands our astonished admiration. He was a botanist, a
zoologist, a biologist, a geologist. His curiosity was all-embracing;
he applied the same fervent attention to the reproductive cycle
of microscopic marine creatures as to the origins of the Andes
mountains. He revelled in the discovery of strange new species,
in the unearthing and analysis of giant fossil remains, in exploring the wild, unknown regions of the earth. He revelled too in
the dissection of some obscure mollusc, in the setting of a butter-
fly's wing. He littered the *Beagle*'s decks with his samples —
bones, skins, rocks — and crammed his tiny cabin with bottles
and jars, to the despair of the officers. They called him The

Philosopher. It was an apt nickname; because from all the
multifarious strands of his studies during the voyage of the
Beagle, he wove an Idea. It was the Theory of Evolution.

Darwin returned home. He married. He shut himself away
from the world, he buried himself in the green Kentish countryside. He worked at his Theory, scrupulously and impartially
testing it against any known scientific fact that might disprove it.
On November 24th 1859 he published *The Origin of Species* and
exploded the greatest intellectual bombshell of the nineteenth
century or indeed any century.

Now that Darwin's ideas have been almost universally accepted
—(though there are still one or two splendidly silver-tongued
fundamentalists fighting the good anti-Darwinian fight, mainly
in the Deep South of the U.S.A., always a rich source of fanati-
cism) — it is almost impossible to imagine the savageness of the
controversy they caused. What was it that made Bishop Wilber-
force so vehement at the meeting of the British Association
at Oxford in 1860? Why were Darwin's ideas considered so
revolutionary?

If Darwin was right, if the natural world as we know it had
evolved over millions of years, if species, including Man himself,
had assumed their present forms through a process of natural
selection, then the Bible was wrong because the Bible said that
the world had been created by God, whole and immutable, with
the balance of animal and vegetable life divinely established,
some four thousand plus years ago. And if the Bible was
wrong . . . well what?

Darwin seemed to be attacking the very roots of religion, of
the religion on which not only Society but accepted scientific
thought was based. He was also, by suggesting that Man and
apes shared a common ancestor, offering an appalling affront to
the dignity of his fellow men, who believed that they had been
created in the image of God. Unless he was saying that *God*
was a *monkey* . . . No wonder Bishops thundered from their
pulpits, no wonder the scientific establishment raged and
trembled, no wonder the cartoonists got busy depicting a simian-
featured Mr. Darwin swinging from a tree.

There is no evidence that Darwin himself was anti-religious
or even agnostic. Far from denigrating the work of the Creator
by his ideas, he showed for the first time the almost unimaginable complexity, scope and symmetry of the Creation. Religious
men could go on believing that the awesome scheme of things

revealed by Evolution was the work of God with an added sense
of wonder. Scientists, believers and atheists alike, were released
from the rigidities imposed by a fundamental belief in the Bible,
and could look at the world in a completely new way.

All this stemmed, in a large measure, from Darwin's voyage in
the *Beagle*. Columbus, Magellan, Cook, all the great explorers,
in their voyages, discovered new continents, new islands, a New
World. Darwin too discovered a New World — a way of looking
at the world which made it new. In this sense, the voyage of the
Beagle is one of the great voyages of discovery of all time.

It is also a spanking good story, full of drama, incident, con-
flict and — occasionally — farce. The story has been told many
times in books but never on film.

In 1976 the BBC decided to film the story of the *Beagle* for
television. They decided to film it as a dramatised documentary
in seven parts; in other words, to reconstruct, with actors in costume, the principal events of the voyage in, as far as possible,
the original locations — Brazil, Patagonia, Tierra del Fuego,
the Andes, the Galapagos. It was an awesome prospect but one
worthy of a great theme. The very idea of taking a full film
crew and actors to Tierra del Fuego, still one of the emptiest,
remotest, most inhospitable parts of the globe, must at times have
seemed preposterous.

The man to whom the responsibility of realising this grand
design was given was Christopher Ralling who, with similar films
like *The Search For The Nile*, had virtually invented and certainly established the genre.

The BBC had a superb story, they had an outstanding producer, a fine director ; they could put together a film-crew of
unrivalled technical brilliance ; their design and costume department was the envy of every television company in the world ;
some of the best acting talent around was available to them ;
all they needed was a *Beagle*.

They must have a three-masted, wooden sailing ship, rigged
as a barque, with square sails on foremast and mainmast and
fore-and-aft sail on the mizzen. The vessel must have engines,
so that the tight filming schedules should not be jeopardised by
the incalculables of wind and weather, but she must also be able
to be sailed effectively. She must be capable of making a twenty
thousand mile round trip. Her conversion, provisioning and
charter must not bankrupt the BBC.

It sounds like a tall order, but there was such a vessel available.

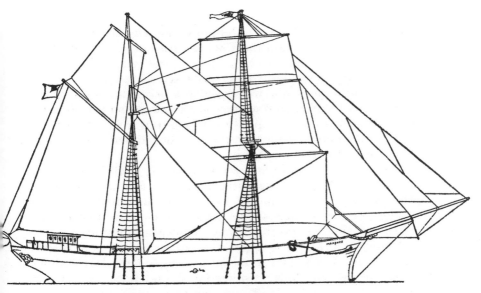

The *Marques* before conversion

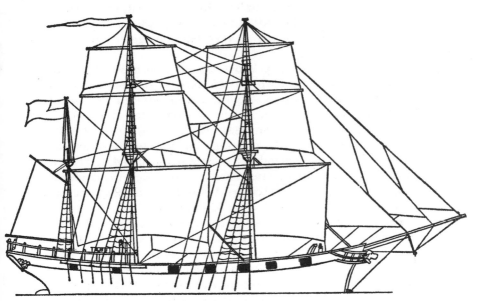

The *Marques* as H.M.S. *Beagle*

Figure 1

She was called the *Marques*. Her home base was the tiny Cornish port of Charlestown, and the BBC had used her before on series like *The Onedin Line*.

The *Marques* was built sixty years ago in Spain, well built, out of Spanish pine. She was rigged as a brigantine, with square sails on her foremast, and a fore-and-aft gaff sail on her aft mast. She was a cargo vessel, originally carrying fruit from the Canaries to northern Europe, later transporting almond-nuts from Palma, Majorca, to Tarragona in Spain.

Seven years ago, a slightly eccentric young Englishman called Robin Cecil-Wright bought the *Marques*. She was dismasted but her hull was sound and two of the most temperamental engines in the Mediterranean made her more or less mobile. First in Spain, later on in England, he began to restore her.

Restoring a ship so that you can sail away to remote islands with a few friends and a movie camera, (which was Robin's intention), is one thing. Converting a ship into a reasonably accurate replica of H.M.S. *Beagle* and preparing her for a twenty thousand mile voyage through the most dangerous waters on earth is quite another. When Robin agreed to charter the *Marques* to the BBC he faced two major problems immediately: a very tight schedule and a very tight budget. There was so much to do.

First the rig of the ship had to be changed from brigantine to barquantine with the addition of a third, mizzen mast and square sails on the main mast, exactly the same modifications which had been made to the original *Beagle*. A completely new poop-deck had to be built, the deck-house remodelled, new hatches fashioned for the main saloon. As time began to run out the exigencies of historical accuracy demanded a mass of detailed and highly skilled work, the exigencies of safety and seaworthiness demanded new engines, radar, radio, extensive re-caulking, treating the entire hull with anti-fouling and so on ad infinitum.

Curiously enough it was largely as a result of this huge programme of renovation and reconstruction, and the fact that it had to be done at an impossible speed and to a limited budget, that the crew of the *Beagle* was formed. Robin needed men with skills — carpenters, shipwrights, riggers, plumbers, engineers — who were prepared to work eighteen hours a day for a pittance. All he could offer in return was a berth in the *Beagle*. It was a powerful inducement.

A professional crew was out of the question; the wage-bill

would have been prohibitive. Scores of people wrote offering to pay large sums to participate in the voyage but, at sea, discipline is vital and how do you call the tune if the pipers are paying you?

The result was that the crew of the *Beagle* was composed mainly of amateurs who knew little, or in some cases — my own for instance — nothing about the sea. There were exceptions, of course ; the enterprise was not *totally* crack-brained. The sailmaker, Alf Readman, was a serving Petty Officer in the Royal Navy, on loan to the *Beagle*. Robin's partner, Mark Litchfield, the navigator, had been an officer in the Navy. Jason Ralph, the Mate, had solid experience of square-rigged sailing ; Roger Scales had rounded the Horn in the Sydney-London yacht race ; the boatswain, Dick, had been with the *Marques* almost from the word go (while hitch-hiking round Spain, he had joined her for a one-day cruise and never quite got around to leaving).

I should add that Robin himself is a seaman of great experience with an encyclopaedic knowledge of his own ship. He also has that quality, vital to any commander, of taking decisions and sticking to them.

Every member of the *Beagle*'s crew, in fact, was highly competent in some skill vital to the maintenance, safety and running of the ship. The only person who had no qualifications of any kind was myself, and the question may well be posed: what in the name of lubberliness was I doing on board?

The original plan was that I should be the ship's cook and at the same time produce a chronicle of the voyage. This would have meant taking a year off to make the round trip. At the time it seemed possible. When actors are out of work they 'rest'. When screen-writers are out of work they 'concentrate on that novel they've been meaning to do for years'. I was concentrating on a novel. Then suddenly I was busy again. It would have been professional suicide to disappear for a year. By this time Robin had found a cook who was also a qualified doctor, but it still seemed important to have some sort of written record of such a unique voyage and so it was agreed that I should join the ship for as long as possible and bring my typewriter along.

Captain Fitzroy had his own description for people like me: 'shore-going fellows'; and no doubt when he so described someone it was with a disdainful curl of his aristocratic lip. I am — or was — strictly a land-based creature. Even on so harmless a stretch of water as a river, I was supremely incompetent. At school I succeeded in demolishing a valuable rowing-eight when, acting as coxswain, I became suddenly incapable of remembering which tiller-rope you pulled to go left or right and steered the delicate, expensive craft slap into a granite bridge. On the rare occasions thereafter when I was cajoled into messing about in boats I found the experience hectic, bewildering and always saturating. I was convinced that by far the best way of experiencing the joys and perils of life on the bounding wave — or anything else, it could be argued — was by reading a good book.

However, even the most sedentary can rarely resist the lure of adventure and, as I will show in the appropriate place, all my life I have longed to visit Tierra del Fuego, and what better way could there be than in a square-rigged ship called the *Beagle*? I was also interested by the literary challenge of deserting the familiar, fictional territory of novels and television action-adventure series and attempting a personal narrative.

And so, in a state of profound ignorance and not a little apprehension, I went to sea.

Part One

GOING SOUTH

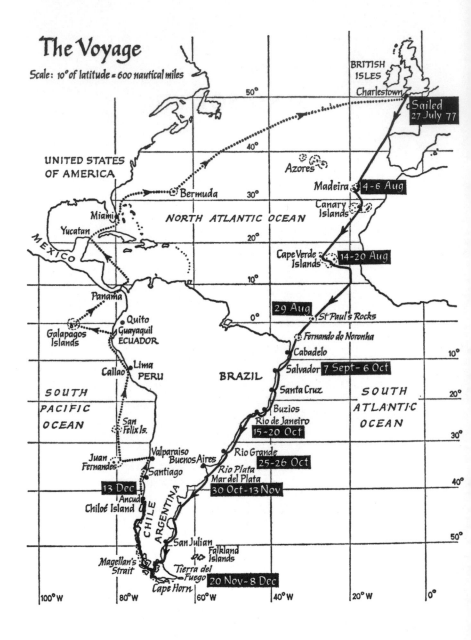

The Voyage

Scale: 10° of latitude = 600 nautical miles

BRITISH ISLES
Charlestown
Sailed 27 July 77

UNITED STATES OF AMERICA

Azores

Madeira **4-6 Aug**

Bermuda   30°

Miami

NORTH ATLANTIC OCEAN

Canary Islands

Yucatan   20°

MEXICO

Cape Verde Islands **14-20 Aug**

10°

Panama

29 Aug   St Paul's Rocks

Quito
Galapagos Islands

Guayaquil
ECUADOR   Fernando do Noronha

Cabadelo   10°

Callao   Lima
PERU   BRAZIL   Salvador **7 Sept-6 Oct**

SOUTH PACIFIC OCEAN   Santa Cruz   SOUTH ATLANTIC OCEAN   20°

San Felix Is.   Buzios
Rio de Janeiro **15-20 Oct**

Valparaiso   Rio Grande   30°
Juan Fernandes   Buenos Aires **25-26 Oct**

Santiago   Rio Plata
Mar del Plata
13 Dec   **30 Oct-13 Nov**   40°
Ancud
Chiloé Island

ARGENTINA

San Julian   50°
Falkland Islands

Magellan's Strait   Tierra del Fuego **20 Nov-8 Dec**
Cape Horn

100° W   80° W   60° W   40° W   20° W   0°

SALVADOR, BRAZIL

28 September – 6 October

WHEN the young heroes of *The Coral Island* or *Mr Midshipman Easy* or *Treasure Island* joined their ships, the scene always smacked resoundingly of the romance of the sea—walnut-faced old salts lounging along the quays, a constant scurry and bustle of fish-porters, errand-boys, merchants and traders ; and, of course, one-legged sea-cooks heaving along the dock followed by a boy with a barrow and an iron-bound, salt-stained chest.

When I joined the *Beagle* in September 1977 she was in dry dock in the Brazilian naval base at Aratu, near Salvador. A drenching, drowning tropical rain was falling. The humidity was dreadful. I felt as if I were in a steam-room in Hell and all I could see were sentry-boxes, Nissen huts, military vehicles and barrack-blocks.

Preconceived notions die hardest of all. I suppose that, in spite of the cryptic and ominous telegram I received the day before I left London, I still expected to find the *Beagle* anchored in some luscious bay with the jungle rising, dark, tangled and mysterious, from a white beach. Or perhaps she would be moored in some picturesque harbour, her tall masts and elegant yards standing up proudly amongst a huddle of yachts and high-prowed fishing boats.

As it was, I could not see the *Beagle* at all or even the sea ; just a waste of tarmac, a red and black striped barrier and a gate-sentry with a machine-gun. The gate-sentry glowered at me.

Like all fundamentally law-abiding citizens, I am terrified of uniformed officials. Even a commissionaire outside an hotel or cinema, if his manner is sufficiently forbidding, can arouse a sort of guilty panic. One normally masks this feeling with an attitude of exaggerated heartiness or hauteur, depending on the circumstances. In the circumstances under discussion, such play-acting was almost beyond me. I was addled.

The last weeks in London had been frenzied. In the space of

about fourteen days I had moved house — twice — written a television script, paid a flying visit to Copenhagen, rushed round buying apparently vital bits and pieces for the *Beagle* in impossible locations in E.23, paid a flying visit to Cornwall and bade what seemed like a thousand fond farewells. It really only remained for me to mislay my passport. Which I did — with about two hours to take-off.

The flight across began with scenes of mob-violence at Heathrow, the result of a strike by air-traffic controllers. There followed a highly technical and extremely vituperative argument between myself and sundry airline officials about the precise nature of hand-luggage.

At Casa Blanca airport, a place remarkable for the size and agility of its cockroaches, at about three in the morning, all Brazil-bound passengers were invited to identify their luggage which had been strewn about the tarmac in confused heaps. Bewildered and exhausted travellers stumbled about in the dark, cursing and peering.

At Rio airport the plane for Salvador conked out two minutes after take-off and had to make an emergency landing. At Salvador airport there were violent cross-winds amounting to little local hurricanes. As we came in to land, the American beside me, a World War Two fighter pilot, went white and tightened his seat-belt. I asked if anything was wrong.

'The guy's just made two course corrections,' he said.

'Is that bad?' I enquired.

'Bad? It's forbidden — within five miles of the runway.'

Ten seconds later we touched down in a series of juddering crashes, leap-frogging along the runway with the engines howling and the tyres shrieking.

Welcome to Salvador.

And so the sight of that gate-sentry, with his sub-machine-gun, his sleazy uniform and his air of menace, seemed just about the last straw. It may sound absurdly tautologous but it's true that, in any kind of journey, the great thing is to keep going. However impossible or debilitating the situation is, resist the temptation to stick your bags in the left-luggage locker and slump in the nearest hotel. Struggle on.

So I flashed the gate-sentry a warm, human smile and tried to explain. This was no easy matter since I myself had only the haziest notions about what the hell the *Beagle* was doing in a Brazilian naval base, if she was there at all, and knew exactly and precisely one word of Portuguese, namely 'obrigado' which means 'thank you'. (And this was sadly irrelevant, I felt, since, so far, I really had very little to thank anybody for.)

I can only suppose that the sentry had got it into his head that I was some sort of advance hit-man for the Cuban guerrillas, because I made very little progress with him. Or with his superiors ; sergeants, lieutenants and captains in their turn. But in the end, possibly because I have an honest face, probably because they eventually unearthed a man who spoke a smattering of English, I was admitted into the naval base.

The *Beagle* was in what looked like a gigantic metal box, open-ended and lidless. She was propped up with huge wooden wedges and blocks and beams. Among the grey sheds and hangars of the naval base, in the tumbling rain she seemed like a battered old toy ship discarded by the spoilt child of an over-indulgent giant in favour of one of the sleek, metal warships moored along the quays. A few familiar figures, in soaked shorts and tee-shirts, were loitering disconsolately under her hull. Among them I recognised Robin, the Captain and joint-owner of the *Beagle*. I don't remember the exact wording of his greeting, but it was suitably British and laconic, something along the lines of:

'What kept you?'

The role of new boy is always difficult, often unpleasant, and this is especially true of joining an established ship's company. There is no tighter community than the crew of a ship. In my case, things were made much easier by the fact that I had met almost everyone on board at least once and some of them, like Robin, his wife Virginia (there on holiday — some holiday!), Robin's partner, Mark and the boatswain, Dick were old friends. On the other hand, I was painfully conscious that what I knew about ships and the sea could be written on the back of a postage stamp and that I was over-weight, totally out of training and probably quite unfit for the rigours of life at sea. The crew could quite justifiably have regarded me as an interloper, an outsider. If some did, they masked their feelings very effectively, but I think that in the days that followed I was accepted as a possibly somewhat bizarre but nonetheless welcome addition to a motley crew. At any rate, I was the (happy) recipient of the leg-pulling, studiously offhand treatment that constitutes accept-ance among English people and which makes them appear, to foreigners, more truly enigmatic even than the Chinese.

A berth was found for me in the aft cabin. When the mound of junk — clothes, boots, about a ton of assorted film stock and a great deal of other, unidentified tackle — had been removed, my home for the next few months was revealed as a coffin-like place about seven feet long, three feet wide and four feet high with some storage lockers whose doors were either shut so tightly that you needed a screwdriver to prise them open or not shut at all so that when the ship rolled they were likely to give you a sharp crack on the head. There was a light that dimmed and glowed according to the ship's whimsical electrical system and a horse-hair mattress, slightly damp. (Later on, in a brilliantly cunning manoeuvre, I managed to replace this with a sheet of foam-rubber — ingenuity coupled with a touch of ruthlessness are the qualities required to acquire creature comforts on a ship.)

I unpacked my battered suitcases, deriving some reassurance, in these strange surroundings, from the sight and feel of familiar possessions. It is odd how comforting one's tatty old items can be in such situations, especially books and, for some reason, shirts.

The decks of the *Beagle* were chaos. I picked my way gingerly through a welter of tangled ropes, paint tins, jerry-cans, blocks and shackles, carpenter's tools of every size and shape, outboard motors, half-inflated dinghies, gas-bottles, hunks of equipment whose purpose defied speculation and the remains of the ship's deep freeze, a mountain of splintered wood and polystyrene which oozed clinging, black bitumen. I thought, Ye Gods.

The rain eased up and night fell with the suddenness of a power-cut. Most of the crew had lunch and dinner in the base canteen and slept in a bleak and evil-smelling barrack. Robin and Mark, being classed as officers, ate in the Officer's Mess, and so did Virginia of course. This was to comply with the strict military regulations governing the base. And very strange regulations they must be since I found myself officially classified as an officer, a distinction which, in the circumstances, was science fiction.

I suppose the mess was fractionally more civilised than the canteen but it had one serious drawback. It was a twenty-minute walk from the dry dock. Later on I learned to loathe this twice daily hike which, coming in the middle and at the end of a day of gruelling physical work, had all the worst elements of a medieval penance. On my first night, though, it was a revelation.

In tropical Brazil, even in large cities, even in a modern naval base, the jungle is never very far away. The sky had cleared and sparkled with unfamiliar constellations. Large areas of the base had been cleared but already the jungle was reclaiming the ground. All along the concrete roadways there was a dense, burgeoning tangle of green from which rose an unceasing night-orchestration of insect and animal sounds, strident, pervasive and, because so unfamiliar, wildly exciting. I began to cheer up.

A few hours later I lay in my bunk, slightly tipsy on duty-free whisky and encased in a stifling film of my own sweat. The heat and humidity in the cabin were choking but I could not sleep up on deck because the rain had returned. Five or six mosquitoes whined above me. I knew that during the night I would be eaten alive. I tried to read a book, not one of the solid, informative tomes I had brought, but a familiar, undemanding thriller-fantasy I had read many times before. It was impossible. The only practical use for the volume was as a mosquito-destroyer. I selected my victim, stalked it for a minute, then struck. I crushed it between pages 52 and 53 of Dornford Yates's *Cost Price*. I turned out the light. The mosquito whines intensified. A steady drip of water from some defective caulking in the deck above was now added to the other barbarities of the night. I thought — what the hell am I doing here?

The reader may well be asking, what the hell was the *Beagle* doing in a dry dock in a Brazilian naval base?

If the reader has dipped into the Prelude he will recall that the *Beagle*, otherwise known as the *Marques*, had been chartered by the BBC for location filming in South America for *The Voyage of Charles Darwin* and that throughout the latter part of 1976 and the first half of 1977 the crew was working sixteen hours a day to prepare for the voyage.

By the end of June these preparations were well enough advanced to make a departure date somewhere around the second week in July feasible. The *Beagle* was moved to a dry dock at Turnchapel, near Plymouth, so that her hull could be treated with anti-fouling paint. This dry dock was a world away from the metal monster of Aratu which could be lowered and raised hydraulically. The slip at Turnchapel was tidal. At low tide, the ship was left high and dry, her whole weight resting on the bed of the dock. It is obvious that the bottom of such a dock must be absolutely sound, as was allegedly the case at Turnchapel.

On the evening of Friday, 1st July, the tide was going out and, as the water receded, the *Beagle* began to settle on the bottom of the dock. But she was settling not on to firm sand or mud but on to a bed of loose rocks. As the tremendous weight of the ship, over two hundred tons, concentrated into the narrow line of her keel, bore down on the rocks, they shifted. The *Beagle* slipped sideways — literally keeled over — and crashed against the concrete wall of the quay.

For a steel-built modern ship such an accident would have been extremely dangerous ; for a sixty year old timber ship it was catastrophic.

I happened to be down in Cornwall that weekend, staying with Robin and Virginia. We returned home late on Friday night to find a message from the ship which stated briefly what had happened. We were perturbed but, since we had no details about the extent of the damage, not unduly alarmed. We had no way of contacting the ship directly and so, in the early hours of Saturday morning, Robin and I drove over to Plymouth.

It was one of those cool, blue, hazy mornings which herald a day of blistering heat and which imparts a feeling of immense well-being to the early riser who sees the dawn come in.

There could not have been a greater contrast to the freshness and brightness of the morning than the atmosphere on the *Beagle*. I have rarely encountered such an air of utter despondency, amounting almost to despair.

The damage to the ship was extensive. Along the port side the rail and stanchions were split ; we could only speculate on what further disasters we would find when we examined the hull. As it was we could see that the *Beagle* was in for a major repair job which might take months and which would certainly cost thousands of pounds. It was not so much the thought of the cost which cast such a profound gloom over the normally ebullient crew but the *time*. The ship had to be in Brazil in early September. If she could not meet this deadline then the whole idea of filming her in South America, of re-enacting the original voyage, would have to be abandoned and alternative locations found in Scandinavia and Portugal. A delay even of a few weeks would simply kill the entire expedition stone dead.

And, standing on the quay at Turnchapel, looking at the great splits in the *Beagle*'s side, the fresh wood like yellow wounds in the dark, weather-stained paintwork, we knew we were looking at a major operation. We knew that the second voyage of the *Beagle* was over before it had begun.

My own reaction was one of deep disappointment. Although I

had planned to participate in the voyage only for the central section, from tropical Brazil south to the Magellan Straits and then up the coast of Chile, I was already revelling in the prospect of fulfilling a life-long dream of visiting the remote, uninhabited islands of Tierra del Fuego, and had extensively re-organised my life to make it possible. But my own case was trivial compared with that of the crew. I had lost a unique opportunity of exploring Tierra del Fuego in a square-rigged sailing ship ; they had lost everything, everything they had worked for in month after month of gruelling labour. For me the voyage was an excursion— hard, uncomfortable, dangerous perhaps — but nonetheless a temporary diversion from the mainstream of my life ; for them, it was their life, they had staked their all on it. The *Beagle* was their home, their job, their future. And she was smashed.

Necessity may be the mother of invention but the capacity to achieve the impossible also requires that most mysterious and powerful human attribute, will. By working round the clock, by refusing to be beaten by time, the crew of the *Beagle* repaired the damage to the ship and made her fit to go to sea. It was an extraordinary effort which owed a great deal to the drive and determination of Robin.

I have never seen Robin admit defeat in something he believes in, and I have seen him in some fairly bleak situations. He is a man of vision. Sometimes his visions consist of wondrous Schemes — a gigantic night-club suspended over Hyde Park in a barrage balloon, a system for generating electricity involving numerous windmills, artificial waterfalls and turbines, a fleet of agricultural tricycles, a plover's egg farm and so on — which never go beyond the scribble and scrap paper stage but provide an endless source of amusement for his friends and family ; sometimes his visions become a reality. I admit that I was one of the prime scoffers when, years ago, he declared he would buy an old sailing ship, restore her and enact spectacular voyages in her. I have since eaten indigestible quantities of my own words. When Robin really wants to achieve something, he generally achieves it. If he particularly wanted to sell a million electric fires to countries situated exclusively along the equator (a Scheme he is more than capable of conceiving) the wretched inhabitants would have little alternative but to pay up and prepare to swelter.

Through a succession of daily miracles of hard work and ingenuity, the *Beagle* was more or less prepared to leave England by mid-July. More or less is an understatement (and I am almost

never guilty of *that*). There were still a thousand and one things
to do and it is important to emphasise this fact since, during the
subsequent voyage, the crew had not only to sail the ship but
also to complete a formidable programme of conversion, renovation and repair. She was always a very hard-working ship.

Captain Fitzroy wrote of the first *Beagle*: 'Never, I believe,
did a vessel leave England better provided, or fitted for the
service she was destined to perform.' It is tempting to draw a
reverse parallel and say that almost exactly the opposite was true
of the second *Beagle*. It would be wrong, however, to give the
impression that the *Beagle* did not have a reasonable chance of
surviving her voyage. Had that been the case neither Robin nor
the BBC would have consented to her setting off. On the other
hand there is no doubt that her condition was somewhat groggy.

One factor, in particular — a factor which led directly to the
dry dock at Aratu — added an element of danger to the already
formidable perils of an Atlantic crossing. The surveyor who
examined the hull after the accident at Turnchapel warned
Robin that the terrific impact of the ship's crashing against the
dock might have weakened the whole construction of the hull
and that, in heavy seas, she might start to leak from the garboard
strake. The garboard strake is the first line of planks above the
keel.

The danger was not such as to prevent the *Beagle* putting out
to sea but it was something to watch out for.

On 23rd July the *Beagle* set sail from Charlestown, the cheers
and farewells of the large crowd which had gathered to wish her
bon voyage echoing round the tiny, grey port.

Which is to say that she *officially* set sail from Charlestown,
the cheers and farewells of the large crowd which had gathered
to wish her *bon voyage* echoing round the tiny, grey port.

In fact, by ten o'clock the same day she had sneaked back into
Charlestown, and when she did eventually put out to sea, from
Falmouth, on the 27th, after sundry technical hitches, it was
almost in secret: people had become somewhat bored with endless goodbyes.

But it must have been a brave sight as the flying jib was raised
to pull her bow away from the mooring and the fore and main
topsails followed by the main lower staysail, the mizzen and the
outer jib were broken out. Like her predecessor, the *Beagle*
quitted England under a good spread of canvas. There was no
racket and clatter from her engines to mar the departure.

For the first eleven days the seas were calm. The *Beagle* was certainly making water and the bilges had to be pumped twice a day but there was nothing alarming in this. She had not been at sea for months and it would take time for her dried-out timbers to expand. There was also a defect in the domestic plumbing system and fresh water from the showers was leaking into the bilges.

Far more depressing, at this stage of the voyage, was the demise of the ship's deep freeze. This, on the advice of experts, had been installed in, of all bizarre places, the engine room — where the temperature rarely drops below a hundred degrees Fahrenheit. The deep freeze contained the entire supply of fresh meat for the Atlantic crossing. It was an awful lot of meat, as I knew only too well. On departure day I had been given the task of transporting it all from a butcher's shop in Bodmin to Charlestown. It was in a semi-frozen condition and oozed with a kind of thick, frosty gore which soon seeped into every cranny of the boot of my car. A few weeks later, during a spell of hot weather, I opened the boot and a vast cloud of flies swarmed out.

As a result of the deep freeze breaking down — it would be more accurate to say that it melted — the crew lived on roasts and steaks for several days until the bulk of the suppurating meat was thrown to the sharks.

On 8th August the *Beagle* experienced the first rough seas, and the next day it was clear that what the surveyor had feared would happen had happened. The heavy weather had strained the garboard strake and the *Beagle* was beginning to leak like a colander.

Robin decided to alter course and put into Porto Grande, on San Vicente in the Cape Verde Islands where, according to the Admiralty Pilot, there were excellent repair facilities. What he did not know was that the Cape Verde Islands had just declared independence from Portugal, that all the Europeans had been kicked out and that the islands were in a state of anarchy.

The shipyards in particular were chaotic since all the people responsible for manning and working them had fled. Robin did not feel inclined to entrust his ship to a lot of bewildered revolutionaries. The nearest reliable shipyards were in Salvador, Brazil, which was in any case the *Beagle*'s destination, so the only thing to do was press on.

Although at no time was the ship in danger, the leak grew steadily worse. On the day before the *Beagle* made her landfall at Salvador, the bilges were pumped five times.

The leak was worrying enough but, a day or two out of the Cape Verde Islands, Robin discovered another potential hazard. This was that the area south of the Cape Verdes is where hurricanes come from. And the prime spawning season for these devastating winds just happens to be August.

Robin has said that, for him, the most terrifying moment of the whole voyage was a day when three of the classic signs of an approaching hurricane materialised. First of all the sea and air temperatures were within half a degree of each other and above the danger level of 75° Fahrenheit. Next, there was a heavy swell coming in against the direction of the wind. Finally, the wind began to veer steadily round the points of the compass, increasing alarmingly.

One, two, three.

Robin decided to alter course towards the coast of West Africa and took the *Beagle* in a long loop round the danger area. It was not a question of avoiding a risk, it was a question of avoiding certain obliteration. Hurricanes reduce coastal towns to rubble in a few minutes. The *Beagle* would have about as much chance of surviving one as an egg in an avalanche.

Robin and Mark decided not to advertise the fact that the course alteration had been made to avoid a hurricane; but men with some experience of the sea have an instinct for danger. As Robin and Mark were poring over their charts, Dick came quietly into the charthouse and said:

'Expecting a blow, then?'

There was a silence, an exchange of half-averted looks, an attempt at a casual reply. By tacit consent the subject was not referred to again.

Leaks and hurricanes provide one sort of drama, people and places provide other kinds.

The most notable human drama during the Atlantic crossing occurred on 25th August at 11.30 p.m. when something very nasty happened to the only female member of the *Beagle*'s crew.

Yes, there was one lone woman among sixteen men, but the nature of the nastiness that occurred was *not* a factor of that interesting proportion. What happened to Suzanne, the ship's cook and doctor, was that she fell out of her hammock — the result, I am assured of the motion of the ship — and her head hit a metal ring-bolt on the deck.

Physician Heal Thyself.

All very well in theory; but when the physician in question is dazed, bruised and streaming with blood, it is no easy matter. Happily, Suzanne is a woman of remarkable fortitude. Swaying in front of a diminutive glass, with the ship pitching and rolling, she gave herself a local anaesthetic and stitched herself up. It was not for some days that she realised that she had broken her jaw.

She had to wait until the *Beagle* reached Salvador before her jaw could be set. This involved wiring her teeth together so that she could neither eat (a curious predicament for a cook) nor talk (a dreadful fate for an Irishwoman).

On 29th August there was an excitement of a different kind.

At precisely 0925, the look-out on the masthead sighted St. Paul's Rocks.

St. Paul's Rocks, a minute islet in mid-Atlantic, is one of the loneliest places on earth. Situated approximately one degree north of the equator and 540 miles from the coast of South America, the land area is not more than 1400 feet long by 750 feet wide and, since it is far away from the main shipping routes, it is very rarely visited ; indeed it is so dangerous that most ships give it a wide berth. The original *Beagle* anchored there on February 16th 1832 and the *Challenger* in 1873, by a curious coincidence on the very day that the second *Beagle* arrived, 29th August.

To have successfully made a landfall at such a miniscule spit of rock was a considerable feat of navigation and represented a major triumph for Mark Litchfield whose calculations were based entirely on star-sights. It was, in fact, he who first sighted the rocks from the masthead. He had declared that unless the rocks were sighted over the starboard bow within twenty minutes, they would not be sighted at all ; and he was probably the only one on board who believed they would find the rocks.

St. Paul's Rocks made a deep impression on everybody. Months later, people in the *Beagle* were still talking about the day they spent there, and from such descriptions and reactions I was able to form my own picture.

The rocks are white from the guano of the thousands of birds, mainly boobies, who inhabit the place. These boobies, having no contact with man, are completely without fear. The sailors from *Beagle I* were able to kill hundreds of them, perhaps for meat, more likely for sport. The sailors from *Beagle II* merely photographed them. Apart from a few spiders and insects the only other inhabitants of the rocks are crabs. The waters round the rocks, especially in the central lagoon, teem with fish. All these creatures, birds, crabs and fish, prey on each other in a ruthless cycle which is a vivid example of the natural balances in nature.

The only sign of man's influence is the ruin of a navigational beacon, crumbling and derelict, half buried in guano. When parts of the beacon were discovered to be made of copper, the souvenir-hunters got to work. It is probable that, had the *Beagle* spent longer at the rocks, this last trace of human interference in the life of the place would have disappeared altogether. As it was, only one day could be spared.

But it was a magical day—snorkelling in the clear green water among the multi-coloured tropical fish, with the sea-birds wheeling and screaming overhead—and when it ended and the *Beagle* sailed away, a great moon rose over the rocks. The *Beagle*'s crew had left no mark of their visit, no names scratched onto the rocks, none of the graffiti and detritus with which visitors are usually tempted to litter remote places (I did it myself later on in Tierra del Fuego), in obedience to some compulsion to leave behind them a physical sign that 'A man was here'. The solitude of this almost lost islet, the perfect self-sufficiency of its life, had, perhaps only subconsciously but nonetheless powerfully, humbled them, abated for a moment the pride we humans feel as lords of our world. Every political leader should be compelled by International Law to spend at least one day of his life on St. Paul's Rocks. Except that one of them would be bound to annexe it and turn it into a missile base.

The *Beagle* arrived in Salvador on 7th September and I think the BBC were secretly surprised that she had made it. But there she was. The crossing had been accomplished in 43 days. The first *Beagle* had done the same journey in 63 days. The filming, which, since I was not present, I am unable to describe, took place among the bays and islands where Darwin had first experienced the thrill, in his case amounting to ecstasy, of the Brazilian jungle.

'Delight,' he wrote, 'is a weak term to express the feelings of a naturalist who, for the first time, has wandered by himself in a Brazilian forest.' He added: 'Such a day as this brings with it a deeper pleasure than he can ever hope to experience again.'

It was when the filming was over and the *Beagle* was lying in the inner harbour at Salvador that the leak reached a sudden

Beagle at sea, with all square sails set

Heavy swell in the Magellan Straits

Rio de Janeiro from the Sugarloaf Mountain,
with the *Beagle* (ringed) at her mooring

Anchorage at Mar del Plata

climax. It was a hot, soporific afternoon and the ship was deserted except for the duty watch. The sound of rushing waters was heard, as if someone had carelessly left a tap running. The watch checked and found that all the taps were firmly closed. They began to check the whole ship. When they reached the engine room they found it flooded. The water was rising fast and was just below the level of the starter motors. A minute more and the starters would have been under, making it impossible to fire the engines and thus impossible to operate the main pumps. The *Beagle* would, shortly after, have sunk like a stone.

It was now imperative to find dry dock facilities as quickly as possible.

You can achieve almost anything in Brazil if you know an Admiral or two. Luckily Mark Litchfield's wife Marcia is a Brazilian with potent connections in Rio. Admiral called to Admiral like aunts in a novel by Wodehouse, and all was magically arranged.

The *Beagle* limped off to Aratu and she was still there when I joined her.

Having, with difficulty, prepared myself mentally for becoming a sailor, I now found I had to re-adjust to becoming a kind of sub-nautical navvy.

The day at Aratu began early, at about six o'clock, when Virginia, standing in for the speechless Suzanne, would fry dozens of eggs for those members of the crew unable to face breakfast in the base canteen. We would work all day, with an hour's break for lunch, and, later on, most of the night too, with great flood-lights attracting every stinging insect for miles around, the thick, insulated wires cunningly placed to trip you up at least five times an hour. The pressure was on. The naval authorities kept reminding us that the entire Brazilian fleet was due to go on important manoeuvres in a few months and that we were occupying vital dry-dock space. Indeed, every day new warships arrived in the base, and it was subtly hinted that Ministers and Admirals were more or less hopping up and down and tearing out their hair in their anxiety to see us gone.

Naturally I was not allotted any tasks that required skill. Scraping the hull was about my mark or ordering supplies from the quartermaster's department. I managed to turn even this latter activity into farce one humid morning, owing to my ignorance of the fact that, in Portuguese, 'paint', the liquid you apply to surfaces with a paint-brush and 'to paint', the verb which describes this activity, are quite different. What I wanted was twenty or thirty litres of anti-fouling paint. What the patient, courteous Brazilian lieutenant thought I wanted was thirty or forty painters. It took an hour, fifteen little cups of coffee, well over a hundred diagrams and drawings and some brilliant mime, worthy of Marcel Marceau, to unscramble the situation. All became clear amid much back-slapping and hand-shaking, and all would have remained clear if I hadn't also required twenty or thirty paint-brushes . . .

One of the first things I learned about myself as a result of my voyage in the *Beagle* was that God did not intend me for a painter. Given a litre of paint, a large brush and a ship's hull, I find I can cover my clothes and myself with about five coats in a matter of minutes. And of that litre of paint I would estimate that about one per cent goes on the hull and the remainder goes on me. It was small comfort to think that if I should fall off the dock and drown and if my body should not be recovered for some months — highly likely in a country like Brazil where procrastination is the national sport — at least my corpse would be entirely free of barnacles, limpets, weed and marine termites.

After a few days at Aratu I looked like a lobster with leprosy. My skin glistened repellently with sun-tan lotion; it glowed with a carbuncular red because the sun-tan lotion was completely ineffective and I was horribly burned ; it was splotched and blotched with the anti-fouling paint which was also red, but not the kind of red which suggests tribal rites and spirited war-dances, rather one which was reminiscent of the terminal stages of a fourteenth-century plague.

Washing was not easy. The showers on the *Beagle* were, of course, inoperative while she was in dry dock. So were the lavatories. There were cold showers in the bug-infested barracks and hot ones in the Officer's Mess, except that the water was invariably stone cold. The lavatory problem was not helped by the fact that half the ship's company went down with stomach upsets. I escaped this particular torture. I can't imagine why.

However, it was not all scraping and painting and cursing and frying. There was a beach by the Officer's Mess with palm trees, white sand and warm water. There were shopping expeditions into the nearby village, a shanty-town full of crippled dogs, sleazy shops and vast, evil-smelling puddles. There was an excursion into Salvador itself with a roaring lunch preceded by many ice-cold, lemony cocktails and one night there was a genuine

Darwinian happening when one of the crew caught a gigantic moth of a type observed by Darwin. The pigmentation on the wings is such that when they are extended they look exactly like the face of an owl. A vivid example of defensive colouration.

But at last the damage to the hull was repaired, the hull was painted, and all was ready for the great re-floating of the *Beagle*. Before lowering her into the water, a simple precaution was taken to test the soundness of the new timbers. The holds inside the hull were flooded, on the principle that if the water was seen to be flowing *out*, we could be quite sure that it would flow *in*.

Officers and ratings arrived to organise the lowering of the dry dock. They looked grim. There was a long queue of ships waiting to use the dock. We were scurrying about, frantically trying to clear up the accumulated debris from the floor of the dock which would otherwise float and further pollute the already foetid water of the base. The dock began to go down with a rumble of hydraulics. The floor of the dock was awash.

It was then that we noticed that water was indeed coming out from the new timbers in the hull. It wasn't dripping out or even trickling out, it was gushing out like a mountain stream in a Spring spate.

I turned to Robin and said feebly:

'Is it, er, all right?'

He looked stricken for a moment then replied, with an air of great detachment:

'I must say I've never seen a ship put into the water leaking quite so badly.'

I turned to the officer in charge. He gave a massive Latin shrug of his shoulders, and a firm twist to the wheel which controlled the dock's rate of descent. It began to go down like an elevator.

'But,' I said to Robin, 'surely she'll sink.'

'Eventually,' he replied.

In fact, she didn't. What had happened was this: the Brazilian shipwrights responsible for fitting the new timbers had cut a corner, probably by order of the authorities. The timbers are fixed to the hull with enormous nails, called spikes. The shipwrights had cheated by drilling holes slightly larger than necessary for the spikes, which were thus driven in more easily but were not tight to the wood. Robin explained all this to me and added that, when the timbers expanded in the water, doubtless the spikes would 'take up'. For the next few days I confess I went around asking nervously:

'Do you think she's taking up?'

The next day, we left the naval base, several hours late, as usual. The cause of the delay was the engines and this is as good a point as any to introduce these two thundering, fire-breathing monsters; after all, I did sleep with them for many months. A pair of 127 horse-power Gardner diesel marine engines make exacting bedfellows.

The engine-room on the *Beagle* is right next to the aft cabin; only a door, a particularly thin, flimsy door, separates the two. It is a feeble defence against the heat, the noise, the fumes and the vibrations, especially as, all through the night, at regular intervals, members of the duty watch crash down the stairs, fling open the door and unleash the full fury of the inferno, as they carry out routine checks or operate the bilge-pump. In addition to this, the main drive-shaft of the port screw passes right under the berth and leads a strange internal life of its own. When the sea is calm it hums and grumbles to itself and the sound is almost soporific. When the sea is rough and the ship is plunging and rolling it mutters and groans and grinds and quivers and the sound is not in the least soporific. When the engines are silent and the ship is under sail the forward motion of the vessel keeps the screw turning and then the sound that it makes is a doleful lament that rises and falls in the cadences of a lullaby.

Many people, especially those whose ownership of a fibreglass cabin cruiser or a small sailing dinghy for use only at weekends and always within hailing distance of the yacht club makes them, in their own eyes, the lineal descendants of Drake, Frobisher and Nelson and thus purists in matters nautical, have expressed surprise and shock that the *Beagle* had engines at all. Captain Fitzroy, they say rather frostily, didn't have engines, seeming to imply that some sort of fraud was being worked.

Such an attitude is so patently absurd, it is not worth answering; but I have sometimes wondered whether, if Fitzroy had indeed had engines, and if they had caused the same endless delays, frustrations and expenses as ours did, he would ever have completed his voyage.

However, late in the afternoon of 5th October, the said engines were at last coaxed into life and the *Beagle* left Aratu. As we steamed away from the quay, a trail of dry-dock wedges which had been stuck to the hull bobbing merrily in our wake, you could almost see the surge of relief and joy we all felt at finally quitting that place of purgatory. We headed out into the bay in bright sunshine. Our destination was, first, a re-fuelling dock, then the inner harbour of Salvador. But once on the open sea we hove to for a swim. As I dived from the starboard rail into the crystal water, I felt I was taking part in some kind of ritual purification, cleansing myself in the warm, stinging sea of all the accumulated sweat and grime of Aratu, in preparation for the real voyage which was about to begin.

In this spirit, I took over the wheel for the first time and had a lesson in helmsmanship. Helmsmania would be a more accurate description of my performance, as, like most beginners, I tended to over-correct wildly, spinning the wheel in a furious panic, the bowsprit swinging from port to starboard, and outraged yells emerging from the chart-house where Captain Robin was attempting to plot a course.

Naturally, since this was Brazil and since we had made meticulous arrangements to take on fuel at an appointed time in an appointed place, we found the fuelling dock was swarming with fishing-boats and had to proceed to Salvador dieselless. By the time we moored in the inner harbour, it was night.

I recently read an article in an English newspaper which reported that 35 children and old people died of thirst this summer in Salvador, Brazil. The information shocked me but did not surprise me.

Salvador is the oldest city in Brazil. It was founded by Thomé de Souza in 1549 and is now the capital of the province of Bahia. The teeming life of its large port, the lush modern hotels that loom and glitter along its beaches, the traffic that clogs the broad avenues of its business section, all give it an atmosphere of solid prosperity, of standard, modern dollar-chasing bustle. But the beggars dying by inches in dark doorways, the hordes of ragged, hungry boys who haunt the markets and the quays and pounce on bewildered tourists in pleading, jabbering swarms, these tell a different story, of extreme poverty being forced to co-exist with extreme wealth.

In fact, in Salvador, this state of affairs which is endemic in virtually all Latin American countries, regardless of the extreme left or right politics of the prevailing dictatorship, does not appear to be so blatant. I was told by one of the BBC crew that a few hundred miles inland famine conditions are evident in the stick-like limbs and distended bellies of children. In Salvador's port there are enough pickings to support a vast population of have-nots in that degree of discomfort, just above the level of absolute destitution, which does not unduly embarrass the haves or spoil the booming tourist industry.

It is not so much the actual poverty of Brazil which is so striking, it is the universal indifference to it. In Salvador, I felt that just below the surface of life there was a dark current of Haitian barbarism.

The first building pointed out to me by the taxi-driver who had taken me from the airport into the city, was an ancient, stone structure with tiny, square windows and a thatched roof, which, he said, was where the slaves used to be confined after their hideous passage across the Atlantic from West Africa. The building seemed to me to be in a suspiciously good state of preservation. Later that same day I learned that Salvador is the centre of a curious religion which combines the more regrettable aspects of voodooism and Christianity. In the markets, in the back alleys, especially in the bars and brothels, there is an atmosphere of primitive violence, of ancient spells and superstitions, ancient terrors and hatreds, as if the spirits of those terrible African petty Kings who chained their own subjects and lashed them through the swamps of Senegal to the barracoons of the white slavers and who built palaces out of human skulls, still permeate the life of modern Brazil.

I had a sense of this underlying violence and brutality when Virginia and I attempted to rejoin the *Beagle* after she had moved from the inner harbour to the re-fuelling dock, which turned out to be a slaughterhouse. We had spent a gruelling afternoon in a vast and squalid fruit market, buying supplies for the trip down to Rio. This market was a Public Health Inspector's vision of Hell. The ground was covered in a thick pulp of rotting vegetable matter which would have looked septic on a compost heap. The place was a labyrinth of sagging stalls and huts made out of scrap metal and orange crates. One stall, where we bought a hunk of bacon, stands out in my memory: a rickety trestle table spread with lumps and gobbets of meat and tripe with—as a glorious centrepiece—the flayed head of an ox, complete with eyes, whose compelling gaze induced a fit of nervous hilarity.

We dispatched our mountainous purchases of fruit and vegetables and the evil-smelling bacon by taxi and proceeded to the dock/slaughterhouse on foot. It began to rain. At the entrance to the dock stood the inevitable armed guard. Almost every building of a faintly institutional kind has an armed guard

in Brazil. It would not surprise me if even the public lavatories
were provided with sentries. I never summoned up sufficient
courage to visit one and check on this. We explained who we
were, Virginia displaying an impressive command of Portuguese.
So far so good. We now had to gain access to the quay itself, and
here we encounterd yet another guard ; but this one might well
have been the reincarnation of King Gezo of Dahomey, so
arrogant was his attitude, so menacing his demeanour.

He began by denying that any such vessel as the *Beagle* was in
the dock. Patiently we pointed to the fore and main mastheads
and t'gallant yards quite visible above the roof of the slaughterhouse. But apparently in this gentleman's scheme of things, the
evidence of his own eyes was inadmissible. Gently at first and
then more pressingly, we explained that the *Beagle* was taking
on diesel, that when she had done so she would be putting out
to sea and that it was absolutely vital that we join her as soon as
possible. Our friend barely troubled to listen. He just glowered
at us, shook his head and waved us away. We began to walk past
him, towards the metal gates that gave to the quay, in the hope
of contacting someone on the other side who could vouch for us.
King Gezo's reaction was not only instant, it was instinctive.
Like Goering at the mention of culture, he reached for his
revolver.

I stared at him. He was shouting at us, waving the gun at us,
working himself up into a frenzy. He seemed to be the very
embodiment of unreason. There was something shocking in the
sight. It was not just the spectacle of a pettifogging minor official
suddenly armed with a dangerous weapon, though this in itself
was alarming enough, it was something else. Here was a slave-
driver showing us the whip, or a rebel slave with the hated
overseer suddenly at his mercy. Here was a man whose automatic
reaction to a couple of patently harmless strangers was to draw a
gun, assuming, I suppose, that we would be instantly cowed and
humbled.

Well, as a matter of fact, we were. Or appeared to be. We
retreated hastily, seething with anger, to seek some higher
authority. We trudged through the deepening puddles to the
other end of the slaughterhouse building, grimly determined to
wreak havoc amongst those responsible for the running of the
dock. As it turned out we were spared the trouble. We found a
gate similar to that guarded by King Gezo near which some
friendly slaughterhouse workers were lolling. They sent for the

key, opened the gate and that was that. I made enquiries and discovered that there were no regulations governing access to the dock, that King Gezo had not a shadow of right to stop us ; but I was advised not to remonstrate with him, as I wanted to, and it did seem the better part of wisdom. I felt he was quite capable of shooting me. I am certain that he would have fired at Virginia and me if we had persisted, probably over our heads, possibly not.

In a way, it was a trivial incident. Far worse things happen in Brazil every second of the day. I have seen much more extreme acts of violence—in Paris in 1968 with the cobble-stones and tear-gas grenades flying merrily about as the Fifth Republic tottered—but I had never seen before, in the eyes of a man, a light so primitive and mindless.

Salvador contains a great many fine churches, some particularly handsome eighteenth - century buildings, spacious parks and gardens and a multitude of other monuments that no tourist should miss. I missed them all. I was not a tourist but a sailor, or a dim approximation of one, and a sailor sees a place from a completely different perspective, from the underside and, usually by night.

My ship-mates had been in Salvador long enough to discover all the most louche clubs and bars and to establish complex commercial and non-commercial relationships with a variety of girls, the most notable of whom was a plump, determined, emotional and hilarious harridan called Marijuana Lil. She was the colour of a hand-made chocolate and, judging by her impressive girth, chocolates may well have been her staple diet. Her laugh was like a death cry of an intoxicated cockatoo and she was all woman.

Most of the places we visited in our night-long roister through the low-life quarters of Salvador were the more depressing types of brothel-bar, dimly lit caverns where the strobe lighting, the harsh music and furious dancing give a surface impression of gaiety and abandon but where you soon realised that it was all strictly for business. An exception was the celebrated Tom Jones Bar, of hallowed memory to all members of the crew of the *Beagle*. Here, the tiny dance-floor shook and whirled with people in love with movement and rhythm. It was a bright, happy place with some genuine joy about it.

The great thing about a foray into the underside of a big port—known on the *Beagle* as a rape and pillage party — is to take with you only so much money as you are prepared to lose, because it will all go—teased and wheedled and conned out of you, or simply stolen. Easy access to large quantities of anti-biotics is also advisable.

I was still nursing a massive hangover when we left Salvador at ten o'clock of a black, streaming night and to make matters worse I had elected to join the crew as an ordinary, very ordinary, seaman and had been assigned to a watch. My first spell of duty was due to start at four in the morning.

2

SALVADOR – RIO

6 – 15 October

KIPLING may have imagined that he wanted to roll down to Rio, some day before he was old, but I can hardly believe he understood the full implications of the word 'roll'.

I was awoken at 3.45 in the morning. The *Beagle* was rolling all right. The aft cabin was chaos. Loose objects bounced and slithered from one side to the other. Insecurely fastened locker doors slapped and slammed. Even louder than the racket from the engine room were the creaks and cracks and groans from the ship's timbers. Only utter exhaustion could have allowed me to sleep through any of it.

'You'll need wet weather gear,' I was told.

I crawled out of my bunk. In a horizontal position I had felt faintly queasy; upright, or nearly upright, I realised that I felt distinctly ill. I groped for various articles of clothing. The ship lurched violently. I found myself skipping unsteadily across the cabin, cursing. I began to dance a strange fandango, half crouched, in which boots, trousers and sweaters became hopelessly tangled. Later on, when I had become accustomed to the way the ship moved in a heavy sea, I was able to dress swiftly and without bumping my head and cracking my elbows. But that first night I seemed to be locked in an impossible struggle with drawers that refused to open and objects that performed Irish jigs or imitated the escape tactics of eels. I couldn't remember where I had stowed my brand new wet-weather gear. All I knew was that it was buried under a pile of other stuff because I had, with pathetic naiveté, assumed that it would not be required in the tropics. I rummaged and fumbled as the world rocked and plunged round me and my stomach churned. I gave up. I wanted air.

I tottered up on deck, suitably dressed for a stroll in the country perhaps, but totally unprepared for the rain which was sheeting down.

I found my two fellow watch members huddled by the wheel.

There is no wheelhouse on the *Beagle*. The helmsman is exposed to all the elements, the principle being, I suspect, that he is thus less likely to doze off.

The watch leader, Mike Freeman, a rigger by trade and an experienced seaman, was got up in a voluminous black oilskin which streamed and glistened with water. He was grinning and cracking jokes, evidently revelling in the wind, the driving rain and the violent motion of the ship. Beside him John Truelove was putting a brave face on things but it was clear even to my inexperienced eyes that he was feeling very, very seasick. I suddenly realised that I was feeling very, very seasick and, with a mumbled apology, I clambered up onto the poop deck, rushed to the stern rail and heaved up the *haute cuisine* of a Salvador restaurant into the Atlantic ocean. In retrospect, the best place for it.

I clung to the rail, the sweat like ice on my forehead and neck, and waited to see if I would feel better. Having never been to sea before—unless you count the cross-channel ferry—I had no means of knowing how badly seasickness would affect me. Most people get their sea legs in a couple of days, after horrible suffering. The test is whether you feel better or worse after vomiting. If you feel worse, you are probably one of those unfortunates who never get their sea legs, of whom the most relevant example was Charles Darwin himself whose journals tell of unspeakable misery throughout all his five years in the *Beagle*.

After a moment or two I decided that I was feeling better. So much better, in fact, that I was able to observe the sea itself. There was a heavy swell and the crests of the waves were being whipped into spume by the wind. But it was not the steep, ever-shifting contours of the sea that made me almost gasp, though these were impressive enough, it was the colour of the sea.

I hesitate to write down the next sentence because it seems to be such a banal statement of the obvious. But there it was.

The sea was blue.

Even in that black night, in that blinding rain the sea appeared almost to glow with a kind of blue I had never seen before or even imagined. I cannot find an adjective to describe the colour, which by day, of course, and under a clear sky, was even more intense and resplendent. It was a deep blue yet had no hint of purple or black, it was a light blue but with only the faintest suggestion of green (and I am aware that having deemed it impossible I am now floundering about trying to describe it and

old salts are beginning to yawn), it was, well it was simply an
oceanic blue, the blue of the wide, clean, deep sea. And it was a
revelation to me, accustomed as I was to the grey-green waters
of the North Sea or the cesspit which the Mediterranean has
become. It was unquestionably due to an emotional reaction to
this splendour that I was promptly sick again.

I lurched back to the wheel, clutching various ropes for support
as the deck tilted and slanted. John Truelove had volunteered,
volunteered to do the engine checks. I shuddered at such fortitude. I would not have ventured into the heat and stench of the
engine room for a thousand pounds cash. John emerged, ashen,
and took over the wheel. Mike and I went forward to check that
nothing had broken loose and all was safely lashed and stowed.
At the foot of the steps from the poop down onto the main deck,
the sea was swirling in through the scuppers, then hissing out
again as the ship rolled. The canvas cover over the saloon hatch
was flapping wildly. I had my first experience of how a wind at
sea invests inanimate objects with a savage and unpredictable
life of their own. Loose ropes become threshing snakes which
twist and dodge and, when captured, try to strangle you. After
ten minutes I was bruised and panting and clammy with nausea ;
but I was able to reflect that I was receiving a true baptism as a
seaman. I was soaked to the skin.

I shall always believe that it was a malign joke of Mike's—his
sense of humour is as black as it is dry—to ask me to go below
to the galley and make some hot coffee. As a new boy, eager to
please, I complied. (A month later I would have damned his
soul to hell.)

In the saloon the light was dim, the atmosphere was close and
humid and I thought I detected a faint but familiar and noisome
smell. The galley was in a state of wonderful chaos—by far the
most accurate indication of heavy weather is the first, inevitable,
crash from the galley as the ship begins to roll—but one object
in particular almost immediately began to mesmerise me. It was
a metal roasting dish, and it slid back and forth with the motion
of the ship with a pendulum regularity. In the dish was the slab
of bacon Virgina and I had bought in the market. The fat had a
horrible yellowish tinge and it exuded an odour of festering rot
which pervaded the whole saloon and, in the galley area, was
particularly strong and particularly reminiscent of the Salvador
market and the skinless, staring ox-head.

It would be paltering with the truth to say that my stomach

churned. My stomach performed three somersaults and began to scrabble frantically up my throat. I scrabbled frantically up the stairs on deck, flung myself over the rail and hung there, empty, cold and miserable, miserable because I realised there would be no relief from the plunging movement of the ship, that I could not switch off the wind and the sea, that I would have to go on suffering until nature decided otherwise, and that there was absolutely nothing I could do about it.

But there was. I could concentrate on something and, on Mike's advice—John was by now prostrate in his berth—I concentrated on steering the ship.

The night dragged on and dawn came but I kept my eyes fixed on the illuminated face of the compass and gradually began to get the feel of the wheel and of the sea, began to learn that a few spokes to port or starboard achieved much more than three or four panicky turns, that when you put helm on you had to correct it the minute the ship responded. In my determination to keep the needle of the compass at 210 degrees (that was the course—I will never forget it!) I forgot that my clothes were soaked and that I was shivering with cold and I quite forgot to feel seasick. By eight o'clock in the morning, when we were relieved by the forenoon watch, I was even a little hungry.

But in the end, I couldn't face breakfast. It was eggs and . . . bacon.

The watch system on the *Beagle* was unorthodox and, since it was the routine under which we all lived, I will describe it.

It was based on a four-day cycle, three days of work and watches, the last day off. Most people spent their day off sleeping. Work was divided into 'ship's duties', any tasks, from carpentry to caulking, from painting to rigging repairs—there always seemed to be a million things to do—which were vital to the repair, maintenance or continuing conversion of the ship ; and 'general duties' which sound harmless enough but in fact entailed washing up the three main meals of the day, cleaning the galley, saloon, showers and lavatories, organising tea and coffee breaks and preparing vegetables. One day in the four was devoted to these dreadful chores.

The crew was divided into four watches, small teams of three or four, with a watch leader acting as the equivalent of a petty officer. These four watches were called Darwin, Fitzroy, Wickham and Sulivan, in pious memory of the original *Beagle*. Wickham and Sulivan were respectively first and second lieutenants in the

Beagle and close friends of Darwin and both went on to the most distinguished careers, Wickham becoming Governor of Queensland, Australia and Sulivan, having organised the re-settlement of the Falkland Islands, becoming an Admiral and gaining a Knighthood.

The day was divided into the following watches: 2400 to 0400, the middle watch ; 0400 to 0800, the morning watch ; 0800 to 1230, the forenoon ; 1230 to 1600, the afternoon ; 1600 to 2000, the dog watch ; 2000 to 2400, the first watch. Of these, by far the most enjoyable to me, curious though it may sound, was the morning watch, from four in the morning to breakfast time. For a start it was absolutely peaceful ; the only sounds were the wind and the sea and the regular breathing of the exhausts, like an old giant snoring. For the first part of the watch, when it was dark, there were the spectacular night-skies of the southern hemisphere and the sudden excitement of sighting another ship, spotting a cluster of tiny lights on the horizon, watching them grow as, as so often happened, the anonymous skipper altered course to take a look at the strange nineteenth-century ship scudding along. Then the dawn would come, often with fantastic effects of crimson light and cloud, always with the special grandeur observed only at sea or in deserts. And then the gradual stirring and awakening of the ship, people wandering up on deck, still half dazed with sleep and usually wearing bizarre combinations of clothing. And then breakfast, made all the more pleasurable because one was alert, alive and hungry.

The worst watch was unquestionably the dreadful middle watch, from midnight to four in the morning. If you went to bed early and snatched a few hours sleep before being called you spent the first hour and a half of the watch in a haze. If you didn't go to bed early you spent the last two hours of the watch half dead. Whatever you did, your sleep pattern was broken and, over a few weeks, a permanent fatigue settled on you.

The dog watch was not, as in the Navy, designed to vary the cycle and ensure that the crew is not stuck with the same routine. Variability was achieved through the day off system which some thought a good idea and others, including myself, regarded as dubious. A day off at sea is really a non-event. As I have said, most people used it to sleep, but I never could, partly because I can never sleep during the day in any case, partly because it seemed such a waste of a unique experience. It is also difficult to be entirely idle when everybody else around you is working and even more difficult not to resent being roped in on your due and lawful day off.

The prime duties of a watch-member were to steer the ship, write up the log and keep a look-out. If the engines were running then there were hourly and half-hourly checks to do and every so often it was necessary to look at the bilges and pump them out if the water was above a certain level. If we were under sail, one had to watch the wind and the set of the canvas. In rough weather one was responsible for seeing that everything was securely lashed.

Look-out duty was in many ways the most important. It is amazing how, with a million square miles of ocean in which to miss each other, two ships will inevitably collide.

One night, I was on the wheel, concentrating on the compass, when Mike came up and said quietly:

'Could you go to starboard, please, John?'

I gave the wheel a couple of idle turns, then took a squint round the side of the quarterdeck. An enormous ship was looming on our starboard bow. I began to turn the wheel furiously but, I hope, without panic.

Mike and I never panicked. Before each watch we would have a couple of minutes of hopping up and down, running round in circles and wringing our hands so that if we did encounter a crisis, we could remain calm, having already had our panic.

When not on watch my duties were many and various. The worst were the ghastly general duties, all that washing-up in tacky sea-water and, running them a close second, was caulking. Oakum is one of the most disagreeable substances I know. It does not surprise me that prisoners were made to pick it as a punishment. But to try to induce a length of this oily cotton waste into a gap between the deck-planks about a tenth of an inch wide with a mallet and a caulking iron is the refinement of torture.

The only job I refused point blank to do was painting. Otherwise my days were spent in a mass of faintly nautical and usually fiddly tasks, most of which I botched. A few hours each day were spent with my journal and my typewriter and Robin had a habit of roping me in for clerical jobs.

It is important never to be idle at sea. Idleness breeds boredom and boredom breeds feuds, quarrels and mutinies. Perhaps one of the reasons why the *Beagle* was such a happy ship, was because she was such a busy one.

This is the appropriate moment to introduce the various characters who made up the crew of the *Beagle* and to describe the conditions in which we lived below decks. The simplest method of establishing the *dramatis personae* of the voyage would be to reproduce the crew-list, adding such personal comments as would be within the laws of libel and not likely to result in outbreaks of assault and battery. However, I have for a long time been convinced that very few people ever read lists in books any more than they read Prefaces, Introductions, Appendices or Footnotes. Similarly, in describing conditions below decks I find myself in danger of producing one of my own literary *bêtes noires,* namely the topographical description.

I loathe them.

Nautical topography is the worst. How often has one struggled with this sort of thing?

' "Avast there, you bilge-rat" cried the boatswain. But Black Jake took no heed. Leaping nimbly over the larboard gunwale, and snatching up a marlinspike, he ran towards the taffrail, felling two tars who came at him with belaying-pins. Now forced amidships by a rush of hands from abaft the jolly-boat, Jake took to the ratlines and began to climb towards the fore-top. But a shot from Captain Lanyard's musket caught him on the futtock shrouds and he fell to his death, impaled on the starboard fish-davit.'

The only thing that is reasonably clear here is that Black Jake probably died from the shot in the futtock.

A truce to lists and topographies. Let us pretend that the *Beagle* is anchored in some sheltered bay, that it is early morning and everyone on board is asleep except you and me, who are on watch. It is 7.15, time to start shaking all hands for the start of a new day.

We begin in the aft cabin because that is where Suzanne, our cook-doctor, sleeps and she is the first to be roused as she has to start preparing breakfast. Her berth is a cabin within a cabin with its own door—unheard-of luxury in the *Beagle.* The interior of the cabin is orderly and she has managed to create an atmosphere of feminine comfort in these extremely spartan surroundings. A row of fat books with terrifying titles like *Haggenblatt's Tropical Diseases, Amputation At Sea* by J. Hacksaw, M.D., R.N. and *Know Thine Enema* by the same author cause us to shudder. We shake Suzanne gently and she emerges from sleep muttering something incoherent about being in a

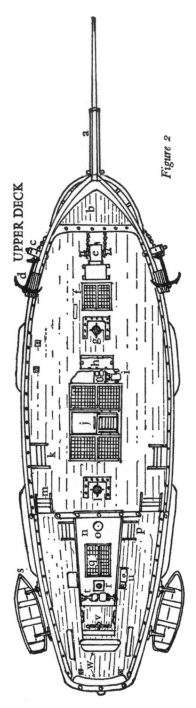

d UPPER DECK

Figure 2

UPPER DECK

a. Bowsprit, b. Foredeck, c. Cat-head, d. Anchor, e. Winch, f. Fore-hatch, g. Foremast and fife rail, h. Chippies' bench, i. Auxiliary bilge-pump, j. Main hatch, k. Access ladder, l. Mainmast and fife-rail, m. Ladder up to poop-deck, n. Chart-house, o. Standard compass, p. Ladder up to 'bridge', q. Bosun's locker, r. Mizzen mast, s. GRP Boat on davits, t. Stowed out-boards, u. Portable generator, v. Cockpit and Wheel, w. Seats

'TWEEN DECKS

'TWEEN DECKS

1. 'Lazarette': stowage areas, 2. Aft cabin: four berths, 3. Seat, 4. Ladder to cockpit, 5. Stowage area (BBC cannons, etc.).

Engine room

6. Main engines, 7. How water tanks, 8. Workbench, 9. Generators, 10. Bathrooms.

Galley

11. Aga cooker, 12. Sink.

Saloon

13. Seats, 14. Bar, 15. Freezer, 16. Galley serving bar, 17. Dining table.

18. Ladder to upper deck, 19. 3-berth port cabin, 20. 4-berth centre cabin, 21. 2-berth starboard cabin, 22. Collision bulkhead, 23 Fuel tanks (900 gallons each), 24. Hatch to coal-hold, 25. Ladder to upper deck, 26. Foc's'le: five berths, 27. Hatch to cable locker, 28 Heads

panic over the eggs.

We nip up the steep flight of wooden steps out of the aft cabin into the well, below the level of the poop deck, where the wheel is housed, and walk along the poop deck, down, left and towards the chart-house, because we have forgotten to take a barometer reading. We step into the chart-house and

SPRING BACK WITH A STRANGLED CURSE.

In the nick of time we have observed that there is no floor but a gaping void and a six foot drop into the engine-room below.

One of the many titles suggested for this book was: 'Where the bloody hell's the chart-house floor?' This was a *cri de cœur* uttered by Robin one dark and stormy night when he nearly took a step into the burning, fiery furnace of the engine-room. The idea of having a moveable floor is, officially, to provide extra ventilation for the engine-room. I have long suspected more sinister motives and consider that Robin was hoist with his own petard.

The chart-house itself is everybody's idea of a nautical interior. There is a big flat chart-table, piled with charts and flanked with neatly-stored instruments—slide rules, set-squares, calipers, sextant. There is the radar screen and, above it, the main depth-sounder. There is the radio, pale green, a mass of dials and knobs and—during the most critical section of the voyage—totally inoperative. There is the flag-locker, crammed with all manner of mysterious bunting. There are stacks of the Admiralty's invaluable blue-backed *South America Pilot*—in my view, a classic. And, in and amongst the serried heaps of paper, on the Captain's little desk, is my typewriter.

We return to the aft cabin. It is now time to shake the whole ship's company. Behind Suzanne's cabin is the berth of David Langley, the Chief Engineer whose exact age is a matter of dark secrecy but who can be safely described as over twenty-one. He is a Scot. Until joining the *Beagle* he was a racing-driver and now gets his kicks on the t'gallant yard. To distinguish him from the ship's other David, he is known as Haggis. His berth represents a sense of order and tidiness temporarily overwhelmed with clothes and boots and bottles of mineral water.

If Haggis's berth is a little disorderly, the one opposite—mine—is ancient chaos, so, with a mental resolution to have a clear-up, never to be fulfilled, of course, we pass on to Mark Litchfield's cabin which is exactly like Suzanne's, private and luxurious. We pop our head round the door and the expression 'ship-shape and Bristol fashion' immediately occurs to us. We recall that Mark is ex-Navy. His rows of books reflect a passion for Naval history and his neatly hung and folded clothes his talent for indestructible elegance in all circumstances.

We now proceed to the main saloon which is roughly in the centre of the ship, where we eat, cook, drink and occasionally perform pantomimes. The saloon is lined with banquette seats and on the starboard side is a long built-in table at the end of which is a large bar. Behind the bar is the galley (which I was never able to think of as anything but the kitchen). The galley is narrow and cramped and is dominated by a large, solid-fuel Aga which also provides domestic hot water. The Aga is festooned with frayed trousers, old socks, threadbare sweaters and other less respectable clothes hung up to dry. These, combined with innumerable pots and pans and cauldrons, make you think of a combined slop-shop and soup kitchen in the slum quarter of the most wretched town in the poorest country in the world.

In the galley Suzanne is practising kung-fu with a frying-pan. The egg-panic appears to have reached crisis point.

Everybody complains about food on a ship and everybody, because he is always hungry, eats it. I will not pretend that Suzanne's food would have always produced a round of applause from the gourmets at Maxims, but she contrived to produce a meal, three times a day, in all weathers and in all climates, however rough the sea or scanty the supplies and nobody, so far as I know, died of botulism. She was famous for two revolutionary inventions. One was a form of glutinous adhesive, guaranteed to bind any two objects together, especially the walls of the stomach, and it was called porridge. The other was a dense, heavy substance, not unlike ferro-concrete, useful as ship's ballast, or to form the foundations of a bridge or as a handy form of dumbbells for weight-lifters and it was called a loaf of bread.

Behind the galley are the showers and lavatories, sometimes coyly referred to as 'heads' ('tails' would have been more appropriate I always felt) which interconnected for that extra lack of privacy. We will not linger in these dreadful regions. The lavatory known as 'The Throne', which works on a complex sequence of pumping, tap-turning and valve-releasing, is prone to the most alarming blow-backs, the results of which make strong men blench and faint.

Opening out of the saloon are three cabins, port, centre and starboard. In the port cabin we find Jay Pilley, ship's carpenter, a gentle, dozy soul who plays the guitar and paints pictures. Below him is Nigel Radcliffe who is soon, though he doesn't know it yet, to achieve stardom in pantomime. The third occupant of the cabin is David Martin, known as Dave the Rave, and we will find that it is totally impossible to wake him. His nose is always buried in a book and his head in a cloud. He is a professional Cornishman who believes the Duchy should announce U.D.I. as soon as possible.

In the starboard cabin we discover, to our horror, Robin and, to our delight, his wife Virginia, object of universal but clandestine desire, life and soul of the party. We take a certain pleasure in rousing Robin, yelling into his ear: 'It's another wonderful day in your life.'

In the centre cabin we find Alf Readman, the sailmaker, whose life I was destined to save. Alf, whom unkind people have described as main prop of the rum industry, is an early riser. He is also a master of his craft, a spinner of wonderfully subversive yarns about naval life, a singer of lewd songs who once squeezed a concertina to death. Below him is John Truelove, whom we have already met, braving the horrors of the engine room.

Opposite, we discover Jason Ralph, the Mate, who, with his massive build and great, bushy beard is a true sea-dog. The image doesn't lie. He loves the sea and he understands it. He is also a skilled shipwright. Below him is Roger Scales whose berth is modestly draped with a black curtain. Roger is the ship's Australian (what is a crew without an Australian? You might just as well try to build an Empire without Scots) and the inventor of a unique braking system which actually causes cars to accelerate.

Passing on through the centre cabin towards the sharp end of the ship, we enter the most exclusive quarters of all — the abode of the Fo'c'sle Fairies. Here, where the motion of the ship is always the most violent and the creaks and shrieks from the timbers most deafening, fantastic depths of sleep are achieved. Tenants of the fo'c'sle form a club whose membership is limited to five.

There is Geoffrey Ridpath (known as Blond Geoff) who has deserted farming for sea-faring. Little does he know it, but one day he will have the honour of being my watch-leader. His berth is notable for the profusion of earphones, cassette players and tapes. He is, after all, the ship's electrician. Below him is the youngest member of the crew, Jonathan Jackson, whose nickname, Teapot, is a source of constant speculation to me. Jonathan should have gone to sea four hundred years ago. He would undoubtedly have discovered several continents which he would have been too modest to have named after him. He is a born explorer and adventurer.

Opposite, we find Mike Freeman, the rigger, whom we have also met before, bandying witticisms in the teeth of a gale, and we wish we could think of something particularly nasty to do to him in the way of a practical joke to get our own back for all the jokes he has played on us. We can be sure that when we shake him he will tell us to bugger off. However, beneath his rape-and-pillage personality is something very complex, sensitive and charming.

Below Mike, Manchester Geoff is buried in blankets. We shake Manchester Geoff very gently because we don't want to cause any damage to what is left of his right lung.

We can say of Manchester that he breathes cigarettes and occasionally takes a puff at a bit of air. His breathing sounds like an orchestra tuning up. Up in the rigging, he performs acrobatic feats like an intoxicated monkey and down on the deck his dry wit crackles like static.

Finally, in a berth built into the very bow of the ship, we find Dick Farnsworth, called Dabbler, boatswain, oldest inhabitant. Dick is to the morale of the crew in general what the barometer is to the pressure of the air, an infallible guide. It would be as difficult to imagine the first *Beagle* without Fitzroy, as the second *Beagle* without Dick, though I am not sure how he and Fitzroy would have got on. Dick has always been with the *Beagle* and I hope he always will be. He too is destined to star in pantomime, dressed in rubber diving-gear and waving an unusual kind of wand.

Our tour now over, we return to the saloon where Suzanne has routed the frying-pan but is being strangled by her own porridge.

We sit down on one of the banquette seats and think to ourselves that, while the room cannot be reckoned to be more than just tolerably comfortable and while aspects of it can only be accounted squalid, it is cosy. In the coldest weather, it is warm from the Aga ; at night, its dim lighting is intimate and friendly ; it is, to say the least, 'lived-in'.

In those first days at sea, I learned to live in it. I had had enough experience of communal existence to know that minor irritations can flare up into savage and irrational rows when fifteen or sixteen are gathered together, and was able to suppress the petty rages I inevitably felt from time to time. My biggest problem was a craving for cheese — a commodity apparently unobtainable in Brazil.

The weather continued bad, with squalls and rain, but about noon on the third day out, it cleared, a steady breeze sprang up and we were able to set some sails — the mizzen, or spanker, if you prefer, inner, outer and flying jibs and the main staysail. At once the ship felt more stable and became easier to steer. There was another benefit. The main staysail is situated directly above the main hatch and a deliciously cool downdraught aired and sweetened the somewhat foetid atmosphere of the saloon. We altered course with the intention of putting in at a tiny port called Santa Cruz and at about five in the afternoon sighted land.

We anchored off a beach about two miles from Santa Cruz. It was dark. The night passed quietly and in the morning, after a surprisingly chilly swim, I was eager to go ashore. The place looked so wonderfully like the setting for a coconut and chocolate bar advertisement — a wide, golden beach, palm trees, jungle. Ashore we went. The sand proved to be remarkably fine, as yellow as primroses and with the texture of brown sugar. It gave rise to one of Robin's schemes. He would fill the *Beagle's* holds with this high-grade sand, export it to England and sell it for vast sums to various South Coast municipalities.

Robin and Virginia had gone on ahead to buy fresh stores in Santa Cruz. Suzanne and I decided to follow. It began to rain in the torrents I had loathed in Salvador. We trudged disconsolately along the road which ran parallel to the beach. The rain and the grey light seemed to blot out the beauty of the jungle. The dripping green leaves conjured up a picture not of romantic tropical wilds, but of Aldershot on a wet Sunday afternoon ; soggy laurels, dingy evergreens and cold left-overs for supper. Not at all what I had come four thousand miles to see. The only comfort was the thought that Robin would be getting equally drenched, though I suspected he would be propping up some warm, dry bar and knocking back *batida* cocktails.

One day I will write a treatise on the subject of blame-transference, the curious dynamic by which we transfer the blame for some minor, or indeed major misfortune, on to another individual or institution.

You find the perfect spot for a picnic. Slavering with thirst, you remove the bottle of white wine from the ice-pack . . . and

discover you have forgotten the corkscrew. If you have made
yourself responsible for seeing to the drinks side of things, you
cannot blame the inefficiency of your wife or your girl-friend —
or can you? 'If you hadn't started panicking about the hard-
boiled eggs at the last moment, I would have remembered the
corkscrew.' Or if that doesn't work, you can proceed to the
extreme of blaming the nameless people who bottled the wine.
'It's ridiculous, in France they have those little plastic caps. Why
they bother with corks in this day and age I can't imagine.' Or
even, at a most basic level: 'You know I loathe picnics. I never
wanted to come in the first place.'

When you are hopelessly lost, in a strange country, at night,
through your own inability to read a map accurately, the transfer
of blame is automatic. 'I told you this map was completely out
of date. Anyway, how do you expect me to read the damned
thing when the interior light isn't even working?' You then
progress to: 'Absolutely typical of this Godforsaken country.
Not a sign-post anywhere,' by which time the blame for your
plight is firmly attached to some anonymous Rural District
Council.

The most profound and universal example of blame-transference is a belief in a Divine Power.

On the principle of blame-transference I naturally attributed
the fact that I was soaked, weary and depressed, to the malice
of Robin. It had been *his* idea to stop at Santa Cruz, *his* idea
to go shopping, *his* idea to come on this ridiculous voyage in the
first place. All I wanted was revenge. And I got it.

It came in the shape of a gigantic sort of Cadillac Vista-Cruiser
Phaeton Mark VII limousine. Suzanne and I had been hoping
to hitch a lift but we really didn't expect to see a car in this
remote part of the country. We certainly didn't expect to see
one of Detroit's most extravagant masterpieces of gleaming
chrome, with a bonnet as long a bowling-alley and seats like a
club chesterfield. We subsided gratefully into these and made
nervous conversation with the vehicle's owner who appeared to
be the local Mr. Big. The windows were probably bullet-proof.

We arrived in Santa Cruz, a desolate little town of squat,
peeling buildings and squat, peeling people. Sure enough, we
sighted Robin and Virginia, drenched, struggling along the street
with bulging carrier bags. I asked Mr. Big to stop. He drew up
right by Robin and Virginia who looked round, gazing with
wonder and envy at the great, sleek car — a vision of comfort

and ease. The expression of baffled rage on Robin's face as he saw me emerge superciliously from the interior of the vision, was worth all the rain in Brazil.

The people in Santa Cruz appeared to be friendly and warm-hearted. As stray members of the *Beagle*'s crew arrived at a modest house where we had been invited to drink coffee and eat home-made cakes, we all remarked on the spontaneous gener-osity of these simple folk, unspoiled by the crass commercialism of a place like Salvador. When the meal was over, and we were debating whether our kindly hosts would be insulted if we offered them some sort of modest payment, we were suddenly presented with an enormous bill. Even by South American standards, it was inflated. All the jollity and good cheer ended up in an acrimonious haggle. So much for simple, spontaneous generosity! On the other hand, it may have been a punishment for a ghastly gaffe I committed. Wishing to compliment our hostess on the excellence of her cakes but unable to communicate verbally, I made a gesture, forming the thumb and index finger of my right hand into a circle, which in England indicates that something is absolutely superb but in South America means roughly: 'Up yours'.

I suppose it is impossible to visit any half-forgotten port on the coast of Brazil without encountering a middle-aged American in old shorts, sandals and a threadbare shirt who looke like Ernest Hemingway. We certainly found one in Santa Cruz. His name was Frank, he had been everywhere, done everything and had finally dropped out in Brazil. He gave us all a lift back to the beach in his lorry and I mention him not because he was such a classic example of the escapist but because his description of how he first saw the *Beagle*, riding at anchor off the beach, gave me an understanding of the strange effect the ship had on people when viewed at a distance in a remote place where the landscape has remained unchanged for centuries.

Just after dawn, Frank had been beachcombing along the sands. He turned a corner — and then stood stock still, blinking, trying to come to terms with the fact that he had stepped through a gap in time. There, before him, was a pirate ship, perfect and complete, its masts and yards looming through the early morning mist. At any moment, he expected to see the Jolly Roger run up to the mast-head and a boat-load of ruffians, with cutlasses in their teeth, hauling towards the shore.

'I'm telling you,' Frank said, 'it was eery.'

It was some months before I was able to appreciate this eery quality myself. As part of the crew I was only too familiar with the non-period aspects of the *Beagle* — the engines, the radar, the electric light, the radio — and, in ports, alongside modern ships, she looked like a curiosity. But there came a day when we anchored in a bay in Desolation Island, at the Pacific end of the Magellan Straits.

It was a remote enough place and certainly unchanged in thousands of years. I doubt if the area we visited has ever been inhabited, even by Alacaloof Indians. I scaled a steep cliff by the side of a plunging waterfall and when I reached the summit and got my breath back I looked down into the bay. It was a startling picture — the brave little barquantine at anchor in the glass-calm water ; great rocky cliffs rising sheer around her, their bareness relieved here by the silvery vein of a stream, there by a deep gulley choked with the dark foliage and contorted boughs of the Antarctic forest ; above the cliffs, the jagged, snow-covered peaks of Tierra del Fuego. The illusion that I had been transported back to the early nineteenth century was overwhelming. There was nothing in the scene that remotely suggested 1977. If I had come across such a sight unexpectedly, I would probably have fallen off the cliff in amazement.

We left Santa Cruz late in the afternoon. During the night we passed through the notoriously treacherous Abrolhos Islands without mishap, thanks to radar, but with a great deal of nail-biting suspense in the chart-house. Fitzroy felt his way through these dangerous rocks with a longboat going ahead and a man taking soundings every half minute.

The next day brought hot sunshine, a fair breeze and whales.

It was about mid morning when some merry satirist shouted 'Thar she blows!' and we all rushed to the rail. But thar they were, two of them, less than a quarter of a mile away. I had a glimpse of a great, glistening hump in the sea and the flash of a mammoth tail and, even among the clicking cameras and inaccurate quotations from *Moby Dick* I felt a surge of excitement. After all, a voyage is not a voyage without one or two whales.

I will spare the reader the kind of poetical ravings usually inspired by the subject of whales which invariably begin: 'These monarchs of the oceans' darkest deeps . . .' However, it is worth saying that it was not until I saw these mighty mammals in their natural habitat, from the deck of a ship, that my blood began to boil significantly at the thought of what man is doing to them, viz. systematically exterminating them.

Unquestionably the most moving recorded sound I have ever heard is that of the Great White whale calling to his mate — a weird, high-pitched moan whose cadences evoke an infinite sadness. (I don't imagine that a female whale finds them anything but thoroughly exciting.) I believe that recorded whale-sounds have been included in the bizarre bric-a-brac on the American Voyager II space-craft which will travel beyond our own solar system into hyper-space and, hopefully, let other civilisations know what's going on on planet Earth. It is blackly ironic to think that by the time Voyager II has flown beyond the reach of our tracking instruments, the likelihood is that there will be no whales left on Earth ; or that a fraction of the money that was devoted to the space programme would be enough to finance the sort of international policing required to protect threatened species of whales — and a great many other creatures. I only hope that the superior intelligences of space will be able to interpret whale-language and that the whales have something pithy to say about the follies of their fellow-mammals, mankind.

Whales were not the only excitement of the day. At a quarter to four in the afternoon, we switched off our engines and set all our sails. It may not sound terribly exciting, but it was to me, as this was my first experience of *sailing*, as opposed to motoring along with a few sails set.

There is as much pleasure to be derived from the sound of a thing as there is from the look, touch or smell of it. We all have our favourite sounds. Mine include the crunch of thin ice on a puddle in mid-winter, the flutter and crackle of a log fire, the dry, metallic zip of a sheet of paper being pulled from a type-writer, the murmer and hum of insects in an English wood in August, and the squeak-pop of a cork being pulled out of a bottle. I now have to add to this list the sound of a square-rigged ship under full sail. Or should I perhaps say sounds, in the plural, since the air is filled with a myriad subtle creaks and whispers from the rigging and the sea chuckles and gurgles and occasionally a sail flaps with a testy slap like a man swotting a fly with a newspaper. Below decks, the lap of the sea against the hull sounds exactly as if someone is splashing about in a bath nearby.

The utter peace of it, after the incessant, unvarying thunder of the engines, altered the whole atmosphere of the ship. The sharp-tongued became mellow, the severely practical became philosophical, the over-energetic became quiet and easy, the habitually melancholy became merry and the habitually merry became quiet and thoughtful. Even Robin seemed human.

We ate our dinner and drank our beers on deck, revelling in the cool breeze, in the gentle motion of the ship, in the dazzling night sky. We were only making two or three knots but suddenly the urgency of the business seemed to have receded.

I had the best night's sleep I ever enjoyed on the *Beagle* and arose, like a giant refreshed, for the morning watch, during which, owing to a sudden veering of the wind from north to west, I managed to achieve an error in course of seventy degrees, a feat equalled only by Manchester Geoff who once contrived to heave the ship to alone and unaided, or Robin himself who was discovered to be over one hundred degrees off course. I should add, in his defence, that the ship was virtually stationary at the time, as we were all swimming.

The daily swim was one of the great pleasures of this section of the voyage. Even well out to sea the temperature of the water was over seventy and there was something rather exciting about the thought that one was splashing about in the middle of the Atlantic.

I was soon initiated into the mysteries of the 'Geronimo'. A Geronimo is the nautical equivalent of Tarzan's unique method of getting from place to place in the jungle via conveniently placed creepers. A rope is attached to the end of the course yard (the course is the lowest and largest square sail, the yard is the cross-timber from which it hangs), so that it dangles out over the side of the ship. The Geronimo-freak takes the free end of the rope and works his way along the side of the ship, away from the yard. He then grips the rope as high up as he can and launches himself out over the sea in a dizzying parabola. It is essential to let go of the rope when it has completed its semi-circular arc otherwise one is liable to be dashed against the hull as it returns to the vertical. True Geronimo experts time their swing to coincide with a roll of the ship to achieve extra lift. The reason why this exercise is called Geronimo is that as you fling yourself into space you yell 'Geronimo-o-o-o'.

Now that we were sailing, I was faced with a tricky personal decision, namely whether I was brave enough or indeed strong enough to go up the masts. When I first joined the ship, I took one look at the masts towering over seventy feet above the deck

and thought, There's no way they're getting me up there. I am
no good at heights. When I was a boy I was a fanatical tree-
climber and liked nothing better than to perch for hours on a
couple of twigs at the top of a cedar tree. But somehow, in the
process of reaching man's estate, I became prone to vertigo.

I comforted myself with the thought that nobody could *force*
me to shin up the rigging and I was assured that there would be
'plenty of deck work'.

It was this 'deck work' that convinced me that I should master
my fear of heights and get up those masts, out of harm's way, as
quickly as possible. I had simply no idea that setting a few
square sails involved such a nightmare of rope-hauling or that
there was such a bewildering variety of ropes to be hauled.

(Old hands, who know about these things should find something else to do for the next few paragraphs. Read a good book,
perhaps.)

Each square sail is attached to a yard and each yard has to be
raised before the sail can be set, with the exception of the course
yard, which is fixed. The ropes for raising the yards are called
halyards. The *Beagle* carries three square sails on two of her
masts ; in rising order, these are the course, the topsail and the
t'gallant. Many square-riggers carried square-sails above the
t'gallant and these were, again in rising order, the royal, the
sky-sail and the moonraker. Alf, our sailmaker, swears there was
also something called a star-straker. On the *Beagle,* thank God,
we were spared anything more vertiginous than a t'gallant.

Apart from the halyards, each yard also has two ropes called
braces, used to alter the angle of the yard to the mast, in
nautical jargon, to 'brace the yards round'.

Each square sail has two ropes called clew-lines, which are
attached to the foot of the sail to haul it up and two more
called bunt-lines which prevent the sail from bellying when it is
being furled. There are two ropes called tacks attached to the
bottom corners of the sail . . . and so it goes on. The point is
not to deliver a treatise on square-rigged sailing — a subject of
which I have an imperfect understanding — but to give some
idea of the complexity of it all. I should add that the *Beagle*
also carried four jibs, three staysails and the gaff-rigged mizzen
and that all the hundreds of ropes attached to these various sails
were secured to belaying-pins along the sides of the ship and that
they all looked the same to me.

So that when suddenly requested to release the main topsail

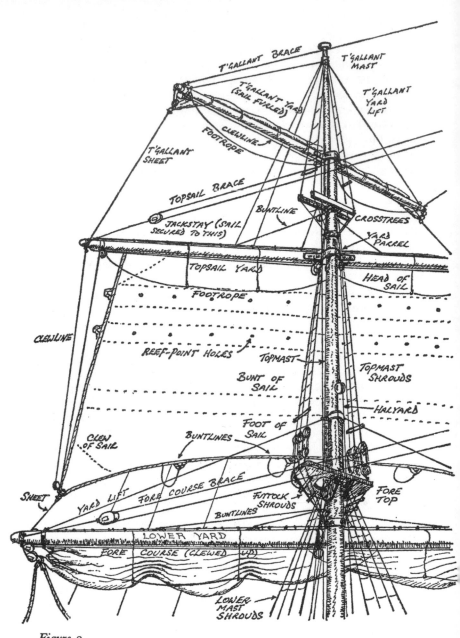

Figure 3

SKETCH OF FOREMAST (viewed from aft)

Ship on the port tack, close-hauled, i.e., yards braced sharp up to catch the wind. The fore course is shown clewed-up. The t'gallant furled and the yard braced square. The topsail is shown set.

bunt-line or pull on the fore t'gallant port tack I found myself in a state of hopeless confusion. Nor were these requests couched in polite terms ; they usually took the form of impassioned yells from up the mast. I have sworn never to use the expression 'learning the ropes' again. It conjures up painful memories of being shouted at, jostled, cursed, pushed about and generally trodden on.

I did my best. I tried a logical approach. I thought that if I learned the *principles* of the business, all else would follow. It didn't. I decided that the matter was beyond my comprehension. I would, like Black Jake, take to the ratlines.

My mentor in this hair-raising activity was Mike Freeman. On his advice I rejected the 'in at the deep end' approach in favour of 'breaking myself in gently'. In the weeks that followed I gradually became accustomed to the height and to the motion, which, the higher you climb, becomes more exaggerated so that what, on the deck, seems a gentle roll, on the t'gallant yard gives you the feeling that you are a flag being waved in a patriotic demonstration. There was one aspect of mast-work I never learned to enjoy and that was the moment when, having furled a sail into a sort of sausage, below the yard, you have to reach down and heave it up on top of the yard. At that point everything conspires to push you backwards which is thoroughly alarming since the essence of staying safely on a yard is to push forwards, with your stomach pressed on to the yard and your feet behind keeping the foot-rope taut.

There are some golden rules. You never move your feet unless your hands are secure and, whatever the circumstances, you keep one hand for the ship and one for yourself. When going out on to the yards, you always warn anyone already there that you are about to step on to the foot-rope. I had one rule of my own which was never to go to sleep. *Go to sleep?* Hardly likely, you would say. But on a hot day there is nothing more pleasant than to shin up to the fore-top, a sort of crow's nest halfway up the fore-mast, with a good book. You settle yourself comfortably. It is quiet and, above all, private. The roll of the ship is soporific. Even the albatross perched on the main-mast opposite you appears to be a trifle dozy. How easy to drift off into sleep . . . and end up a squashed statistic on the deck below.

In the early days I thought that going up aloft would be the most terrifying aspect of the voyage. By the time I left the *Beagle,* I regarded it as one of the greatest pleasures.

The winds continued to be favourable and we sailed on. One night we achieved eight knots, a remarkable speed for the *Beagle*, one knot less than the maximum the engines could produce. On the morning of the 13th we arrived at Capo Buzios.

Ten years ago Buzios was a miserable fishing village. Today it is considered by some to be Brazil's answer to Saint Tropez, mainly, I suspect, because Brigitte Bardot has, or once had, a house there. I don't think the Mayor of Saint Tropez would feel flattered by the comparison.

Certainly it did not take me very long to discover that it was impossible to obtain a piece of edible cheese. My craving for cheese had by this time become an obsession.

As far as I could see Buzios consisted of a few pleasant houses on the beach, inhabited by surrealist artists and well-heeled drop-outs, some particularly squalid shops, a dreary bar or two and a staggering quantity of pot-holes. The main street looked like something left over from the Battle of the Somme, a waste-land of trenches and rubble, all part of a wonderful new sewerage scheme which, judging by the tempo of work in progress, will be completed in about 2021. There was no sign at all of the hordes of beautiful girls, the cream of fashionable Rio, who, it had been alleged, made the beaches of Buzios a paradise on earth.

However, Buzios has one distinction. It was there that I saved a man's life, an act of superlative courage and selflessness which has since become the subject of some controversy as certain malicious persons, motivated no doubt by jealous envy, have maintained that, far from nobly diving into the water to save a drowning man, I merely fell in, incapably drunk.

I would like to take this opportunity of setting the record straight in the hope that my heroism may be rewarded by some public honour — the Lord Wardenship of the Cinque ports would do.

We had met some holidaying Americans, an artist and his wife and some other congenial souls and we decided to have a beach party with a huge driftwood bonfire, guitars and revels.

Now, both Alf Readman and I allege that we are almost total abstainers. I attribute the fact that, during the aforementioned beach party, I apparently danced like a dervish, flung off all my clothes and plunged into the sea, either to food-poisoning — the calcined lumps of chicken and sausage on which we feasted tasted most peculiar — or to withdrawal symptoms caused by cheese

Furling sails

'Geronimo'

Painting the hull,
with the author,
reluctantly, at work

a

b

c

d

Wildlife: *a* boobies at St. Paul's Rocks; *b* jackass penguin guarding an unusually large clutch of four eggs; *c* iguanas at the Galapagos; and *d* dolphins, our most frequent and welcome visitors

deprivation. I claim that though my actions that night might have given rise to the suspicion that I was as gassed as a rat, I remained completely clear-headed throughout. Similarly, there is a perfectly simple explanation for why Alf was discovered, towards dawn, stretched out on the sand, totally unconscious. The effort of constantly refusing the bottles of rum which well-meaning shipmates kept pressing on him had completely exhausted him. So much so that when Jay and I decided to transport him back to the *Beagle*, we had to half-carry him to the rubber dinghy.

We started up the outboard and set off across the bay to where the *Beagle* was anchored. It is surely proof of my absolute sobriety that I am able to remember clearly that the sea was phosphorescent, or, more correctly, bio-luminescent. When the outboard packed up, as it inevitably did, and we had to paddle, this bio-luminescence produced a startling effect. Each time one dipped the paddle into the water, it was as if a powerful light had been switched on under the surface of the sea. We made slow but pyrotechnic progress towards the *Beagle*, Alf snoring peacefully in the bottom of the boat.

We came alongside the *Beagle* and were now faced with the problem of getting Alf out of the dinghy and up onto the deck. We managed to rouse him and guide him to the steps. He was muttering incoherently, as people in the last stages of exhaustion tend to do.

'I'm all right,' he murmered, 'I'm all right.'

He was about to roll over the rail onto the deck when he lost balance and fell into the sea. I realised in an instant that he would probably sink like a stone and I did not hesitate to do the manly thing. I dived in after him, grabbed him and hauled him to the side of the ship. He was making vague swimming motions with his arms and was still burbling :

'I'm all right, I'm all right . . . '

Between us, Jay and I managed to manhandle him onto the *Beagle*.

I do not want to be accused of giving a one-sided view of this incident so I will briefly outline the version put about by my enemies and detractors : which was that when Alf fell in, I was so weak with laughter that I fell in on top of him.

The intelligent reader will be able to judge the truth of the matter.

We left Buzois, appropriately named, you may think, on the following afternoon and, quitting the shelter of the bay, encountered the worst seas so far on the voyage, including the Atlantic crossing.

The waves were so steep that the ship was soon imitating the motion of a big dipper. Convinced that, by now, I was immune to seasickness, I watched the faces of our American friends, to whom we were giving a lift down to Rio, go white, then grey, then green, with a feeling of smug superiority. But nemesis is always at hand to smite the patronising. After half an hour, to my horror, I felt myself becoming queasy. Cramming anti-nausea pills into my mouth, I went and hid in my berth. I was not actually sick but I was quite unable to face the fresh mussels Virginia was lovingly preparing in the galley. Judging by the fact that vast quantities of the mussels were thrown over the side the next day, most of the ship's company was in a similar state. Even Robin admitted to a twinge of nausea.

By four o'clock the next morning, when I arose for the early watch, the seas had abated. The sun rose in a haze of scarlet and purple and, to starboard, we could see outline of the coast north of Rio. Soon the strange configurations of the mountains under which Rio sprawls became clearer and I was given the improbable but romantic-sounding order: 'Just steer for the Sugarloaf.'

3
RIO
15 – 20 October

THERE is a sense of occasion about entering Rio de Janeiro from the sea, especially in a sailing ship. Even the most ignorant landlubber (I refer to myself) must appreciate that this is one of the finest natural harbours in the world.

Certainly Captain Fitzroy, in the original *Beagle*, regarded this as a special moment in the voyage because he went to considerable trouble to make his arrival as theatrically effective as possible. The *Beagle* arrived at night but Fitzroy lay to, determined to enter the great bay in dazzling sunshine. He had something to show the crews of the numerous men-of-war anchored in the harbour. The *Beagle* sailed right up alongside the British flagship and proceeded to perform what was, for a vessel of her class, a spectacular manoeuvre. All her sails were taken in and then immediately set again with a speed and a precision astonishing for a mere survey ship. This was one of the few occasions when we know that Darwin himself lent a hand with the ropes. He claimed afterwards that the *Beagle*'s remarkable display of seamanship would have been impossible without his aid!

Probably unconsciously, we on the second *Beagle* wanted to do as Fitzroy had done and cut a dash on entering Rio. The best we could manage was to set as many of our sails as possible in the hope that the people of Rio would be suitably awed by the handsome sight.

We entered the bay at a decent clip, our white canvas billowing elegantly, passed the base of Sugarloaf and cruised up and down near a curious, green Moorish-style palace built by one of the Emperors of Brazil in emulation of the Brighton Pavilion, congratulating ourselves on the fact that we must be the talk of the town.

Rio yawned.

In every port the *Beagle* had visited, in every port where she subsequently put in, she was headline news. But the editors of Rio evidently regarded the *Beagle* as a drag.

However, we weren't to know this as we paraded up and down, waiting for the customs' officials to meet us.

There are two methods of docking in a South American port. You can do it strictly according to the book or you can simply toddle in, tie up and deal with all the red tape when you've had a hot shower and a decent drink.

The first method is an appalling waste of time and a severe trial on the temper. You heave to and contact the customs, police, immigration and all the other minions of South American bureaucracy on the radio. There is a great deal of excited and incomprehensible jabbering in and amongst the crackles of static which inevitably leads to the most exasperating misunderstandings. Hours later, cross, complaining officials arrive, breathing threats and brandishing rubber stamps. Eventually a launch escorts you to your mooring (at a price, of course) and then you find it is the wrong mooring and you have to get another launch (at another price) to take you to the right mooring by which time you are nicely softened up for the rapacious shipping agents waiting for you on the quay all ready to sell you bottles of coca-cola for a knock-down price of about two pounds each.

Such is method one.

Method two, the toddle-and-tie approach, is infinitely to be preferred. You can select the mooring that suits you and you are not bewildered by some incoherent pilot shouting contrary orders to the helmsman. You secure the ship to her mooring in your own time and to your own satisfaction, fortify yourself with a tot of whisky and face the wrath of officialdom with a bland and convincing air of injured ignorance. Since you have presented the rubber-stamp brigade with a *fait-accompli* you find that for some curious reason all the stamping and ticketing and docketing is over in a fraction of the usual time and you are free to sally forth and find a supermarket which sells coca-cola at two pence a bottle.

I should emphasise that method two is only practicable with a ship of modest size which can claim to be classed as a yacht.

It had been decided that when we arrived at Rio we should adopt method one, for the good reason that Mark's wife, Marcia, is a prominent citizen of Rio and we wanted to avoid any official embarrassments. We felt too, that the kind of brazen cheek that worked so well in smaller ports might not go down so spinningly in the former capital of Brazil. Mark had in fact flown on ahead from Salvador to arrange every detail of our arrival in advance and had, with the utmost efficiency, pre-lubricated the official machinery. But, of course, bureaucracy knows no law. For all the good our meticulous arrangements did we might just as well have motored into Rio stern first, flying the Cuban flag, with the crew dangling naked from the yards and feeding heroin to the fish.

All the trouble stemmed from the fact that, though we had arranged a specific time for the bureaucrats to meet the ship, they simply didn't turn up and we had no alternative but to continue cruising up and down. In doing so, we allegedly sailed too close to the naval base, thus infringing some arcane regulation.

The result was that a military launch came alongside, its decks bristling with machine-guns, and the very last person we could have expected — or indeed desired — to see, stepped on board the *Beagle*. It was Idi Amin.

Well, of course, it wasn't actually Idi Amin but it was his exact double, a great, fat, glowering sergeant who immediately began to carry on in a manner that can only be described as Ugandan.

I am sure that what the man was really after was a bribe. A couple of hundred cruzeiros, two hundred cigarettes and a bottle of whisky would have settled his hash for sure. But it is fatal to start handing out bribes. Grease one palm and the word spreads until every petty official is inventing infringements of the regulations and expecting his little pay-off. The only safe course to pursue is solemn British incorruptibility.

Idi Amin stalked about the deck, uttering threats and snarling. Portuguese-speaking negotiators approached him timidly, ingratiatingly, politely. He stamped and raved. Everybody was anxious to keep Robin away from him, because Robin has a healthy loathing of all officialdom and the combination of his forthrightness and Idi's righteous wrath would have been dynamite. Robin was immured tactfully by the wheel, where, in the hot sun and as the minutes crawled by, he began to seethe.

Negotiations continued and, under the thinly-veiled mockery of the crew, Idi began to seethe as well. After an hour or so of hot air, it began to be clear that Idi's only real bone of contention was the fact that we were flying the Brazilian courtesy flag below the Red Ensign — which is correct practice, though Idi denied it.

It was conveyed gently to Robin that perhaps it might be wise to humour him.

'Absolutely not!' roared Robin. 'You can tell him to get stuffed.'

Well, this kind of sentiment, when uttered in ringing tones, makes light of all language barriers. Idi didn't speak a word of English, but he understood. His expression became even more malign. He produced some sinister-looking documents. There was further negotiation while Robin stalked the poop deck and Idi fiddled with his ball-point pen and the upshot of it all was that the entire ship was placed under arrest.

Welcome to Rio.

Time passed, as Idi waited for his ploy to take effect. Surely he would get his money now?

'The ship's been arrested,' I said to Robin.

'Good, splendid.'

'But we've been *arrested*. Don't you think . . . ?'

'I don't give a damn. They can do what they like.'

So that was that. More time passed and then another launch came alongside the *Beagle*.

It contained the long-overdue officials.

A fat, little man in a shiny suit clambered on board. He carried a big, black valise, which he plonked on the deck.

Then another fat, little man in a shiny suit clambered on board. He had a big, black valise too and he placed it beside the other.

In quick succession what seemed like five hundred men in shiny suits with big black valises climbed aboard—short ones, tall ones, thin ones, bearded ones, moustachioed ones, young ones and old ones. They all carried big black valises and soon the deck of the *Beagle* looked like the left luggage office at Waterloo station.

'My God,' I said to Robin, 'who are all these people?'

But he didn't answer. There was a gleam of triumph in his eyes and he was gazing at Idi Amin.

'Look,' he said.

Idi was visibly shaken by the massive invasion of officialdom. In the face of so many and so varied bureaucrats, he was completely upstaged. An immigration officer, calling imperiously for crew lists and passports, shooed him impatiently out of the way. Poor Idi was in the position of the urban guerrilla who, having kidnapped an ex-President, is conducting negotiations at the highest level with the Government when the USSR and the USA simultaneously declare war on the country. Suddenly, from being an important threat to national stability he is reduced to the level of a minor irritation to be dealt with by the Assistant to the

Assistant Secretary to the Under Minister of the Interior. Idi slunk back to his launch, defeated and deflated.

The invading army who had thus put him to flight turned out to be composed of immigration men, customs men, chandler's representatives, agents, radar experts and two morose individuals who had come to inspect the engines.

Hours later, when we had got rid of them all, we were allowed to proceed to our mooring at the Yacht Club, in spite of the fact that we were still technically under arrest.

I never did learn what the outcome of our brush with Idi Amin was. I know that Mark had to go off to some terrifying office, but what he did there, whom he saw, remains a mystery. However, he managed to extricate us from the situation and it would be indelicate to inquire exactly how. Or how much.

Marcia's powerful influence in Rio had procured for us a prime mooring at the Rio yacht club, no less than the President's own personal mooring. (I refer to the President of the Yacht Club.)

One of the most hallowed traditions of the *Beagle* is that she should run aground on entering any harbour, preferably in circumstances of maximum embarrassment.

In Rio, I am proud to say, we excelled ourselves. It was really not our fault, we were being guided by others, but, as Robin remarked afterwards, we did have two depth-sounders, neither of which anybody thought to turn on.

It was not so much the running aground that caused us problems, the bottom was soft and we quickly stuck up a couple of jibs to take us off when the engines failed to do so ; it was the manoeuvres we had to perform amongst the trim little pleasure boats and bobbing yachts. If the *Beagle* had seemed like a toy ship among the destroyers of Aratu, in the yacht basin of Rio she seemed to be a potential destroyer of toy ships. Her bowsprit, as it swung through 180 degrees, threatened to hole and sink several sleek and gleaming gin-palaces whose owners, frozen in the act of pouring champagne or lighting cigars, gaped in horror.

As soon as we went ashore we realised we were in champagne and cigar country, or more accurately whisky and cigar country since the smart drink in Brazil is Scotch, the very rich quaffing 20 year old malt, the not-so-rich having to be content with blended whisky at £35.10 a bottle.

A single bomb placed strategically on the terrace of the Rio yacht club on a Saturday afternoon would wipe out a fair proportion of the richest and most prominent citizens. And they must be aware of this since the whole area is sentried and patrolled by armed guards in white uniforms.

In the five or six days we were there I observed very few members actually venturing onto the sea. The purpose of the club appeared to be more social than nautical and the vast majority of the yachts remained firmly battened down under custom-made canvas covers.

It occurs to me now that the reason for this may be linked to the fact that the water in the yacht basin was the filthiest and most polluted I have ever seen. It was little better than an open sewer. In fact several large sewage pipes discharged a noxious flow directly opposite our mooring. It struck me as curious, at the time, that a club whose financial resources appeared to be bottomless and whose membership included powerful politicians could not have insisted on more civilised arrangements. As it was, we all lived in terror of falling in.

The sanitary arrangements inside the club were equally baffling. The men's lavatories were sumptuously constructed of solid marble and, on a cursory inspection, looked like something out of the pleasure dome of an Arab oil sheik. But any attempt to use these luxurious facilities shattered the illusion. The marble was splendid, but the plumbing simply didn't work. The floors were permanently awash and handles and taps tended to come away in your hand.

The subject of plumbing is not entirely frivolous. Ineffective plumbing is generally found in countries which lack a well-established class of skilled artisans ; a sociologist could do worse than to begin his inquiries amongst the pans and porcelain.

By far the greatest tourist attraction in Rio de Janeiro is Mr. Ronald Biggs, the well-known train-robber, who holds court in a bar called The English Pub where the olde oake beams are made of fibreglass.

However, Sugarloaf mountain, Copacabana and Ipanema beaches still retain a little drawing power and, though this is not a guide-book, Ipanema is worth a mention.

On a hot Sunday afternoon the whole of Rio parades there in a splendid display of near-nudity. Every square inch of sand is occupied but, curiously enough, the atmosphere could not be less like Brighton on a Bank Holiday or Coney Island in August. There is nothing static about the scene. People do not sit in a heap, they walk up and down ; and Rio women walk in a very special way, with a graceful, provocative swing of the hips seen nowhere else. Life on the beach combines elements of a cocktail party, a marriage bureau, a mannequin parade and a striptease joint. The only disappointment is that the sea is freezing cold.

At night, thousands of tiny lights twinkle on the hill over-looking Ipanema—a charming spectacle. Except these are not electric lights, they are the gas and candle lights of the *favella*, the slums and shanty-towns that are the disturbing counterpoint to Rio's somewhat garish, neon-lit prosperity.

It is a good city for the affluent motorist. I was walking down a street one morning when I saw a car blatantly shoot the red lights under the very nose of a policeman. The policeman blew his whistle and the car drew in to the kerb. The policeman approached the car, fingering his revolver. There was a rapid rustle of five-hundred-cruzeiro notes, the policeman saluted and the motorist went on his happy way.

Copacabana beach is interesting at night. It is several miles long and separated from the high, white hotels and apartment buildings which rise behind it by a broad highway, so that during the hours of darkness the vast expanse of sand becomes a place of remoteness and mystery. Small fires flicker among the dunes and strange rites are performed. A small army of prostitutes roams up and down, turning the beach into an alfresco brothel.

The atmosphere of Rio encourages one to drink, to eat, to spend, to dance and to make love. What it doesn't encourage one to do is to work.

In the streets of Rio there was music and merriment ; in the *Beagle* there was tumult and affray.

Port fever is a disease that affects all ships' companies and the most obvious symptom of it is drunkenness, and the consequences are always the same—missed watches and massive hangovers that render the sufferers unfit for any duties.

Darwin was shocked when, during the first two days of the *Beagle*'s voyage, Fitzroy had four men flogged for misdemeanours arising from drunken revels in Devonport. Seamen are not flogged these days but port fever is the same and always will be.

In the second *Beagle* in Rio there were none of the excesses committed by Messrs. Bruce, Russel, Phipps and Davis, the four seamen flogged by Fitzroy, but it is no good blinking the fact that a holiday air gripped the whole ship's company which, com-bined with a profound lassitude induced by the humid climate and the after-effects of pleasure, meant that work on the ship virtually ground to a halt.

And why not? You could argue that such a dedicated and hard-working crew deserved a little leisure.

The problem was that though the *Beagle* was basically a working ship, it was understood by everyone from the outset that there would be elements of the pleasure cruise, opportunities for sight-seeing, and exploration. But the area between these opposed elements was ill-defined and, in Rio, the situation got out of hand.

I do not want to exaggerate this. By and large the *Beagle* was a happy ship, a miraculously happy ship, in fact, given the natural frailty of human relationships. And in this event nothing very terrible happened unless you count the spectacle of Captain Robin rampaging up and down, breathing fire and brimstone and performing his celebrated impression of Captain Bligh while groups of potential Fletcher Christians muttered darkly in corners or tried to suppress giggles.

If it had not been for an unfortunate coincidence the whole episode would have passed as an interesting example of a port fever epidemic. The coincidence was a decision to return one member of the crew home to England. This was John Truelove and the reason was simply that he suffered from chronic sea-sickness which would have been a serious handicap to him in the rough seas of the Southern Ocean.

In the circumstances it appeared to be an action deliberately taken by Robin *pour encourager les autres,* and further increased the HMS *Bounty* atmosphere. I wish I could record that it all ended in a mutiny with Robin and Mark cast adrift among the floating faeces of the yacht club or dangling from the yard-arm. Alas there was no mutiny. Life soon returned to normal. From time to time we toyed with the idea of an insurrection with technical discussions as to the superior advantages of plank-walking or marooning but all my own hopes for a dramatic incident were dashed when Mike Freeman, a natural mutineer if ever there was one, pinned the following notice up in the saloon.

'The Mutiny scheduled for 8 a.m. today has been cancelled due to lack of interest.'

Rio wasn't all tension and internal politics of course. The whole crew was lavishly entertained by Mark and Marcia in an apartment roughly the size of Blenheim Palace and there were several amusing outrages which went some way towards puncturing the somewhat pompous atmosphere of the yacht club, but by and large it was a relief to everyone when, again with all sails set, we left. We had lingered so long in Rio because our engines needed repairs. After a week of investigating local facilities we decided to postpone the work until we arrived in Argentina.

By a curious coincidence, the original *Beagle's* stay at Rio was similarly marred by internal dissension, the sending home of an officer and other gloomy happenings.

First, Darwin and Fitzroy, who messed in the same cabin, had one of their rare quarrels which temporarily destroyed the friendly atmosphere of what everybody from Captain to cabin boy attested was an extraordinarily happy ship.

The row was about slavery. Darwin had been visiting a jungle plantation belonging to a man called Lennon. In Darwin's hearing Lennon had had a violent dispute with his manager during which he threatened to separate all his female slaves, with their children, from their husbands and fathers, march them off to Rio and auction the lot. Darwin was appalled that a civilised man could even contemplate such barbaric action and he was still seething when he returned to Rio. Now he discovered that the old woman who lived opposite the cottage he was renting at Botofogo kept thumb-screws and other instruments of torture for use on her slaves. So when he went aboard the *Beagle* he was burning with indignation and poured out all his loathing of slavery in an impassioned oration to Fitzroy. Darwin's relatives, the Wedgwoods, it must be remembered, were early and prominent supporters of the anti-slavery lobby.

Fitzroy's attitude to slavery was equivocal. While there were many aspects of it which distressed him, of course, he thought that by and large it was beneficial to the economies of the colonial countries and, after all, there was nothing in the Bible that condemned it . . . One can imagine his clipped, level, aristocratic voice and the slight hint of superciliousness as he added that he thought that much of the outcry against slavery, from comfortable liberals who had never run a plantation, was little more than what we, in modern terms, would describe as radical chic.

And one can imagine how this dig at Darwin's own family further enraged him. Hotly, he described Lennon's behaviour. Fitzroy, himself becoming heated, said that he too had visited a plantation where the slaves lived in excellent conditions and were quite happy. Indeed, the owner had asked numerous slaves, in Fitzroy's presence, whether they were content with their lot and they had all answered in the affirmative.

At this point, of course, Darwin had Fitzroy on toast. He could combat superciliousness with sarcasm. What on earth did Fitzroy expect the slaves to say in the presence of their master? That he was a cruel and vicious tyrant and that they were all miserable and about to shoot the overseer and burn down the hacienda?

Fitzroy flew into a rage and told Darwin he could find somewhere else to mess. Darwin, full of righteous wrath, declared he would leave the ship altogether.

All the *Beagle*'s officers sided with Darwin and the atmosphere was tense and strained—I know exactly what it must have been like—until that able diplomat Lieutenant Wickham smoothed down everybody's ruffled feathers.

It was at Rio too that a member of the *Beagle*'s crew was sent home, as with the second *Beagle,* the only instance of this. The officer in question was the surgeon, Robert MacCormick, and the reasons for his dismissal remain obscure.

Finally, it was at Rio that three of the crew died, casting further gloom over the *Beagle*'s stay. The three were young Charles Musters, a protégé of Fitzroy's, Boy Jones and a tough old seadog called Morgan. All three contracted a fever after swimming in the River Macaú.

Fortunately in this instance I cannot claim an exact parallel with our own experiences in Rio, though I have no doubt that if any of our crew had swum in the festering waters of the yacht club, I would be in a position to do so.

4

RIO — MAR DEL PLATA

20 – 30 October

W E were now heading out of tropical waters into more temperate and more dangerous zones.

But for the first few days there was enough sunshine and delight to lull us into a false sense of security.

One day we anchored at a beautiful island called the Ilha das Couves. The sea was as green as vine-leaves and the jungle which rose some 350 feet behind the beach was full of exotic, unfamiliar bird-cries. Near the beach in the burnt-out ruins of a primitive shack we found evidence that the island had once been inhabited. The profusion of banana trees suggested that this might once have been an outpost of the Fyffes empire.

The conditions for snorkelling were perfect. I spent hours swimming just off the rocks watching the shoals of brilliantly coloured fish moving in perfect formation and with an almost balletic precision as if their darts and dives and flips were controlled by some mysterious underwater choreography. Only when I dived or splashed the surface with my flippers would they scatter and even then their movements seemed to be part of some sophisticated emergency drill.

Another day I was able to astonish the entire ship's company with a positively Darwinian knowledge of marine biology, genuinely Darwinian in fact since my information came directly from his *Journal*.

It was just after lunch, a period of siesta when everyone lazed about the decks and basked. We were under sail, making a modest two or three knots. Someone noticed a large, reddish-brown stain on the surface of the sea.

'That,' declared Robin, 'is an oil slick.'

'That,' I said, 'is confervae,' adding, with a pedantic air, 'called by the seamen on Captain Cook's third voyage sea-sawdust.'

Hoots of derision from all sides greeted this statement, brute ignorance mocking the distinguished amateur of science.

We altered course slightly to take us into the centre of the discoloured band which was about seven or eight yards wide and at least a mile long, and I dipped a bucket over the side.

(Note: there is a right way and a wrong way of doing everything at sea and the novice invariably chooses the wrong way. There is an art even in so simple an action as collecting a bucketful of sea-water. One's natural instinct is to chuck the bucket aft on the assumption that the forward motion of the ship through the sea will naturally cause water to *flow* into the bucket. This is wrong. All that happens is that the bucket drags, the rope on which it is suspended jerks and tautens and you are in danger either of losing the bucket or falling overboard. The correct method is to chuck the bucket forward and *dip*, raising the bucket swiftly out of the water the minute it is drawn back level with you. Watch out for further hints: How To Tie a Sheepshank, What is a Futtock?)

Anyway, I collected a bucket of sea-water and there were the confervae, a species of minute marine algae, cylindrical in shape and exactly resembling chaff or sawdust. Vast bands of these tiny creatures abound in the Red Sea, hence its name. Darwin first observed them near the Abrolhos Islands.

Then there were dolphins. At least once or twice a day we would be visited by a school of these graceful, merry creatures, of all mammals the most intelligent, the most humorous, the most perfectly adapted to and integrated with their environment.

I began to look forward to the arrival of dolphins alongside in the same way that one anticipates a weekend visit from old friends. This was not simply because their leaping, swirling acrobatics provided such a marvellous spectacle but because of the sheer joy they communicated.

The best place to observe them was up in the bow, lying face down in the bow net. Four or five of them would swim just ahead of the ship, apparently gliding through the water without effort, using the shock waves from the dipping prow to propel them, with only an occasional shudder of their streamlined bodies to give them extra speed. They would play elaborate formation games, criss-crossing, passing swiftly over or under each other. Then they would be off with a sudden, breathtaking surge of speed and away, round the stern of the ship and back to the bow, blowing and laughing, yes laughing. I swear I once saw a dolphin wink, a saucy, conspiratorial wink, as he surfaced for a moment, then dived right under the bow and emerged the other side.

I have never visited a dolphinarium, where these boundlessly free creatures are confined in tanks and taught, as if a man could teach a dolphin anything, to perform tricks. I cannot see that there is anything very edifying in the sight of a dolphin balancing a rubber ball on his nose or being made to 'stand' in the water while a piece of fish is dangled in front of him any more than I can derive the slightest pleasure in the spectacle of elephants, dressed in tutus, being made to dance in a circus ring. Are we so unsure of our own superiority in the mammalian hierarchy that we need to make fellow creatures perform such ridiculous and shameful antics?

Even as a child I hated circuses and once shocked a doting godmother by piping up loudly, when the lion-tamer put his head in the lion's mouth: 'I hope he bites it right off.' Twenty-five years later, I am still optimistic.

Scientists now assure us solemnly that dolphins can talk. Several million dollars' worth of research has proved what anybody who has ever observed dolphins intelligently can see almost at once. Not only do they talk to each other, or, more accurately, communicate with each other, they quite patently crack jokes. Further millions are now being expended in an attempt to interpret dolphin language. I would be all for this if I thought that the intention was to learn something from them. It is far more likely that, once in touch, Man will feel it incumbent on him to teach the dolphins a thing or two, like the principles of nuclear fission or the history of the First World War.

Cases have been reported of dolphins saving the lives of marooned swimmers or ship-wrecked sailors, allowing them to cling onto their fins and towing them to shore. What is amazing about such tales is not the intelligence shown by the dolphins, but their forbearance and charity in wishing to save a man's life.

Dolphins were a delight but, above all, it was the pleasure of being at sea again that made these days sailing south so enjoyable. Darwin remarks somewhere that, if it were not for seasickness, every man would be a sailor because ships are the best homes imaginable. There is a lot in this.

After the dissensions and dislocations of Rio it was a relief to return to the steady routines of the sea, the regular watches and especially the meals when we all gathered round the table in the saloon and there was a sense of community.

I began to love the life and to dread putting into ports with their dubious metropolitan pleasures and their fragmenting effect on the spirit of oneness that is the most enjoyable aspect of a happy ship.

But it is not good to fall in love with the sea. People who do so may find themselves clutched to its bosom in a fatal embrace, for the sea is always dangerous, always unpredictable.

Five or six hundred miles south of Rio we were entering a region in which the local danger to shipping goes under the misleading name of a *pampero*. A *pampero* is a violent squall from the south-west and the last thing it does to ships is pamper them.

There came a day when the classic sequence of events which heralds a *pampero* began to unroll in a manner which swiftly put paid to any feelings of complacency.

The first sign was a steady fall in the barometer from 1016 in the early morning to 1010 by late afternoon. For the past two days we had had steady northerly winds with a high temperature and humidity. Now the wind veered to the north east. All this conformed to the onset of a *pampero*. The wind became stronger, about force five and gusting six to seven.

For the first time, the *Beagle*'s alarm siren was used. This has two notes, a warble and a continuous whine. The warble means all hands on deck but put your trousers on, the continuous noise means all hands on deck and forget about your trousers. In this instance all hands appeared on deck trousered, in obedience to the warble.

All the sails had to be taken in as quickly as possible and everything on the decks securely lashed. Even in a moderate sea a loose object on deck becomes a potentially lethal missile.

I had my first experience of furling sails in a highish wind and it was terrifying. It was not so much the force of the breeze which threatened to sweep you off the yards ; it was the urgency of the situation and the fact that the rigging was crowded with bigger, braver and more nimble men who jostled you on the foot-ropes, climbed past you on the shrouds and blared vivid descriptions of severed spines and shattered limbs into your left ear.

After half an hour of frenzied activity the decks were safely lashed and battened and the yards bare. As if to mock our efforts the wind now died and the sea grew completely calm. The air was suddenly smotheringly oppressive. There wasn't a whisper of a breeze coming off the land beyond the starboard horizon. But this was all part of the pattern of a *pampero*. We waited for the rolls of cumulus cloud, followed by cumulo-nimbus which would precede the onset of the south west wind.

The sky clearly indicated that there was a *pampero* in the vicinity. The only question now was whether it would hit us or not.

By early evening it seemed likely that the storm would miss us. Tentatively we set a few sails. But by 2000 hours the sea was beginning to mount alarmingly and we took them all in again. It was no joke clinging to the extreme end of the topsail yard which was imitating the action of a dipping-stool, scrabbling for some sort of purchase on the hard canvas with one hand while groping for the end of the gasket—the thin rope you bind round the furled sail to keep it in position—with the other. I still had a lot to learn.

Towards midnight we were hit by a nasty beam sea which made the ship roll violently and it was obvious that we were catching the edge of the storm. And sure enough there was a loud crash from the galley to prove it.

I reeled down below and found the galley floor awash with salad cream. I have never been fond of salad cream and now that I have had to mop up about ten gallons of the stuff in conditions where it oozed and slopped and eddied, I will certainly never insult a lettuce leaf with it again.

Next day we had another mild scare. This time it was an invasion of insects which seemed to presage a strong offshore wind. Thousands of insects ranging from huge dragonflies with spider-like legs, bulky thoraxes and six inch wing-spans, to flying beetles, gnats and flies of every kind, moths, butterflies and one monstrous green creature which looked like a winged toad infested the rigging, in fluttering swarms. I am sure that Darwin would have seized on the green giant with delight and instantly dissected it.

Again, the expected danger did not materialise and I was reminded of something people often said about the *Beagle*, that she was a 'lucky ship'.

Seamen, as a breed, are famous for their superstitions. They don't shoot albatrosses. On a sailing-ship they don't whistle unless they want a wind. They don't paint their hulls green. Underlying such nautical taboos—and they are legion—is a secret belief that there is a force which watches over ships and which it is folly to offend.

You pace the deck alone at night. You look down at the sea

which is as smooth and calm as milk in the moonlight. But you know that it is a potential destroyer of men and their puny vessels. You look up at the night sky, at the millions of stars, the unnumbered solar systems in an infinite universe and you have a sense of your own littleness in relation to all this vastness. You know that between the sky and the sea you are a nothing. It is of no comfort to you to reflect on Man's achievements in probing the mysteries of space or, through his endless capacity for invention, mastering his own little world. You know that the sea is no respecter of human genius, that no ship has ever been built or even devised that the sea could not destroy.

But you look up at the sky again and you see the planets and constellations fixed in a perfect order. And you feel that in that order, incomprehensible though it is, there may lie a power even greater than the power of the sea. You think perhaps there might after all be some justification for the feeling which few, even the most entrenched atheists, can escape, the feeling that you matter.

Mystical claptrap? Religious bogosity? If it seems so it can only be because it is ill-expressed. All men who have had a long experience of the sea have witnessed miracles which some may ascribe to luck, whatever that is, some to God, others, with a shrug of their shoulders and a quick glance up at the sky, to something they cannot define.

On the *Beagle* we had a minor miracle of our own which, though not particularly dramatic, is interesting in that, had it not happened, the voyage would have ended in a welter of stove-in timbers in a somewhat desultory port called Rio Grande.

We put into Rio Grande on the night of the insect invasion (running aground at one point, it goes without saying) and left the following evening in blinding rain. The approaches to the port are a navigator's nightmare, nothing but sandbanks, unmarked shallows, currents and a quantity of fishing boats and other shipping to add to the jollity.

A look-out was posted on the bowsprit and we began to feel our way gingerly out towards the breakwater at the end of the channel. Suddenly the look-out came roaring down the deck, shouting that we were about to hit a buoy. Whether, in the confusion, the wrong order was given to the helmsman or the right order was given and the wrong helm put over (an error frequently made by the most experienced seamen) was never established. It makes no difference. A fifteen-foot metal buoy

was looming up on our starboard bow. It was heavy enough to
do terminal damage if we hit it at the speed we were making.
Instead of going hard to port, the helm was put hard to starboard, a collision course. But there was no collision because, for
a reason which nobody has ever been able to explain, the ship
payed off to port. Slowly but surely the bowsprit swung round
and we slid past the buoy with a few inches to spare.

A sudden freak wind? A strange current? Maybe. The fact
remains that we should unquestionably have been wrecked but
we weren't. The *Beagle* was a 'lucky ship' and later on, she
proved even luckier.

We put into Rio Grande to drop off Robin and Virginia.
Virginia's holiday was over. She would need at least a month
in a health farm to recover from the strain of it. Robin had to
fly on ahead to Argentina to make arrangements for major repairs
to the starboard engine which seemed to be about to disintegrate
entirely.

It is worth noting that our entry into the port was a prime
example of the superiority of the method two, toddle-and-tie
approach. The quays were crammed with shipping and we crept
slowly along in full view of the customs, police and immigration
sheds. We had made no arrangements of any kind. Eventually
we moored alongside a banana boat where we remained for
twenty four hours completely unmolested. At no time did anyone
ask to see a crew list or even a passport.

Rio Grande was a complete contrast to Salvador or Rio. In
southern Brazil there is a large population of German immigrants
and the place had the neat, trim air of some Hanseatic town.
Certainly the dockside bars and discos would have done credit
to the Reeperbahn in Hamburg.

We found a joint where thick banks of marijuana wreathed
and curled fragrantly amongst white, flat-topped pedestals on
which girls performed fantastic stripteases, their bodies phosphorescent in the strobe lights. They were not professional strippers,
they were not even local *filles de joie,* they were just obeying the
pulse and throb of the music.

Having survived the incident of the fifteen foot buoy, the
Beagle, with Mark as Captain during Robin's absence, proceeded
southwards in a blind mist. In zero visibility, with no wind, we
chugged along with one man constantly by the radar, one man
on the bowsprit, one man up the mast and all hearts in mouths.
Even on a clear night, even with an efficient look-out a ship can

appear out of nowhere. In fog there is an ever-present danger of collision.

Like everything else at sea, fog is completely unpredictable. In the morning, at about 10.30, it cleared. There was bright sunlight, a clear horizon. Then, suddenly, when everyone was beginning to relax, visibility dropped from 8 or 9 to 1 in a few seconds. The fog persisted all day and at night, large patches of it lingered on the landward side, thus causing some navigational havoc since the moonlight, shining on them, gave them the appearance of looms—the lights of distant coastal towns—and the looms did not tally with the chart.

The weather became glowering and gusty. The sea was the colour of black ink and lumpy, setting up a strange motion which produced an interesting variety of sea-sickness. This did not take the form of nausea but an overwhelming feeling of fatigue and light-headedness of which several people complained.

The weather cleared and we had a man-overboard drill, the shameful details of which I dare not relate. Suffice it to say that if it had been a man rather than a life-buoy cast into the cruel sea, his only chance of survival would have been a charitable dolphin.

We passed out of Brazilian waters. I reflected that if a general massacre of bureaucrats could be arranged, that vast country, second only to the USSR in size and second to none in the richness of its natural resources, would be a super-power.

We passed the coast of Uruguay—some dingy sand-dunes—and the entrance to the River Plate where the outflow of the great river stained the sea black-green.

We altered course for the Argentine port of Mar del Plata, south-west of Buenos Aires.

It was a Sunday. We could reasonably suppose that the inhabitants might have some leisure to look seawards and so we hoisted all our square sails, mizzen, main staysail and inner jib, to give them a show. If we could have foreseen the kind of flattering but debilitating rapture this display kindled in the generous hearts of the Argentines we might have made a less spectacular landfall.

If Rio had yawned, Mar del Plata raved.

It was as well that only a few people witnessed our attempts to secure a mooring in this port. If we could have proceeded directly to the anchorage Robin had arranged at the yacht club, all might have been well. As it was, officialdom ordained that we should

first tie up at a quay in the outer harbour. We went alongside
the quay with neatness and precision. Robin now came back on
board and took over command. He was followed by several
shipping agents with their usual bankrupting bargains. Then an
angry policeman arrived and began to shout. He was angry
because the shipping agents had come on board before we had
received customs clearance. We explained that we had not
invited the agents on board and pointed out that a man in
pursuit of a 20% commission is an unstoppable force. The policeman summoned three or four other policemen who stood on the
dock and levelled their machine-guns at us.

Welcome to Mar del Plata.

We ate our lunch under a blistering sun and the infinitely
more blistering scowls of officialdom. After the usual delays ('I
thought Argentina was supposed to be so much more civilised
than Brazil?' 'Don't be ridiculous, it's still Latin America') we
were able to attempt phase two, getting to the yacht club.

Now we found that it was impossible to manoeuvre off the
quay because a ship had tied up behind us and another ship had
tied up in front of us and there was a strong wind blowing us
against the concrete side of the dock. The launch from the yacht
club which should have been there to tow us off had not arrived
so we had no alternative but to go it alone.

I believe that every known method and technique was tried
but the only result was that time after time the *Beagle* was
slammed back against the dock while the whole crew, acting as
human fenders, sweated and grunted, Mark paced up and down,
stricken with the shame of it, muttering 'Oh my God' and the
officials on the dock began to enjoy themselves at last. Machine-
guns were discarded, cigarettes rolled and lit, jocularities exchanged.

It got worse and worse. Iron projections in the wall of the
dock began gouging sizeable rents in the gunwales. The wind
blew harder. Ex-Lieutenant Mark Litchfield R.N. appeared to
be on the brink of a coronary thrombosis. Quite a little crowd
gathered on the dock, agog to see the crazy Englishmen who,
having sailed all the way from Great Britain, were now
determinedly ripping their ship to pieces in some mystifying
Britannic ritual of nautical hara-kiri. I suppose we would
eventually either have sunk or succeeded but happily for our
rapidly collapsing public image, the port propellor shaft seized.
What a bit of luck. Several miles of rusty hawser, churned up

from the depths by our wild revvings, had wrapped themselves round it.

We were left with the starboard engine whose parlous condition was the reason for our being in Mar del Plata in the first place.

At length, the yacht club launch arrived and, a few minutes later, we managed to extricate ourselves from the situation.

We followed the launch round to the yacht club. Well, of course we ran aground, but that is not the point of the story. The point is that the owner of the launch (who was really responsible for leading us to our present doom—and doom it was as we were hard aground and the tide was going out faster than a bathful of soapy water) shouted that he would attempt to push us off. At which Robin rushed to the rail and roared: 'I don't want to be pushed. I want to be pulled.'

However, after some similar ambiguities and two snapped cables, the *Beagle* was snugly secured in what turned out to be the most dangerous anchorage in Argentina.

5

DO YOU LIKE MAR DEL PLATA?

30 October – 13 November

IN South America it is usually true to say that where there is a commercial port there is also a naval or military base and—if the community is sufficiently affluent—a yacht club. At Mar del Plata all three exist, side by side, and the *Beagle*'s anchorage was in the middle.

On one side of us were the fish docks, home of a very considerable fleet of small trawlers and source of some of the most terrible smells I have ever encountered. The most palatable was the permanent reek of rotting fish, the most pervasive, the stink of calcined bones, the most pernicious, a stench which suggested an inefficiently administered tannery.

On the other side was the naval base—electrified fences, arc lights, sentries, pill boxes—partly masked by an artificial mole, composed of jagged rocks and boulders, on which lived a colony of sea-lions. These fat, ferocious-looking creatures were a completely incongruous sight in the bleak industrial landscape. At night their snorts and grunts and hoarse love-cries echoed weirdly round the bay. By day, their huge bodies, suddenly surfacing in the opaque water, constituted a danger to rowing boats, dinghies and other small craft. These sea-lions had an easy life, lazily scavenging for the fish-waste which, in the commercial port, was noxiously plentiful. They provided a useful anti-pollution service and some of the more agile ones had turned thief and could be seen clambering up onto the decks of trawlers and blithely guzzling fresh fish. Nobody seemed to object. The sea-lions avoided human beings and human beings did their best to avoid the sea-lions, who reserved all their aggressive instincts for each other. Especially when the sun was shining—which it didn't much—territorial battles would be waged on the rocks. Each sea-lion appeared to have his own personal basking-rock which he would defend against intruders with raucous grunts, rearing up and baring his teeth. The defeated challenger would be rolled off the rocks into the water, from which he would emerge, hissing and blowing, to renew the attack elsewhere.

Behind the *Beagle*, in an inner basin, was the yacht club. This was a very different affair from the marbled halls of Rio, resembling nothing so much as a large transport café. And there was not a hint of supine luxury about it, rather an air of extreme heartiness of the drill-hall and cold shower variety.

For the first night and day, the *Beagle*'s crew were prisoners in the yacht club, forbidden to go beyond the main gate, owing to some official hiccup regarding passports. And there were armed sentries posted to see that this ruling was enforced.

On the first night, some of us played a ridiculous game with these guards, behaviour which, in the light of subsequent events, was peculiarly asinine.

On our unsteady way back from the clubhouse to the jetty where our dinghy was moored, we realised that we were being stalked by two guards. We stopped, pretended to confer in a conspiratorial huddle, then suddenly split up, diving off in all directions and hiding in the shadows. We were all rather alarmed by the effect of this childish ploy. There was much shouting, torch waving, gun-slinging and calls for reinforcements. Sobered and beginning to take our gaolers more seriously, we all made for our boat as quickly as possible. To our dismay, we saw an officer and one of the sentries, armed with a wicked-looking machine-pistol, get into another boat and start rowing after us. They rowed right out to the *Beagle* and, in spite of our protests, climbed aboard.

The officer was very young and very nervous, a dangerous combination, and his companion was dour, sullen and looked as if he had an itchy trigger-finger. The sight of his gleaming machine-pistol being toted round the decks of the *Beagle* was rather shocking. The ship was our home, after all. The officer now proposed to rouse the crew for a head-count. The thought of Robin or indeed any of our ship-mates being roused from their honest slumbers by armed and uniformed men was appalling. They would not have reacted very favourably to the midnight knock. Diplomacy was called for. Luckily the officer had a sense of humour and was extremely unsure of himself and, in spite of growls from his henchman, eventually consented to leave.

He was back at seven o'clock the next morning with a more senior colleague and *two* armed men. That should have warned us that the military in Argentina mean business, but the unpleasant incident was soon forgotten in the overwhelming warmth of our reception by the people of Mar del Plata.

We found we were stars.

The *Beagle* was headline news in the local papers. Journalists and photographers came out to the ship in exhausting hordes while scores of other visitors thronged the decks and turned life in the saloon into an endless cocktail party. We were interviewed on television, lavishly entertained and generally fêted like con-quering heroes. One result of all this ballyhoo was an invitation from the Rotary Club of Mar del Plata for Suzanne (representing glamour) and myself (representing literature I suppose) to be guests of honour at a banquet.

The occasion is worth recording for two reasons. It provided a curious insight into a certain, very representative section of Argentine society and it was my first real introduction to a strange litany which became the theme-song or dirge of our stay in Mar del Plata and consisted of the question — or supplication — endlessly repeated:

'Do you like Mar del Plata?'

A reasonable enough question, you would suppose. But when you find that everybody from the richest ranch-owner to the shower and lavatory attendant at the Yacht Club asks it over and over again with the kind of bashful eagerness more normally found in a young poet asking a celebrated critic for an opinion of his latest internally-rhyming effusion, you begin to wonder what lies behind it.

It soon becomes clear that what people are really asking is: 'What do you think of Argentina?' and that they are pathetic-ally pleased when, with noncommital politesse, you say that it's splendid. You wonder why they should care so desperately about the opinion of a foreigner who is unlikely to have seen enough of the country or its people to form a balanced judgement and who may, for all they know, be quite incapable of so doing through lack of intelligence.

During the hand-shaking, whisky-drinking, smile-stitched-firmly-onto-face ritual which preceded the Rotary Club dinner, I began to learn how the average middle-class Argentine (Rotarians, I discovered, were all lawyers, business executives, entrepreneurs, doctors — solid citizens) thinks of his country. He regards Argentina as the shining exception to the South American rule of banana republics and squalid dictatorships. He is likely to point out, while denying any personal feelings of racial prejudice, that Argentina is white. He will explain that, in South American terms, it is a young country which began its development long after slavery was abolished, and that its exclusively European immigrants did not intermarry with Indians because there weren't any. (He probably won't mention that this was because they were systematically exterminated.)

Having established the racial purity of the nation he will point out that while the majority of the population is of Spanish origin and the language is Spanish, the predominating influence in manners and customs is British.

Argentines are infatuated with things Britannic, with tweed jackets and cavalry twill trousers, with scotch whisky and Kipling, and of course, with breeding and racing horses. Above all, they look with longing at the Mother of Parliaments and with genuine shame at their own ruling *junta* which they nonetheless support and maintain in power.

The average middle-class version of recent Argentine political history goes like this: Argentina was the most prosperous, civilised country in South America where nobody went hungry, where everybody had a job and where, given stability and time, the admittedly wide differences between rich and poor would have levelled out. Parliamentary democracy, the traditional and cherished form of government, would have had a chance to flourish again. BUT . . . Along came Perón. He was a tub-thumper and a rabble-rouser who gulled or bribed the credulous voters into giving him power and then maintained himself in power by plundering industry and agriculture to provide massive hand-outs for the workers and diamonds for his wife. He bankrupted the economy, bringing ruin to all classes and creating civil anarchy. The army was forced to step in to save the nation. Perón fled. When he returned, in 1973, the pattern was repeated and the situation made worse by the actions of extreme Left guerrilla groups. Perón died. His wife succeeded to the Presidency, again there was anarchy, again the Generals were forced to impose a form of totalitarian rule. Now the economy was picking up, the hyper-inflation was being brought under control, the guerrillas had been suppressed, admittedly by brutal methods which are regrettable . . . And so on and so forth.

Dictatorship, torture, arrest without trial, censorship — the Argentine finds these things embarrassing, but he believes they are necessary. He is anxious to explain why they are necessary, and even more anxious that the visitor should think well of his country. He is your friend for life if you say you think Argentina is infinitely superior to Brazil.

For the benefit of those who have never attended a Rotary dinner (I never had), it consists of a moderate amount of eating and drinking and an inordinate amount of speechifying. At least, in Argentina, it does. I am still not absolutely clear about the origins and purposes of Rotarianism, but it appears to be a judicious blend of mutual self-help for business and professional men and charitable works, in what proportion I am not qualified to judge.

I realised, with alarm, that both Suzanne and I would, as honoured guests, be required to make speeches. A charming bi-lingual lady was placed between us to act as interpreter.

The main speaker of the evening was an eloquent physician who spoke at some length about the dangers of smoking and the horrors of cancer. I was able to understand a great deal of what he said as medical terms, especially those that describe the more harrowing symptoms of terminal disease, vary little in Latin-based languages. He spoke movingly and persuasively, so per-suasively in fact, that, as the minutes went by, the little plumes of smoke rising all over the crowded room, where well-fed Rotarians were enjoying their post-prandial cigars and cigarettes, began to disappear. This process of covert, shame-faced stubbing-out continued until I suddenly realised that the only remaining blot on the tobacco-free landscape was my own cigar. Rather a large one too, I'm ashamed to say.

I did not see how I could hope to follow such effective oratory.

Having had about ten minutes in which to prepare my speech I had resorted to the old technique of devising a good punch-line and building it round that. To pad it out, I turned to that in-valuable source, the genius of Charles Darwin.

What a mercy it was that Darwin made an expedition on horseback, independent of the *Beagle,* from Bahia Blanca to Buenos Aires, through this very region of Argentina.

His guides were *gauchos,* colourful, leathery cattle-men who lived on beef and slept on the ground by their horses. He met General Rosas, the flamboyant and bloodthirsty tyrant who was busy exterminating Indians. He examined the skeletal remains of Megatheroid animals — prehistoric giants — and exploded the long-held theory that they had become extinct owing to climactic changes reducing the vegetation of the pampas. It was a period when he was tireless, fearless and voracious in his appetite for new knowledge.

Some of this I told to the Rotarians of Mar del Plata, who listened to the simultaneous translation of my erudite neighbour with an air of polite bewilderment. I delivered my punch-line and sat down amidst thunderous applause.

'Follow that!' I whispered vilely to Suzanne. Follow it? She overtook it on the inside and left it standing.

Scorning an interpreter, she spoke in Spanish and the burden of her remarks was that she agreed with everything that I had said. You know what shameless plagiarists the Irish are. I say that this was the main theme of her speech but at the time I did not understand a single word of what she was saying. It was clear from a quick glance round the room that nobody else understood a word of what she was saying. Afterwards, she admitted to me that *she* hadn't understood a word of what she was saying. But the effect was electric. The audience was spellbound and, at the end of the speech, erupted. The nicotine-hating doctor and I exchanged looks of mutual sympathy and I lit a consoling cigarette.

One thing that evening taught me was a new respect for public figures. The effort of maintaining an air of bonhomie for five or six hours non-stop is torture. My facial muscles ached from constantly smiling. I longed to scowl or snarl, above all to yawn. The task of producing a moderately intelligent response to the endless refrain of 'Do you like Mar del Plata? Do you like Mar del Plata?' became increasingly difficult as the evening wore on and I began to think, secretly, that perhaps I loathed Mar del Plata.

It is an odd town. In fact, it is two towns. There is the old port, where the *Beagle* was anchored, which is rambling, run-down and pleasantly seedy and there is the new town, a Manhattan in miniature, with streets laid out on a grid system, high-rise office and apartment buildings and the biggest casino in the world.

From December to March Mar del Plata is invaded by over a million holiday-makers from Buenos Aires and it becomes a rip-roaring resort town. Out of season it is a quiet, sober place of shuttered villas and half-dismantled hotels where the permanent population goes about its business in a serious-minded spirit, tries to be as British as possible, tries to resist blueing the housekeeping in the casino (a sight worth seeing — rooms on an epic scale with thousands, not hundreds, of roulette tables and several square miles of green baize — I won £65.00), and puts up with the extraordinary weather.

On our first day in Mar del Plata we had a vivid example of the changeability of the climate. At about half past eight a violent north-east wind sprang up from nowhere. With her masts and rigging the *Beagle* carries a great deal of windage and we suddenly realised that she was dragging her anchor and was being driven towards the rocks. There was a dash to the engine room, the engines were started. Scores of fishing boats came streaming back into the harbour, seeking shelter from the storm which we could see was gathering out at sea. Massive black-grey clouds were blotting out the horizon beyond the entrance to the harbour. The wind died as suddenly as it had arrived. There was a short period of absolute calm and then the wind began to blow again, as hard as before, but from the south-east — a switch of 180 degrees! A few moments later we observed a weird cloud formation over the town. It looked exactly like an elongated swan's head and it had a sinister, opalescent sheen. Half an hour later the sun was shining. This whole phenomenon, we learned, is called a *sudesta* and is not popular among the fishing fraternity.

A few days later, in the afternoon, when the majority of the crew was ashore, a similar freak wind put us within a few feet of the rocks. The minute we saw that our anchor was dragging we started up the engines and began to raise the anchor. To our horror we discovered that a thick cable had become snarled up with the anchor cable and was preventing us from moving the ship out of danger. The bottom of the harbour at Mar del Plata seemed to be festooned with rotting old hawsers. Only some prompt and courageous action by Boatswain Dick averted a disaster. Grabbing a heavy knife, he shinned down the anchor cable, climbed on to the anchor itself and began hacking away at the obstructing hawser. The water was choppy, the ship was rolling, the anchor on which he was perched was swinging, but he kept hacking away until the final strands of the hawser parted when he clambered back on to the deck, his ripped hand streaming with blood.

Another day there was a violent hailstorm with stones so big we used them to ice drinks. One memorable night an electric storm raged over the town with such ferocity and such violent effects of lightning that it looked as if Mar del Plata was being blitzed and half the town was blazing.

In and amongst all this we were faced with the unpalatable fact that the starboard engine required major repairs which would involve flying out new parts from England. I know as much about the internal workings of engines as about Chinese irregular verbs but it seemed to me at the time that the starboard engine was entirely dismantled, large chunks of it were carried off to the workshops of a loquacious Italian engineer called Oscar while the remains littered the floor of the engine room and vital sprockets and spigots and spindles kept dropping into the bilges. Chief Engineer Haggis appeared to be permanently coated with oil. It was the long-suffering Robin who had the worst of it, though. It was his impossible duty to shepherd the spare parts through customs at Buenos Aires, a process which normally takes three weeks but which Robin managed to expedite in eighteen hours. This, incidentally, inspired another of his Schemes. The parts would be brought in as personal luggage, prominently labelled as modern sculptures with titles like 'Lateral Space Shape III', 'Ongoing Nude', 'Study for Female Figure' and so on. It was thought, however, that Argentine customs men might not be sufficiently *au fait* with the latest trends in European art and might twig that the masterpieces were really a lot of piston rings and crank-cases.

This is perhaps an appropriate moment to say a word about the heart-breaking difficulties involved in conducting any kind of business in South America. We have already seen something of the pettifogging, arbitrary, all-powerful nature of bureaucrats and officials. This is matched and sometimes surpassed by the dilatoriness, inefficiency, rapacity and deeply ingrained dishonesty of virtually everyone else with whom one deals.

You find a man who can sell you what you want to buy. You arrange to meet him. He doesn't turn up. You arrange another meeting. He is an hour late. Swallowing your pride — and your spleen — you explain what you want. He says he hasn't got it. You can see it on a shelf behind him. You point it out. 'Oh one of *those*,' he says pettishly. 'Why didn't you say so in the first place?' You did, but you are so staggered by the price he demands, you forget to tell him so. You say you'll think about it. For the next two hours you flog round various suppliers and take the advice of well-disposed locals and discover that he is asking treble the going rate. You return. You begin to haggle. You are tired, footsore and gasping for a drink. Your Spanish — at the best of times monosyllabic and heavily reliant on mime — begins to break down. Pencils and paper are produced and sums of money are scribbled down rapidly as you struggle to remember the exchange rate and your brains curdle in spasms of mental arithmetic. You know you are bound to lose. You know that he knows that you need what is on that shelf and he knows that you know. In this welter of inter-knowingness you agree a price. Smiles — sickly on your part, sharklike on his — and an exchange of cigarettes. You stagger out, the bewildered possessor of two metres of special radio cable.

Any large bill, especially if it involves a charge for labour, becomes the subject of protracted negotiation, often lasting a whole day, by the end of which you feel you could have settled the Schleswig-Holstein question in a couple of hours — it would have been straight-forward by comparison.

Sometimes you are simply speechless, as when the man who is to supply you with a thousand gallons of diesel turns up with a hand-cart, a pile of jerry-cans and a plastic funnel five inches long and seems positively offended when you mention pumps.

The engine problems kept us marooned in Mar del Plata for two weeks and did terrible things to our finances and our schedule. But we had no alternative. Without two sound engines we could not possibly venture into the tortuous and treacherous channels of Tierra del Fuego.

The surface of life in Mar del Plata appeared to be blandly civilised. It was easy to forget that this was a police state which had only recently emerged from what amounted to a civil war and still faced massive economic and social problems.

Yet, even in the most intimate or lavish entertainments there was a disturbing undercurrent.

The whole crew was invited to an *estancia*, a country estate of some grandeur, belonging to the mother of a young Argentine, Maxi Ganza, who had crewed in the *Beagle* during the Atlantic crossing and had then, alas, had to return to his studies at Cambridge.

The countryside near Mar del Plata reminded me of Wiltshire — lush, rolling downland — with a suggestion of Dartmoor in the stubby, rocky hills. The only alien note was struck by the endless avenues of eucalyptus trees. The house itself was a neo-Basque pile, like an overgrown chalet, set in spectacular gardens which were entirely English in lay-out and appearance. Floridly dressed *gauchos* grilled vast quantities of beef on an open fire in the garden — a whole animal had been slaughtered in our honour — the sun shone. During lunch the talk was highly political but among the trim lawns and spreading cedar trees there did not seem anything impermanent or volatile about life on an *estancia* in Argentina. After lunch, we were treated to a display of spectacular horsemanship as young *gauchos* exhibited their skills at breaking in wild horses. Yet the whole occasion was coloured by a sense of the fragility of this semi-feudal way of life.

There had been a curious incident on the way out to the *estancia* when the driver of the car had been forced to make an emergency stop. The manager of the farm, a White Russian of patrician elegance and charm, had displayed, during this brief and trivial traffic crisis, a panic fear. It was so startling, it could not pass without comment. He explained that until a few months ago he had been accompanied everywhere by body-guards and that, as the administrator of the estates of one of the richest families in Argentina, he was high on the list for assassination by the guerrillas.

The more intimate example of this feeling of ever-imminent danger and instability, was when I went to dinner with the family of a girl I had met.

It was a quiet, civilised evening with quiet, civilised people who were neither wildly rich nor distressingly poor but enjoyed that most blessed state of being quite content with what they had — the backbone, in fact, of any society. In their house there was warmth, intelligence and humour, a complete absence of bigotry and, above all, a sense of security. But in the hall were the visible scars of a bomb explosion. A year before guerrillas had detonated a device designed to wipe out the whole family.

The final, and most dramatic example of the violence and fear underlying the crisp, clean surface of Argentina — I never once saw a beggar or an undernourished mongrel or any other sign of extreme poverty — was when two members of the *Beagle*'s crew were machine-gunned by the military and that doughty old ship herself received a stray bullet or two in her innocent hull.

It was our last night in Mar del Plata. We had been moored in the same position, between the naval base and the yacht club, for a fortnight. Every hour, on the hour, throughout the night, one of the duty watch would run the little rubber dinghy, with outboard, to the jetty at the yacht club to pick up returning revellers or deposit anyone who wanted a night out on the town. This system is standard practice.

On the night in question, at ten o'clock, Jay ran Haggis ashore. Haggis had arranged an assignation with a young lady. They

a

b

Members of the crew in
costume:

a Jason and Jay

b Haggis

c Ravey Dave and Nigel

d Dick

d

Joint owners of the *Beagle*:
Robin Cecil-Wright
following in Darwin's
footsteps in a Fuegan
forest, and Mark
Litchfield dressed for
rough weather by the
BBC's costume depart-
ment

reached the jetty, Haggis disembarked and began walking towards the yacht club, Jay turned the boat round and began to head back towards the *Beagle*. A moment later, from somewhere behind the wire fence of the naval base, machine-guns began firing.

I was lying in my bunk, reading Darwin's views on the virtues of the mule. I heard the distant rattle of the guns and thought that it was an odd time for the military to be indulging in target practice. But there is a difference in the sound of random gun-fire and gun-fire aimed in your direction. I suddenly realised that the *Beagle* was being shot at. Dumping Darwin, I ran up on deck, and, keeping low, peered timorously out over the stern.

The rubber dinghy, with Jay crouched in the bottom, was zig-zagging towards the *Beagle* at full tilt. Bullets were whipping up the water all round it and singing through the air above the *Beagle*'s decks.

Jay slewed the dinghy round behind the *Beagle*, out of the firing line and, white and shaky, climbed aboard, uttering expletives.

In the meantime, on shore, Haggis was proceeding decorously towards the yacht club. Suddenly bullets began kicking up the dust round his feet and whining round his head.

Now people have said a lot of hard things about Scotsmen. Charles Lamb declared he had tried to like them all his life but was finally forced to give up in despair. Other writers have commented unfavourably on their ruthless inclination to make money and their even more ruthless disinclination to spend it. I have often wondered, when tortured beyond endurance by the howls and shrieks of the bagpipes, whether the entire nation should not be deported to Central Asia and their land turned into a vast country park for the exclusive benefit of the English. But one thing nobody would deny the Scotsman is courage ; or a certain sublime capacity to ignore the antics of half-crazed Sassenachs.

Finding himself being liberally sprayed with machine-gun bullets, Haggis did not make a run for the shelter of the yacht club buildings. He did not fling himself on to the ground, mumbling prayers. He did not dive headlong into the yacht basin. He just walked calmly on, fortified, no doubt, by an innate feeling that the marksmanship of a lot of South American sailors could be nothing compared to that of his own native grouse moors. Wondering vaguely what all the fuss could be about, he reached the comparative safety of the yacht club.

Here he found scenes of amazing panic. Waiters cowered under tables. Club officials crawled about in the shadows shrieking at him to get down, take cover. Haggis observed them with mild wonder. Suddenly the world was full of running soldiers. Haggis was slammed against a wall, a pistol was thrust into his face, he was frisked and bellowed at.

Speaking more loudly than usual, enunciating carefully — as if addressing someone who is slightly hard of hearing—he explained who he was and what he was doing. In English, I suspect. Various of his shipmates who were roistering in the club-house now trickled on stage and confirmed his innocence. Exonerated, he proceeded to his place of assignation and his subsequent adventures are not within the scope of this book.

In the *Beagle* there was an atmosphere of slightly hysterical hilarity with many uneasy wise-cracks. We decided that the best thing to do was to send a boat round through the fish-docks from where it was a short walk to the yacht club and pin notices up warning other members of the crew not to attempt to get back to the ship until daylight. This we did.

The next morning I expected an invasion of officers and police. Mystifying as the cause of all the shooting was, I was sure it would result in the arrest of the ship, if nothing worse.

Nobody came.

So the military authorities knew that a mistake had been made, potentially a terrible mistake since both Jay and Haggis could easily have been killed, and were seeking to hush it up. The *Beagle* hummed with outrage. Protests must be made in the strongest language, to the highest quarters. Nobody could remember the correct form of address to a British Ambassador.

Robin went off to do a little fact-finding in and around the port and came back with the following explanation of the drama. I should emphasise that no official explanation was ever offered.

A ship, sailing under the Spanish flag but with an Argentine crew, had put into Mar del Plata the day before. The authorities, suspecting that she was a gun-runner, had placed her under arrest. The crew was confined on board. The military received a tip-off that the gun-runners might attempt to put their contraband ashore at the yacht club during the night. The sentries at the naval base were ordered to keep a special watch. When they saw the *Beagle*'s dinghy approaching the yacht club, a sight which, after two weeks of precisely similar to-ings and fro-ings, might, you would have thought, have been familiar, they opened fire without a challenge or a warning.

If this was true, it was outrageous and we should do something about it. But our friends advised us strongly to let sleeping dogs lie. The military, they explained, was a law unto itself. If we made any kind of protest they would retaliate by arresting the *Beagle* and holding her at Mar del Plata pending further enquiries which might take anything up to two years. Forget it, they said. It happens every day.

They told us that, only recently, a group of red guerrilla frogmen had attacked the naval base with grenades. It was a sensitive area. The sentries were jumpy. Count yourselves lucky nobody was hurt. Forget it.

So we forgot it.

I was offered an alternative explanation of the outrage by a man in the yacht club who was also the only Argentine who ever put the anti-junta point of view to me. His version of recent events in Argentina differed widely from the standard middle-class view. According to him, and his name must be suppressed for obvious reasons, Argentina had been a rich country where the masses were oppressed and exploited by feudal landowners and bloated capitalists. Along came Perón. He was no doubt a corrupt and foolish man, though his wife Evita was adorable, but he stood for the rights and freedoms of the people. Betrayed by his political colleagues, out-manoeuvred by the cunning and conscienceless capitalists, he had been forced to flee for his life and Argentina was once more under the heel of the Army. By the time he returned he was too old for the Presidency and his new wife lacked experience and the only hope for liberty lay with the extreme leftists. But once again the Army proved too strong and went to all lengths in suppressing freedom.

I did not see why the army, or the navy, however brutal they may be, would want to machine-gun an old British sailing-ship. How would that help them suppress the guerrillas?

'It wasn't that', he explained. 'You don't understand. All these young soldiers, they are scared. They are fighting a war you know. All the time they are being bombed and shot at like your soldiers in the Isle of Wight.'

'You mean Northern Ireland?'

'Ireland, yes. It is the same here. The soldiers are nervous, all the time scared they will be killed. So they drink, they take drugs, hashish, cocaine, heroin even. All night, they drink and they smoke drugs and they go crazy and they see a little boat coming across the bay and it has no lights and they think — it's the guerrillas come to kill us. And they shoot at the boat because they are crazy with drugs and with fear.'

It was a bizarre picture of the internal life of the sombre, bleakly orderly naval base — and like most of the views, political and otherwise, of this engaging fantasist, it had its origins in the two bottles of whisky he tipped down his throat every day of his life.

The truth is that we were shot at in Argentina because Argentina is the sort of country where people get shot at all the time. The military authorities *are* nervous, they *are* fighting a war but, until the bullets start flying your way, you are unlikely to be aware of it, such is the apparent order and prosperity of the country and the open, hospitable character of its people.

The final answer to the question: 'Do you like Mar del Plata?' is an overwhelming feeling of gratitude that you live in Britain where the surface of life may have become a trifle tatty in recent years but where the foundations are strong.

6

MAR DEL PLATA — PUNTA ARENAS

13 – 21 November

THE area of the River Plate has proved, on two occasions, to be unhealthy for *Beagles*.

Beagle II was machine-gunned at Mar del Plata. On August 2nd 1832 *Beagle I* was fired on by a guard-ship as she made her approach to Buenos Aires, in the River Plate. She also encountered the same kind of obstructive behaviour from officialdom which, 150 years later, still bedevils the South American voyager and, to crown it all, when forced, by bureaucratic obfuscation, to put into Montevideo, on the opposite bank of the Plate estuary, she found herself involved in a minor revolution.

As the *Beagle* entered the roadstead at Buenos Aires, the guard-ship in question fired a blank warning shot across her bows. When Fitzroy ignored this, she fired again, sending shot whistling through the rigging. The *Beagle* proceeded out of range, Darwin, Fitzroy and all the other officers, fuming at what Darwin described as 'this insult to the British flag'. Fitzroy, in fact, roared defiance at the commander of the guard-ship:

'If you dare fire another shot at a British man-of-war you may expect to have your hulk sunk, and if you fire at *this* vessel, I will return a broadside for every shot!'

Splendid stuff; which got Fitzroy into hot water with the Admiralty (not for the first, or last time). How we on the second *Beagle* wished we could have conveyed something equally pithy to the trigger-happy sentries of Mar del Plata.

Just as we were thwarted in protesting to the British Ambassador in Argentina, Fitzroy was similarly prevented from making his feelings known to the British Resident at Buenos Aires, Mr. Fox. The *Beagle*'s crew was not allowed to land. Darwin and Wickham, with a large party of officers and men, attempted to land but were forced to turn back on the grounds that they might be carrying cholera. Since the *Beagle* was already nine months out from England and, in any case, was not intending to anchor in the port, it was an absurdly officious move on the part of the quarantine authorities. But there was nothing Fitzroy could do about it and he had to cross over to Montevideo.

Here there was further drama. The police and the captain of the port came on board and requested Fitzroy's assistance in quelling a mutiny of negro soldiers who were threatening to seize the town, putting the lives and property of the inhabitants, many of them British, in danger.

Fitzroy landed with a party of fifty men and, without bloodshed, seized and garrisoned the main citadel, which contained the armoury and magazine. He held the citadel for a vital twenty-four hour period which enabled government troops to get to the scene and surround the rebels, who surrendered. His action undoubtedly prevented a general massacre.

On 14th August President Rivera marched into the town to re-establish his government and on the 15th the *Beagle* received some good news from Buenos Aires. An official protest against the action of the guard-ship had eventually been lodged and the Buenos Aires government had responded with grovelling apologies and had arrested the commander of the offending vessel.

I wonder, in the present state of British foreign policy, whether a similar protest from *Beagle II* would have produced a similar result.

Beagle II left Mar del Plata on 13th November and, speaking for myself, I was thrilled to be at sea again. We were already several weeks late for our rendezvous with the BBC film crew in Punta Arenas, as a result of the enforced delays in Salvador and Mar del Plata and our course now lay directly south, through some of the most notoriously dangerous latitudes in the world—the Roaring Forties and the Fearsome Fifties. The statistical chances of being hit by a major storm were extremely high.

It would be appropriate at this point to consider how prepared the *Beagle* was to survive a really big blow in the Roaring Forties and the terrible following seas such a storm would entail. It certainly occupied my thoughts in those first few days and weighed heavily on Robin's mind since, ultimately, the safety of the ship and the lives of its crew, were his responsibility.

The conclusion I came to, rather a gloomy one, was that, if we were 'pooped' we would be in very serious trouble. A ship is 'pooped' when a wave breaks directly over the stern onto the poop deck and this is a standard occurrence in the waters of the Southern Ocean.

In the *Beagle*, all that stood between such a wave and the engines was a sturdy timber coaming behind the wheel, at a height of four feet above the level of the deck, and two flimsy doors, one of which, that leading into the engine room from the aft cabin, actually opened inwards!

Two big waves over the stern and the *Beagle* would be finished. The well by the wheel would fill up immediately. The pressure would burst open the door down into the aft cabin, green water would rush in a direct line down on to the engine-room door, which would hold for about a quarter of a second, and gentlemen at Lloyds would cast nervous eyes at the Lutine bell.

I would add that directly between the raging elements and the engine room, was my berth.

Supposing we escaped being pooped, how were we placed to deal with the other dangers we must expect? Our engines could produce a maximum speed of nine knots which would be utterly useless in the face of an even moderately strong wind in the Forties. If we had to shelter and were then struck by an on-shore wind and had to 'cut and run', in other words, abandon our anchors and head out to sea for safety, again a standard predicament—Fitzroy, the finest of seamen, lost five anchors in Tierra del Fuego alone—we would be left with precisely one spare anchor. Above all, our crew, though lacking nothing in courage, endurance and physical fitness, were largely inexperienced.

It was clear, from the strange atmosphere that now began to build up in the *Beagle*, that the same thoughts were in everyone's mind. The pleasure cruise was over. We were, by venturing so far south, in a ship ill-prepared to face the sort of weather we must expect, placing our lives at considerable risk. And the reason why the ship was so ill-prepared had its origins in the initial, frantic scramble of conversion and preparation back in 1976. Of course we had plans for strengthening the ship's defences against pooping ; we had a hundred plans for making the *Beagle* more sea-worthy ; but there had never been the time to put them into operation. In any case, no amount of planning or preparation could alter the fact that the *Beagle* was a sixty-year-old timber ship, sound enough, but inevitably extremely vulnerable.

The worst kind of fear is that which you experience in anticipating some formidable or dangerous situation. The actor who faces a first night audience suffers his most agonising moments as he waits in the wings. When the curtain rises and he steps onto the stage, he does so with a sense of release. The hours or days you spend waiting for something terrible to happen affect you much more than the terror itself. Your imagination, always more powerful than reality, is at work, your life becomes a waking nightmare which, even if suppressed, colours everything. You experience an almost pleasurable feeling of catharsis when at last the knock on the door you have been dreading echoes through the hall, or the avalanche falls or, indeed, the guerrillas storm the beach and attack the naval base with bazookas.

I do not wish to suggest that, as the *Beagle* passed through the Roaring Forties and into the Fearsome Fifties, everybody on board was consumed with a morbid dread and, like the young sentries in the drunkard's fantasy, went about in a haze of drink and drugs ; but the fact was that, as each new day dawned, bright, icy, breathless and eerily calm, an atmosphere of extraordinary unease pervaded the whole crew.

It was weird. Every morning I would go up on deck and I would see the same thing: a sea like molten glass with a blue-grey metallic sheen and a pale, hazy sky. In the air I could feel a touch of Antarctic ice, but the winds were gentle. I felt that this could not last, that it was a ghastly, silent prelude to a disaster.

There was a tacit taboo on talk about storms and catastrophes. Any such discussions ended in quarrels and arguments. Each night a few people got drunk. Alcohol-induced frolics on the deck suddenly turned into little fights and skirmishes. The tension was beginning to tell in harsh jokes, extravagant behaviour.

Mike found a piece of old sheep-skin, once intended to prevent chafing between the yards and the masts but long since abandoned, and turned it into a dog by tying a piece of rope round it. At regular intervals he would take his dog for a walk round the deck, stopping while it lifted its leg against the foremast, patting it and feeding it scraps from the galley.

And, as every day dawned calm, we were denied the longed-for catharsis.

One night in particular stands out as an example not only of the strange atmosphere on board the *Beagle* at this time but as a vivid proof that she really is a lucky ship.

It was Jonathan Jackson's twenty-first birthday. Suzanne baked a cake and we had champagne. We were finishing the celebration dinner when a call from the watch had us all rushing up on deck. Twenty or thirty miles to starboard a fantastic storm was raging.

The entire horizon was blotted out by massive banks of cloud, purple-black but incessantly glowing and blazing with great bolts of lightning. It was on an apocalyptic scale. Billions of volts of electricity were lighting up the sky and tearing through the clouds in forks and zig-zags which looked like the chart of some huge river-system, flashing off and on. It was an extraordinary spectacle, but, in the circumstances, a profoundly disturbing one.

It was silent.

We could imagine the huge rolls and cracks of thunder but we could hear nothing. Around us the sea was flat calm. We were spectators of a melodrama in which, we all knew in our hearts, we should be playing the role of victims—and we were drinking champagne.

In the centre of that terrible storm our ship would founder and go down and we were watching it as one watches a fire-work display on bonfire night.

Nobody said what everybody was thinking—'What if it's moving this way?'

It was.

It did. It passed over us, just a few hundred feet above our idly flapping sails, the clouds streaking overhead as in a crazily speeded up film. But the storm did not touch us. It leap-frogged us.

It was a night of wonders. Much later, towards dawn, we passed through a band of bio-luminescence which turned the sea a translucent pale gold. We could see vast shoals of fish which glowed silver. Dolphins, phosphorescent grey, weaved and plunged in a phantasmogoric under-water ballet. I had a feeling, which was in no manner due to the champagne, that we had sailed out of the real ocean into a dream-sea.

And the next day it was clear and dazzlingly bright and one felt that the *Beagle* was a charmed ship and that no storm could touch her.

At a steady eight knots, day and night, we were eating up the distance to Punta Arenas, rapidly putting some stuffing back into our badly winded schedule. One could not help wondering whether the Director General of the BBC did not have a direct line to the gods.

There were three new faces on board the *Beagle* and the ship's company had expanded to nineteen. Each of the three, in his own way, was a valuable addition to an already stimulating community.

Ned Kelly, the co-producer of *The Voyage of Charles Darwin* in charge of the natural history side of the programme, had abandoned first class air travel to Punta Arenas in favour of getting there the hard way, in the *Beagle*. His wit proved to be even drier than Manchester Geoff's and he stood his watches and slept on a banquette in the saloon with amazing good humour and fortitude. He was also a mine of information about sea-birds, fish and wild life in general and gave some point to our hitherto enthusiastic but limited observations of such things. In fact, apart from Charles Darwin himself, I cannot think of anyone nicer to go to sea with.

Christian Ruhle, who also joined us in Mar del Plata, was equally convivial and besides, being a Brazilian with French parents, spoke umpteen languages fluently, including Maori.

And then there was Victor. Victor was a shining example of how an old sailing ship attracts bizarre personalities. I don't suppose we will ever know whether Victor was a Walter Mitty type of fantasist, a smuggler, a spy or merely eccentric. The facts would fit any of these explanations. His residence aboard the *Beagle* was brief but spectacular.

He was an Argentine from Buenos Aires, a short, thick-set, powerful man with a permanently stubbled chin and the most extraordinary table manners I have ever encountered.

He had been recommended to us by a retired sea captain in Mar del Plata. This agreeable old salt had spent a lifetime in Tierra del Fuego and, while he did not claim to know Victor very well personally, believed him to be a man of solid experience who not only knew the Southern Ocean but was a radio expert to boot.

He seemed like the answer to a prayer. We needed tough, experienced hands and our radio was, to say the least of it, on the blink. By the time Victor had finished with it, it had developed several nervous tics and was well on the way to being blinded altogether.

I claim no particular credit, but I suspected from the word go that Victor might not be all he was cracked up to be, or indeed all that he cracked himself up to be.

He first appeared a few days before we left Mar del Plata and arrived with about half a ton of what purported to be special diving gear. From the quantity of mysterious packages and bundles you would have thought that if it was diving gear Victor was more than equipped to raise the Titanic. He heaved all this stuff on board, stowed it, or rather cached it, in inaccessible places and then departed for Buenos Aires in a panic. Victor lived in a permanent panic. He spoke a variety of languages but at such speed and with such a pronounced accent that Spanish, English or Portuguese were indistinguishable one from another— and incomprehensible.

Victor said that he was desperate to join the *Beagle* not because he needed a job but out of his passionate love of sailing ships and the sea. But he had to go to B.A. in order to sell the lead keel of his own boat. This really was his story. Robin pointed out that he was only waiting for a few last engine parts, which could arrive at any moment, and then the *Beagle* would be off. He would not be able to wait for Victor. With a wealth of gesture, a torrent of words and much splattering of the local scenery with food particles—we were having lunch in the yacht club—Victor said it did not matter. He would go to B.A. and he would return. If the *Beagle* had gone—*tant pis!* But what about all his diving gear stowed away in the *Beagle*?

'So,' cried Victor, removing a large piece of gristle from his mouth with his fingers, examining it briefly and popping it back in again, 'I lose my things. I do not care. I am a man. I can work. I can make money. I can buy new things. But I am in love with your ship. I do not care about the risk. I have a business. I can sell my lead for twenty thousand dollars . . .' and so on and so forth.

I thought to myself, this man is either irrational or dishonest. The idea of his simply abandoning what he boasted was thousands of pounds worth of diving gear because he was in love with the *Beagle* was preposterous. However I kept my peace ; it was none of my business and I averted my eyes as the gristle came out for another airing.

Victor went off to B.A. and he returned bearing an enormous canvas bag, an hour or two before the *Beagle* sailed.

His first task on board was the radio. He claimed to have an extensive knowledge of local call signs and frequencies and guaranteed to put us in touch with coastal stations for weather reports and communication with the BBC, who would by now be installed in Punta Arenas and wondering where the hell the *Beagle* had got to.

One evening I happened to be passing the chart-house, where the radio was housed, and was stopped in my tracks by the most extraordinary noise. It was a gurgling, tweeting, clucking, burring, trilling noise and it sounded like a demented corn-crake. I poked my head round the door and there was Victor, his face solemn, his heavy brows drawn in concentration, burbling into the radio mike. He looked like a bandit doing farmyard impressions. The spectacle was ludicrous enough but I managed to control myself until I saw Robin and Mark. They were gazing at Victor with rapt attention, as if they were in the presence of some wonder worker who was about to turn water into wine. It was too much for me. I staggered away, doubled up with laughter. A very cross Robin followed me.

'For God's sake. You'll upset him.'

'But what's he *doing*?' I asked feebly.

'It's some sort of special Argentine call sign.'

'It *can't* be.'

'Since when were you an expert in radio?'—This with cold hauteur.

'Well, has anybody answered yet? Apart from a love-sick albatross or two?'

'Well, er, not so far. There's something wrong with the aerial.'

So Victor said he'd repair the aerial. For several days he was to be seen hopping about the rigging, swathed in yards of copper wire. It was soon clear that if you valued your life you didn't go up aloft when Victor was around. The man was a menace, bouncing about on the foot-ropes, squeezing you off the shrouds, jabbering hoarsely. To add to his already eccentric manners, he now took to wearing a safety harness. A job lot of these contraptions had been bought in England and everybody was issued with one but, typically, the instruction leaflet had been lost, and nobody knew how they were supposed to fit. Victor wore his where athletes wear a jock-strap and he was never known to remove it, not even in bed. If he had fallen out of the rigging, and I was sure he would, he was even clumsier than me, the sudden jerk on the webbing would have done him unspeakable damage.

There were other peculiarities of behaviour. Every other day he would walk round the decks, fully clothed, shampooing his hair, rinsing it from a bucket of sea-water. In the process his shoulders became soaked and the decks were splattered with drops of foam. But it was at table that he was most fascinating.

He was the archetypal grab-and-guzzle man and a great swiller of other people's drinks. He never seemed to grasp, or didn't choose to grasp, that each individual paid for his own drink. It was unwise to sit too close to him without an umbrella.

The end of Victor was as sudden and mysterious as the beginning. When we docked in Punta Arenas, he was the first man ashore. He was observed deep in conversation with another man who had obviously been waiting for the *Beagle* to come alongside the wharf. Their air was urgent and conspiratorial.

Victor returned to the ship and began unloading all his gear. Robin had been to the police office with all our passports and now came back with them, duly stamped. As he handed them round I saw Victor go ashen and sway slightly as if he were about to faint. He kept his passport in a plastic case and he had discovered that this was empty. He was almost speechless with distress. Robin, slightly bemused by this extreme reaction, said he had probably dropped the passport in the chart-house. And so it turned out.

The next surprise was that Victor announced he was catching the next plane back to Buenos Aires. Robin was amazed and rather annoyed. The whole point in taking Victor on was that he purported to know Tierra del Fuego like the back of his hand. But Victor was adamant. He must go.

He had been with us for precisely nine days. A suspiciously brief love-affair with the *Beagle*. In that time, all he had managed to achieve was an almost permanent radio silence.

It was obvious that he had used the *Beagle* as a convenient way of getting to Punta Arenas. Argentina and Chile are currently at odds—almost at war, in fact—over disputed territory in Tierra del Fuego and it is difficult for Argentines to visit the extreme south of Chile. Was Victor a spy, using the *Beagle* as a cover to get into the Magellan Straits? Certainly his reaction when he thought the police had kept his passport showed that he was in terror of *something*. Or was the answer in those boxes and bundles of alleged diving-gear which were never opened or even removed from their hiding-places? Was Victor a smuggler? The charitable maintain that he was merely dotty. Even if he was up to something, I hope he got away with it. Because in spite of everything, he had a good heart and one couldn't help being rather fond of him.

Victor has made me jump ahead of my story. (A menace to the last!)

As I have said, our progress down to the Magellan Straits was exceptionally steady. We had calculated that it would take over two weeks because we thought we were bound to encounter contrary winds ; now it looked as if we would reach Punta Arenas in eight or nine days. Even so, we did not feel justified in making the stop that we had planned, at the Valdes peninsula, where thousands of whales go to mate.

Accounts of travel are always accounts of opportunities missed. Travellers never have enough time or enough money or enough information. However far you go, however remote the regions you visit, on your return you will always find some infuriating old bore who will say: 'My dear fellow, do you mean to tell me you went all the way to Outer Mongolia and you didn't visit the ruined temple at Kazlwdrprdizan? Good Lord, it's the only thing worth seeing. Walls lined with solid gold, you know, and studded with rubies.' Or even worse, this kind of thing: 'If only you'd told me you were going! The Governor's one of my oldest friends. He would have given you a permit to visit Oggabonga-land—you know, the Oggabonga, supposed to be descended from one of the lost legions of Alexander the Great. Speak a form of Macedonian dialect. Fascinating. Dying out fast, though.'

Of the *Beagle* voyage, people have said to me: 'You mean you didn't go round Cape Horn? Most odd.' It is useless to explain to them that we had neither the time nor the requisite insurance cover to go round Cape Horn, that we went to much more interesting and beautiful and equally dangerous places in Tierra del Fuego ; it is also rather distressing because we all wanted to go round Cape Horn, just as we all wanted to go to Valdes, especially as it was the middle of the whale-mating season. But we weren't tourists or naturalists, we were being paid to do a job and our job was to get to Tierra del Fuego as quickly as possible.

We did, however, indulge ourselves in one brief stop at an island called Tova which is a breeding ground for Magellanic or Jackass penguins.

The penguins are called jackass for the very good reason that their cry is exactly like the hoarse braying of a jackass, a sound which, if heard way out at sea by the uninitiated, causes some alarm and confusion.

Tova is a desolate and lonely place, one of a group of long, flat islands off the coast of Patagonia, which is itself empty and featureless. The only inhabitants of Tova are four kelp-gatherers who live in a rude hut by the shingle beach. They have a radio but no boats. A supply ship makes regular visits to the island but otherwise they are alone with the penguins during the mating season, a few armadillos, some rabbits and carracarra birds. This, apart from insects, is the only wild life of the island. These men must have been astonished to see the *Beagle* sailing into their bay, but they were friendly, if very shy.

The island is covered in low, bushy scrub. The penguins nest in burrows under the bushes and, at the approach of humans, utter belligerent hisses. It is difficult to imagine a more ungainly sight than a large jackass penguin waddling along on land. They look like flat-footed head waiters slightly the worse for drink. When they peer out at you from their burrows they move their heads from side to side, glaring at you first with one eye, then the other as they have monocular vision and are unable to focus both eyes on you simultaneously. Their young utter a wistful, whistling squeak. We examined hundreds of nests, some with young, others with clutches of two or three eggs and one, a rarity, with as many as four. The number of deserted burrows and abandoned eggs was disturbing. We suspected that our kelp-gathering friends were supplementing their diet with penguin egg omelettes and roast penguin on Sunday. Penguin eggs are, in fact, a delicacy, prized in some countries, like South Africa, above caviar. In most countries their consumption is banned—the South African government releases only a few hundred a year—as penguins, like so many other delighful creatures, are threatened with extinction.

If the penguins look like vaudeville clowns on land, in the water they disport themselves with marvellous grace and speed, diving and plunging like dolphins and with something of the same zest.

We saw several pairs of carracarra wheeling about in the sky. Darwin is somewhat disparaging about these graceful, eagle-like birds. He says that since they live mainly on carrion and looted eggs, they cannot be considered true birds of prey. I can vouch for the fact that they are ferocious in defending their own nests. I climbed a disused beacon tower and when I reached the top found myself staring at two carracarra eggs which were about six inches from my nose. I was fumbling for my camera when a most unnerving squawking and shrieking made me look hastily to my right. Two carracarra were bearing down on me. For a split second I thought, This will make a good photograph but then, as the outraged birds began to attack, my enthusiasm for a dramatic snap suddenly waned and I shinned back down the tower, routed.

I found it curious that the kelp-men possessed no boats. They relied on the tides to wash the kelp ashore and then collected it into large heaps. Kelp is a tough, leathery form of seaweed which abounds off the coast of Patagonia but especially in the tortuous channels and inlets of Tierra del Fuego. The roots, thick rope-like tentacles, often extend down two hundred feet and wrap themselves round rocks. The leaves contain pods of air which allow them to float and where conditions are favourable vast, dense, tangled underwater forests of kelp form. These are deadly for a swimmer and as I was soon to discover for myself, almost impossible for the oarsman. Kelp is a rich source of iodine, fertiliser and other useful substances and where you find kelp you also find a profusion of other marine life, fish, mussels, limpets.

I was on the morning watch on Saturday 19th November when we passed by Cabo Curioso, behind which lies the natural harbour of St. Julien, home of historical coincidence.

A brilliant night-sky, in which the Magellanic Clouds, clusters of innumerable stars, showed like streaks of mist, gave way to a noble sunrise, the sky ominously suffused with red. There was a bitter wind and the ship was rolling fairly heavily and up on the topsail yard your hands soon grew numb as you furled the sails, but none of this mattered in the light of the exciting historical associations offered by the sweeping view of Cabo Curioso.

This was where Ferdinand Magellan anchored at Easter 1520 and where Sir Francis Drake anchored fifty-seven years later in August 1577. And at St. Julien both admirals faced mutiny.

Magellan's great expedition, during which the globe was circumnavigated for the first time, had been bedevilled by politics and sabotage from the outset. Its purpose was to find an alternative route to the rich spice islands of the Moluccas and attempt to prove that, in the division of the new world between Spain and Portugal ordained by the Pope, the Moluccas lay within the Spanish sphere.

Magellan was a bitter, introspective man, at war with himself. He was also a ruthless and dictatorial commander but one of unique drive, determination and expertise. By the time the expedition, which consisted of five ships, reached St. Julien, Magellan's captains were weary of storms, half-rations and their admiral's high-handed methods. Three of them, Cartagena of the

San Antonio, Quesada of the *Concepción* and De Elcano, convinced that the expedition was bound to fail, mutinied on Easter Day.

Magellan's reaction was swift, effective and absolutely ruthless. He seized the *Victoria*, whose Captain, Mendoza, was cut down, then drawn and quartered and the other rebel ships quickly capitulated. Quesada was murdered by his own servant, and Cartagena and a priest who had supported the mutiny, were marooned.

Magellan left St. Julien at the end of August and, after terrible storms, finally rounded the Cape of the Eleven Thousand Virgins and sailed into the Strait which bears his name. It is said that when Magellan received confirmation that the channel did indeed lead to the Pacific, he wept. He named the cape at the Pacific end of the straits Deseado, the longed-for.

Magellan did not live to complete the circumnavigation of the world. Entering the Pacific, the fleet was dispersed and largely destroyed by storms. The flagship, the *Trinidad*, took a hundred days to reach the nearest Pacific island, a long agony of starvation and disease in which the men ate the leather from the cross-trees and only the iron will of the admiral preserved the ship. It has been suggested that the account of this grim passage by the expedition's chronicler, Antonio Pigafetta, was the inspiration of Coleridge's *Rime of the Ancient Mariner*.

Magellan was killed in a skirmish with savages on the island of Mactar in the Philippines on April 27th 1521. Of his fleet, only the *Trinidad* and the *Victoria* reached the Moluccas. As to the untold wealth Magellan and his patron, King Charles of Spain, had dreamed of gaining in the rich, spice islands ; it was estimated that the expedition made an overall profit of £300.00.

Sir Francis Drake's expedition, on the other hand, is reckoned to have made over two hundred thousand pounds in terms of sixteenth-century money values. But then Drake was a professional pirate.

That he too should have had a mutiny at St. Julien is one of those coincidences so useful to writers. Drake's mutiny was neither so extensive nor so bloody as Magellan's. It was really the work of one man, Thomas Doughty, and its causes have ever since been a source of endless speculation to historians.

Doughty was a courtier and a politician, a man of means, a shareholder in the expedition, and the agent of God knows which of the many factions who intrigued for power at the court of

Queen Elizabeth I. It has been suggested that he was an enemy of the Earl of Leicester, who was Drake's patron, and that Drake had been instructed to get rid of him during the voyage. It is more probable that Doughty, who was a man of fashion rather than a seaman, was simply fed up with the hardships and discomforts of the voyage and, considering himself, as an aristocrat, to be the superior of the low-born Drake, decided to turn back. Drake could have construed this as mutiny but it is surprising that he went to the lengths he did.

Doughty was arrested, tried and sentenced to death. And it is at this point that the story ceases to be merely dramatic and becomes bizarre.

An hour before the execution, Drake and Doughty breakfasted together, according to eyewitnesses, chatting away in the most amiable manner. Alas, there is no record of what they said to each other ; but one cannot help admiring Doughty's fortitude and his power as a conversationalist in the face of imminent death.

The *Beagle* rounded the Cape of Eleven Thousand Virgins (which seems like an awful lot of virgins) and entered the Magellan Straits at 0812 hours on Sunday 20th November. We passed a long, low spit of land which is called, with delightful bathos, Dungeness.

During the previous day we had been amazed by a curious effect of light refraction in which a passing ship had appeared as a black rectangle and alarmed by heavy swells which proved to be the tail end of yet another storm evaded by the *Beagle*. Now in the famous Straits, we enjoyed warm sunshine and absolute calm though there was enough of a nip in the air to remind us that we were less than a thousand miles north of Antarctica. Above us was the wide, pale blue, cloud-flecked sky of Patagonia and all around the land stretched away, flat, sandy-brown. In the foreground was a large oil-drilling rig.

We lingered for an hour or so, waiting to see if any vessels of the Chilean navy would make contact. The original plan had been that the Chileans would provide us with a pilot and an escort down to Punta Arenas. Nothing happened. We twiddled at the radio, Victor chirruping away like a one-man dawn chorus, but without success,

We decided to proceed alone.

The first narrows in the Magellan Straits are notoriously dangerous. An exact balance of tide, wind and current is required to negotiate them successfully. We consulted our Bible, the *South America Pilot*, and decided to have a go.

'Shit or bust,' as Mark succinctly put it.

We entered the narrows at 1836 hours and were carried through the danger zone by a fast current, our hearts in our mouths and our eyes fixed apprehensively on the eddies and whirlpools seething on the surface of the water.

In the evening we anchored at the Isla Isabella, having decided that it would be best to put into Punta Arenas at a civilised hour in the morning.

It was no mean feat of seamanship to have passed through these narrows unscathed.

We weighed anchor at 0740 and by 1030 we were in sight of Punta Arenas. We hove to a few hundred yards from the docks and waited. And waited. Eventually a launch was sent out and a pilot came on board.

Studiously ignoring all this gentleman's instructions Robin brought the *Beagle* alongside the jetty with smooth precision. The look of intense concentration on his face showed that there was going to be no running aground or other disasters. This was an important moment.

Our port side gently kissed the wall of the jetty. Lines were swiftly secured to the bollards. The engines fell silent.

We had made it.

The *Beagle* had returned to the Land of Fire.

Everyone was moved and, being English, avoided each other's eyes. The tension of the last ten days evaporated. We were happy.

And blissfully unaware that we were the most wanted ship in Chile.

Part Two

TIERRA DEL FUEGO

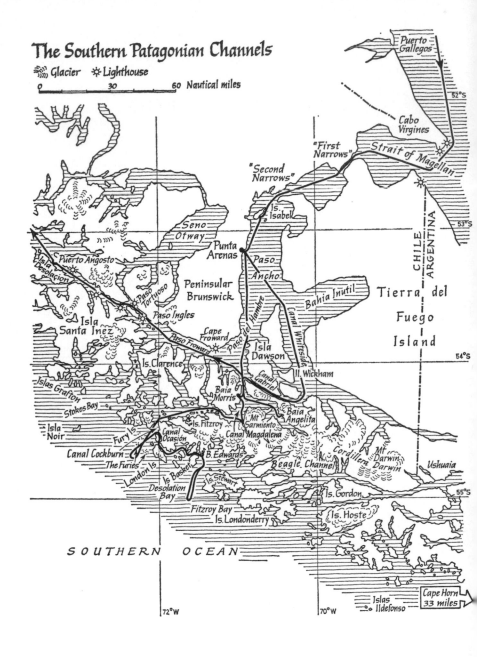

The Southern Patagonian Channels

≋ Glacier ☀ Lighthouse

0   30   60 Nautical miles

Puerto Gallegos

52°S

Cabo Virgines

"First Narrows"   Strait of Magellan

"Second Narrows"

Is. Isabel

53°S

Seno Otway

Punta Arenas   Paso Ancho

Puerto Angosto

Isla Desolacion

Paso Tortuoso

Peninsular Brunswick

Bahia Inutil   Tierra del Fuego Island

Paso Ingles

Paso del Hambre

Canal Whiteside

CHILE   ARGENTINA

Isla Santa Inez

Cape Froward   Paso Froward   Isla Dawson

54°S

Is. Clarence

Il. Wickham

Islas Grafton

Canal Gabriel

Baia Morris

Stokes Bay

Isla Noir

Is. Fitzroy   Mt Sarmiento   Baia Angelita

Canal Ocasion   Canal Magdalena

Fury Is

Canal Cockburn

The Furies

London Is   B. Edwards   Beagle Channel   Cordillera   Mt Darwin

Ushuaia

Is. Bosken   Is. Stewart   Is. Gordon

Desolation Bay

55°S

Fitzroy Bay

Is. Hoste

Is. Londonderry

SOUTHERN   OCEAN

Islas Ildefonso

Cape Horn 33 miles

72°W   70°W

7

PUNTA ARENAS

21 November - 1 December

THE *Beagle* had committed three grave crimes.

She had arrived in Chilean waters without flying a courtesy flag. This was bad.

She had come through the Straits without a pilot. This was worse.

She had done these things without the Chilean navy's having been aware that the *Beagle* was within five hundred miles of the Magellan Straits. We had sailed blithely through their entire defence and monitoring system completely undetected and the first they knew about our arrival was when we hove in sight of Punta Arenas. This was appalling.

On the first count, we were guilty ; but there were exonerating circumstances. Naturally we had provided ourselves with what we thought was the Chilean flag. When it was far too late to do anything about it we realised that the flag which we had bought in Brazil was that of the previous régime which it would have been less than tactful to fly from our masthead.

On the second count we had a specious defence in that as we were classed as a yacht the law did not require us to take on a pilot. Since nobody seemed very clear on the exact legal position, the point was not pressed on either side. Luckily the authorities were unaware of Robin's explosive views on pilots.

On the third count, we were innocent. It had never been our intention to elude anybody's navy although we did feel a sneaking pride in having proved that Britannia can still rule the waves, even if only by mistake. But, of course, we were made the victims of a massive blame-transference operation. It was highly embarrassing for the Chilean navy. This remote southern region is, in national defence terms, the country's Achilles heel. It is also their only potential source of oil wealth. The navy is supposed to keep a rigorous watch over the approaches to the Straits. No ships are allowed into Chilean waters without official clearance. How could the *Beagle* have rounded Cape Virgines undetected? Especially as specific arrangements had been made, at the request of the BBC, for a special watch to be kept for her and an escort provided. My private view is that the answer lies in the date. We rounded Virgines on a Sunday, even in these wild latitudes, a day of rest. The official verdict was that the fault lay in the *Beagle*'s defunct radio. Thank you, Victor.

If the Chilean navy was surprised and furious to see the *Beagle* arrive, Chris Ralling, the producer of *The Voyage of Charles Darwin,* was surprised and delighted. The last communication he had received from the ship had given him an accurate estimated time of arrival and had been enough to quell a small Magellan-type mutiny among his own crew, but when no report came from the navy that the *Beagle* had been sighted off Virgines he assumed we were delayed and probably would not arrive until Wednesday or Thursday. He was sitting in his hotel bedroom, tapping away at the script when looking up from his typewriter and gazing out at the sea, no doubt seeking inspiration, he saw the *Beagle* sailing down the Strait. He was waiting on the jetty when we finally docked and I have never seen an expression of such profound relief on the face of any man.

Our first task in Punta Arenas was to form a diplomatic deputation to visit the naval HQ and smooth their ruffled plumes. Robin, Mark and I went along to grovel. We were received by the admiral's ADC. Initially, the atmosphere in the sumptuous, high Victorian room, was glacial. Chileans, however, have a sense of humour, which, in the case of naval officers, many of whom have been trained by the Royal Navy, includes a sense of the ridiculous. Chilean naval officers are also very fine seamen and, as we chatted to the ADC, I began to realise that part of his willingness to forgive and forget the *Beagle*'s sad lapse stemmed from a genuine admiration of the feat she had performed in making it to Punta Arenas intact in the first place. The ADC was deeply impressed.

Until that moment I had hardly been aware that we had performed a feat of seamanship likely to command the admiration of other seamen. I had been too closely involved in the day-to-day farces, frights, minor calamities, crises and the sheer physical strain of it all to have any perspective. Now I began to wonder whether the reason for the navy's failure to keep a watch out for the *Beagle* might not have been simply because, understanding the problems, they never really thought it likely that she would arrive at all. Catching sight of myself in one of the looking-glasses which formed part of the decor of the *fin-de-siècle* mansion in which the navy was housed, I thought that even I looked something like a sailor, slimmer, bronzed, with a full beard and generally smacking of salt spray. I began to think less about the times when we must have appeared like a bunch of lubberly lunatics, more about our achievement in having arrived at Punta Arenas in a fit enough condition for the gruelling film schedule and with just enough time to complete it. I thought of all the obstacles, bureaucratic, mechanical and human which we had overcome and more particularly of Robin, whose determination, drive, energy and unflagging capacity for taking decisions had turned a Scheme into a reality.

Good relations having been established with the Chilean navy, we now proceeded to fall out with the BBC.

There has never been, and there will never be, a large-scale enterprise involving travel to remote regions which has not, at some point, been threatened with internecine dispute. A perceptive analysis of any major expedition from Magellan and his mutinous captains to a twentieth-century assault on a mountain or indeed the voyage of the *Beagle* itself will show that such disputes are an inevitable, if unpalatable, ingredient in the mixture. It would have been a miracle indeed if something of the sort had not happened during the second voyage of the *Beagle*.

The nature of the dispute is neither very interesting nor particularly relevant, though there are some curious parallels in Captain Fitzroy's dealings with the Admiralty when the *Beagle* was at Valparaiso in 1834 which almost led to his resignation. Nor did the dispute, since it was not concerned with any individuals at Punta Arenas, sour any personal relationships, except temporarily. The crews of the *Beagle* and the BBC were very good friends and, after a brief hiatus, remained so.

The effects, in fact, were more comic than tragic. Our only link with the ultimate court of appeal in London was a single telex machine housed in the office of a travel agent. Punta Arenas is a small town and its main square, where the statue of Magellan (one of the very few public monuments to this great man) stands, the admiral himself gazing with grim disapproval at the modern façade of the Cape Horn hotel, has many of the attributes of the parish pump. It is not a situation conducive to secrecy. Members of the temporarily opposed factions kept bumping into each other on their way to the telex office. The following sort of dialogue was a daily occurrence.

A. (having just dispatched a rip-snorting message to London):
'Oh, er, hello B. We're just on our way to, er, to see the consul.'

B. (icy, edgy): 'Really? You're going the wrong way.'

A. (with a nervous laugh): 'We've just got to pop into the
hotel first.' Seeking to gain the advantage: 'Where are you off
to, then?'

B. (patently heading for the telex office, flustered): 'Oh, er,
just thought I'd do a bit of shopping.'

A. (twisting B's tail): 'Come and have a drink.'

B. (wriggling): 'Love to. In, er, about ten minutes? Something to do.'

Moment of mutual embarrassment.

A. 'Yes, of course. See you in ten minutes then?'

B. 'Right . . . well . . . see you, then.'

A's and B's simultaneous thoughts as they part with an
exaggerated air of heartiness:

A.—'He's sneaking off to the telex.'

B.—'He's just sneaked out of the telex office.'

The majority of the *Beagle's* crew considered Punta Arenas a
dump. I liked it.

I liked the streets of trim, corrugated iron houses and the more
pompous Edwardian buildings in the centre. I liked the sharp,
invigorating air and the bright, crystal light when the sun shone.
From the port you could see, in the distance, beyond the Strait,
the snow-capped peaks of Tierra del Fuego.

In many respects Punta Arenas is like an English provincial
town twenty or thirty years ago. There are scores of old-fashioned
drapers' shops. In the windows dummies with short-back-and-
sides or bobbed hair display New Look fashions. The better
shops run to mahogany counters and those fascinating overhead
tramlines on which dusty capsules, containing money and bills,
clatter back and forth to a central accounts office with a frosted
glass door on which the manager's name is prominently stencilled.

The offices of the British consul, Mr. King, were marvellously
evocative—drab cream and chocolate walls, roll-top desks, hissing
gas-fires, cabinets full of brittle, yellowing papers and a huge,
green safe with a brass handle. It made you think of unfashion-
able virtues like courtesy, thoughtfulness and painstaking
kindness and you soon discovered that Mr. King practised all
three.

Another temple of nostalgia was the English club—or the de-

caying remnants of the English club. It was a shrine, created
by expatriates, in which they could read their two week old
copies of *The Times* in the sombre seclusion of a brown,
buttoned leather, chesterfield, drink their whisky-and-sodas in a
gloomy bar with copper-topped tables and large, mahogany
plaques whose faded lettering told of long-dead champions of
golf tournaments and snooker competitions. In the great billiard
room were three tables, now covered in the dust and rubble of
the cracking ceiling but once, in the heyday of British enterprise
in southern Patagonia and Tierra del Fuego, quiet green battle-
fields where merchants and sheep farmers potted and snookered
each other and talked about the price of wool and reminisced
about the Old Country. Today there are few British left in
Punta Arenas. The club is open only for a few hours each night
and its high, deserted rooms with their portraits, slightly askew,
of Edward VII and George V, their Roll of Club Presidents,
their shelves of superannuated reference books, will be gutted to
make way for a bank.

Engine trouble now made it impossible for the *Beagle* to leave
Punta Arenas on schedule and the result was that I had my first
experience of the scenic grandeur of Tierra del Fuego not in the
Beagle but in an ex-Rhine river-boat called the *Argonauta*. The
Argonauta had been chartered by the BBC as a support vessel to
house the actors and film crew while shooting among the un-
inhabited channels and islands. It was decided to send the
Argonauta on ahead to Angelito Bay, an anchorage in the very
heart of Tierra del Fuego's main island near which was a glacier.
Four members of the *Beagle*'s crew were to go on ahead with the
Argonauta to act as costume extras and to handle the boats —
fibreglass replicas of the sort of craft carried on the original
Beagle. I was one of the four.

Having spent two months grumbling about the discomforts of
the *Beagle*, I now felt uneasy in the comparative luxury of the
Argonauta. I had never consciously thought of the *Beagle* as
home but I can describe the misery I felt as the *Argonauta*
steamed away from the dock at Punta Arenas only as acute
home-sickness. At all places we had visited on the voyage down
from Salvador I experienced a strong desire to go off on my own,
to get away from the crowd. I had found all the togetherness
irksome at times. Now that I was being separated from the
Beagle I felt suddenly lonely. The feeling was not entirely
irrational. I did not know the BBC personnel as well as my

three companions and, since the dispute was reaching a climax in a blizzard of telexes, there was a certain, shall we say, atmosphere on the *Argonauta*. It did not help matters that I was suffering from a hangover, and that I was extremely worried about the outcome of the Great Dispute.

In such a situation there is only one thing to do. Go to bed. So that is what I did.

I awoke early the next morning feeling depressed, disorientated and half suffocated by the foetid heat in the cabin which contained four bodies and about a quarter of a cubic inch of air. The ship was silent and still. Suddenly, my sleep-clogged mind registered the fact that *we must be there* and, scrambling into some clothes, I hurried up on deck.

The sight that met my eyes, so stunning was its beauty, evaporated my depression and malaise in an instant.

We were anchored in a small bay which, owing to a rocky point which masked its entrance, appeared to be land-locked. Opposite me was a tiny beach, a smear of grey-brown in the dark rocks which ringed the bay. Behind the rocks rose the evergreen beech forests, impenetrable labyrinths of twisted boughs and moss-grown trunks, rising almost sheer to the snow-line. Through the cleft between the two mountains dominating the bay was a seemingly endless vista of spiked, white peaks gleaming through the early morning mist. It was absolutely calm, the sea a silken sheet of green-black, and absolutely silent.

These were Darwin's 'still solitudes', each detail of sea, rocks, trees, mountains conforming exactly to everything I had ever read about the Fuegan landscape, but the sum of them adding up to a wild beauty beyond anything I had imagined. In the days that followed I walked through the forests, I explored glaciers, I climbed hills, I saw, from the deck of the *Beagle*, immeasurably grander conjunctions of mountain and sea, I even took an inadvertent dip or two in the numbing water, but that first glimpse of Tierra del Fuego in the Bay of the Little Angel remains for me the most magical not because it was the first or even because it cured me of my mental distempers, but because it was the perfect realisation of a dream and the reality was more beautiful than the dream. Facts are better than dreams, Winston Churchill once declared and no doubt he was right ; but when facts conform to dreams, that is better still.

What on earth am I writing, or indeed over-writing about? What was this dream?

It is one that goes back to childhood. I would spend hours poring over maps of Tierra del Fuego, deriving some strange comfort from the fact that there were virtually no towns or roads; just thousands and thousands of uninhabited islands. I was obsessed with islands. I knew about Magellan and Drake and Anson and the terrible sufferings they had endured — the storms that raged for days on end, the williwaws, freak winds that built up to terrifying speeds in the narrow mountain gorges then howled down into the channels and destroyed ships in a minute. I knew about the fierce, shy Ona Indians who had once trapped and hunted in the great, snowbound forests. The horrors of Cape Horn were part of family legend. My great-grandfather lost many of his clipper ships in those legendary waters. At the same time, I knew too that in summer you could find little meadows of an English green in this Land of Fire, that pioneers had carved vast sheep ranches out of the virgin forest.

I was convinced that when the bombs started dropping, when the cities were heaps of radio-active rubble and the remnants of populations scrabbled about in the ruins with their bodies disintegrating, I would be safe on my island in the 'uttermost South'. The generation born under the shadow of the mushroom cloud was prone to such fantasies.

Later on I realised that even Tierra del Fuego would not be far enough away to escape the holocaust and one was probably better off in Piccadilly Circus, liquidised in the first seconds of Armageddon. But the desire to go there never died, rather increased as I read about oil exploration in the Magellan Straits and boat-loads of American tourists slapping back well-iced martinis in well-heated saloons where the Yaghan women had once dived for mussels and the pioneers of the Patagonian Missionary Society had starved to death and the naked Fuegans had plagued the white men with their endless cries of 'Yammerschooner, yammerschooner'. I felt I had better go there before Fireland became Disneyland.

Now that I was here, now that I could survey for myself the invulnerable emptiness and wildness of the land, such apprehensions seemed absurd. Europeans might have wiped out the aboriginal population of Tierra del Fuego but they had hardly touched the majority of its islands. These were still virgin territory. During his own journey south Darwin had longed to walk in places where no other man had trod. We all have such desires. Darwin fulfilled his in Tierra del Fuego. One hundred and fifty years later such an ambition is difficult to accomplish. There is hardly a square foot of earth left, except possibly in the arctic and antarctic regions, which has not been trampled on by a man at some time. In Tierra del Fuego I felt there was a possibility that my own guaranteed water-resistant sea-boots might cover new ground.

I suppose that I have at some time or other worked as hard as I did on that first day in Tierra del Fuego, but I do not remember ever having worked harder. The scene which the BBC had to film was an incident where Darwin was nearly killed by a fall of ice from a glacier. Lieutenant Wickham warned him of the danger of getting too close to the ice-face but, in pursuit of knowledge, Darwin was fearless. There was an avalanche of ice which resulted in a tidal wave and the *Beagle*'s boats were nearly swept away. Darwin's own prompt and courageous action contributed to saving them.

There was a glacier a few miles from Angelito Bay and the plan was to reconnoitre it and, if it proved suitable, to row the whole film crew into the lagoon at the foot of the glacier and shoot the scene. Rowing the boats was to be the responsibility of the four men from the *Beagle*.

First, though, we had to prepare the boats for filming. Non-period features like rowlocks had to be removed and, to replace them, we whittled thole-pins, short pegs which slot into holes and hold the oars in place. We made grommets, rope-rings, with which to attach the oars to the thole-pins. We diligently scraped off the splashes of paint and other non-nineteenth century substances the boats had acquired after being housed on the *Beagle* for a few months and which the camera's sharp eye would pick out. We dressed up in our costumes. These consisted of white canvas trousers, open-necked shirt, waistcoat, short blue jacket with brass buttons, a stringy cravat and a hat. If nineteenth-century sailors really did wear such clothes in places like Tierra del Fuego, it is a wonder more of them did not die of exposure. In my costume I felt I looked perfectly ridiculous.

The *Argonauta* slipped out of Angelito Bay into the main channel and anchored five or six hundred yards from the beach. The recce party was rowed ashore, reported favourably and we began to transfer all the equipment and personnel ashore.

Those readers who did not skip the Prelude will recall that messing about in boats is not my forte. Alone in a skiff on Regent's Park lake with plenty of room and nobody looking, I

can acquit myself reasonably well. In any other situation I find
that, however hard I concentrate, oars leap out of rowlocks,
blades either skim the surface or dig out cascades of water, and
as for steering the damned boat, I normally manage to describe
a series of ever-diminishing concentric circles. I now found that
not only did I have to contend with thole-pins and grommets,
surely the least practical method of keeping an oar in its place
ever devised, but with a choppy sea and the thickest bed of kelp
in Tierra del Fuego.

I had, of course, read about the difficulties of rowing through
kelp but I was totally unprepared for the reality. It was as if
there was some malevolent marine poltergeist playing tricks
with the other end of the oar. If your stroke was too deep, the
blade became instantly entangled. If your stroke was too shallow,
the blade bounced lightly off the floating kelp-leaves and you
were in danger of toppling over backwards. If you got your
stroke absolutely right you became the victim of a double disaster ; first the blade snagged, then, as you pulled harder, it was
suddenly released. I heaved and jerked and sweated and cursed
in a frenzy of blame-transference which included Robin, the
BBC, the ancients who invented oars, Robin, Ferdinand Magellan who had discovered this ghastly place, and Robin.

Add to all this the fact that the boat was loaded with people
and valuable equipment ; that, as always, time was the enemy,
and that I simply couldn't afford to jeopardise the day's work by
a show of utter incompetence and you can imagine what a state
I was in by the time we reached the shore.

Worse was to come.

The first shot the director, Martyn Friend, wanted, was one of
the two boats pulling into the glacial lagoon with Darwin and
Wickham in one, Fitzroy and Sulivan in the other. It sounds
simple enough but there were three factors that made it a nightmare for me. The first was that I had to appear to be a crack
oarsman, the pick, presumably, of Fitzroy's particularly tough and
experienced crew. It was no good catching crabs, or getting out
of stroke with my fellow oarsman or tumbling heels over head
into the bottom of the boat. The BBC had not come thousands
of miles to film the Keystone Cops and any mistake I made
would ruin the take. The second was that, to make the shot
effective, we had to row in a straight line towards an agreed
landmark. We could not afford to zig-zag all over the water.
The third and by far the worst problem was the fact that there

was a savagely fast tide-race running out of the lagoon, against
the direction in which we had to row. This meant that however
hard we pulled our progress against the tide-race could be mea-
sured in inches to the hour. All I could do was keep my head
down, row like hell and thank God for Andrew Burt and Peter
Settelen, the two actors playing Fitzroy and Sulivan respectively
who kept us on course by means of surreptitious hand signals
and who contrived, somehow, to keep straight faces.

To crown it all, I had a horrible suspicion, when we eventually
pulled past the camera and ran on to the beach, that it had been
decided not to use the shot after all. Nobody dared confirm this
to me, of course, but I shall watch *The Voyage of Charles Darwin*
with very close attention.

The next ordeal was a shot of the two boats moving across
the lagoon, away from the beach. Again, it sounds simple enough.
But this time we had to contend with icebergs. The lagoon was
filled with floating chunks of ice, some no bigger than a football,
others the size of a small car. It was the small, submerged variety
that caused the trouble, scraping under the keel with a horrible
rasping, rending sound that convinced you that you were about
to sink.

With all this heaving and sweating I had hardly noticed
the glacier itself. It was only when the rowing shots had been
completed and I was back on dry land again, that I had leisure
to observe it.

It was breathtaking.

It was a towering edifice of ice, opalescent and veined with
long streaks of an extraordinary blue colour. At the summit
sharp pinnacles stood out against the sky, jagged, slender, fragile.
At the base was a dark grotto and the whole face of the glacier
was mirrored in the still, ice-strewn water of the lagoon. From
time to time this glassy image would be shattered as a piece of
ice fell with a crack and a roar like a distant avalanche. When
the ice hit the water there was a sound like an explosion and the
shock-waves stirred and shifted the icebergs along the beach and
one was vividly reminded that a glacier is not a static thing but
a huge frozen river which has been moving, at an infinitesimal
speed, for millions of years.

Naturally, we hoped that the camera would catch one of these
spectacular ice-falls and naturally they occurred at just the wrong
times. Some genius suggested that we might be able to crack the
ice and produce a fall by the action of sound-waves. So we all

Ned Kelly

Rocky

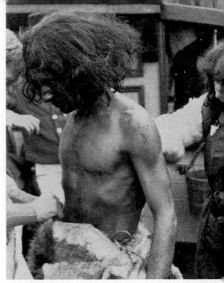

Filming in Tierra del Fuego:

a Captain Fitzroy

b Jemmy Button

c Fuegia Basket

d Mrs. Jemmy Button

stood in a semi-circle facing the glacier, actors and extras in
nineteenth-century costumes, the rest in the bizarre combinations of bright anoraks, bulky trousers and fanciful hats
invariably affected by mountaineers, hikers and yachtsmen, and
we shouted: 'Cut — cut — cut — cut . . .' This curious experiment proved to be a failure. But Dave Whitson, the camera-man,
got his spectacular shot in the end, by accident but with quite
uncanny timing.

It was a shot down the beach towards the glacier. Darwin
steps out of his boat and begins walking briskly down the beach.
Wickham shouts out a warning which Darwin blithely ignores.
He strides on, towards the glacier.

As we filmed this last piece of action—Darwin marching towards possible doom—*it happened.* A great lump of ice detached
itself and fell. And Dave Whitson zoomed in like the master he
is and captured it on film. It was the sort of luck film-makers
pray for and it was a thousand times better than any artificially
arranged fall. The idea of getting the Chilean navy to dynamite
the ice had been mooted at one stage but, luckily for all our
lives, had been abandoned. When Robin and a party visited the
glacier a few days later there was a heavy fall which set up a
twenty-foot tidal wave. Jason, the Mate, was nearly swept away.
He was standing on a rock, near the ice-face, when it happened
and had the sense not to run, but to fling himself face down on
the rock and hang on for dear life. The wave passed right over
him. If we had started blowing the glacier up with explosives
the effect might have been devastating, even fatal.

Towards evening the glacier began to glow pale blue, as if lit
from within. The sky was beginning to darken but inside the
lagoon it was still possible to film in the light reflected—it
seemed almost as if it was *stored*—by the ice. The last shots
were completed and it was time to get back to the *Argonauta.*
Everyone was tired, cold and hungry but still elated by the lonely
beauty of the place, the grandeur of the glacier and the thought
that we had successfully recorded it all on celluloid.

We now discovered that the narrow channel which led out of
the lagoon (scene of earlier agonies) had been turned by the
receding tide into a series of shallow, rocky rapids through which
it was almost impossible to manoeuvre the boats without going
aground.

We did go aground. There was nothing else for it. We had
to roll up our trousers and step into the water which was literally

glacial.

It was a leg-numbing experience. I wondered how the Yaghan Indian women had ever endured water as cold as this — Yaghan men were, by and large, non-swimmers. The women would spend hours in the sea, diving for mussels, their babies tied securely to cradles of frozen kelp-leaves. I began to appreciate what a vital element fire was to the Yaghans who lived in this frozen land almost entirely naked. They never allowed their fires to go out, preserving the precious embers in cocoons of wet moss. They had fires even in the primitive canoes, laid on a bed of wet sand and pebbles. Incidentally this was how Tierra del Fuego acquired its name. When Europeans discovered the country the first thing they noticed were the hundreds of thin plumes of smoke rising from the forests and moving as the Indians carried their fires with them in their ceaseless treks in search of food. So they called it the Land of Fire.

I could have done with a conflagration on the scale of the Great Fire of London by the time we had our boat afloat again but the nearest source of heat was the *Argonauta* and there was some very heavy rowing ahead of us. To add to the jollity there was a strong breeze blowing down the main channel and whipping up the waves. Loading the boats was a nightmare, made tolerable only by the inexhaustible good humour of the actors and film crew, in which the mounting waves, the shallows by the beach, the clinging kelp and dangerous over-loading all played their merry parts. But at last it was done. We were all safely aboard the *Argonauta* and steaming back to the shelter of Angelito and I could seek the universal cure for all ills, without which civilisation would perish, a glass of whisky.

I awoke the next morning to find that the exertions of the previous day had re-activated certain muscles in my neck and back which had lain happily and properly dormant for years. Every movement was agony. But worse than this physical dis-comfort was a sense of *malaise* I could not at first define. There was something potentially bad about the day into which I had just awoken—but what? Then I remembered. The *Beagle* was due to anchor in Angelito Bay this morning. If she did not appear it would mean either that there was serious trouble with the engines or that relations with the BBC had deteriorated to a point where the entire film schedule was in jeopardy. In effect it would mean the end of the voyage. If she did appear, it would mean that harmony had been restored. I fumbled for my watch.

It was five minutes past seven. If the *Beagle* had left Punta Arenas on schedule late last night, she should be here.

I hurried up on deck. It was deserted except for one man, one of the crew of the *Argonauta,* who was fishing off the stern ; the Bay of the Little Angel was completely deserted. The *Beagle* had not arrived.

I strolled gloomily towards the fisherman. He was small, smiling and his high cheekbones and coarse hair denoted Indian blood. He was fishing with a few yards of line which he stored in a rusty old soup tin. I watched him bait his hook with a morsel of clam-flesh and drop it into the flat, black water. Then I saw him react. He turned towards the entrance of the bay and said something incomprehensible. I too turned to look in the direction he was pointing and there I saw, emerging through the mist, the familiar outline of the *Beagle.* Her yards were bare of canvas and, perhaps through some trick of the light breeze, I could not hear her engines. She appeared to be drifting through the white haze like a ghost-ship.

For the second time in Angelito Bay I experienced that delightful feeling of depression suddenly lifting. The fisherman was repeating something to me which at first I could not grasp.

'Beggle, eh?' he seemed to be saying, 'Beggle, eh?'

I recalled suddenly that this was how Spanish-speakers pronounced *Beagle.*

'Si,' I replied, adding in heartfelt English: 'Thank God.'

The *Beagle* hove to about four hundred yards away from the *Argonauta.* I could see figures moving about in the bow and, although I could not at that distance distinguish any features, I knew that two of them would be Dick and Manchester whose responsibility it was to deal with the anchors. No doubt they would be cursing freely at being dragged out of their bunks so early in the morning.

A sudden wave of affection for the *Beagle* and everybody on board swept over me. I had been separated from the ship for a mere thirty-six hours but it had been enough to make me realise, for the first time, the extent to which I had become a part of the life of the ship, how much it had come to mean to me. My rôle on board was, after all, a curious one. I was a working member of the crew but a voluntary one, unpaid and unqualified in the sense that I had contributed virtually nothing to the arduous work of preparation.

In the natural division between officers and crew which must exist on any ship, even one as informal as the *Beagle,* my position was nebulous. I was a free-floater ; and this could have led to resentment and trouble. It did not. I was accepted, or at worst, tolerated ; and, insensibly, day by day, I had become a cog in the machinery of the ship, a cog which would not be found listed in any service manual, which was in no way critical to the running of the machine but which nonetheless had a kind of function. As the *Beagle* anchored in Angelito Bay that cold, hazy morning, I realised that though I was physically viewing her as an outsider, emotionally I was an outsider no longer.

In the afternoon, filming began.

It must surely have been a film-man who originated the ex-pression 'hurry-up-and-wait'. It precisely describes the essentially tedious process by which films are made and applies even more powerfully to a costume drama.

The disguise or elimination of anything non-nineteenth-century on the *Beagle* herself was a ticklish and time-consuming task in itself. It was an obvious though not easily accomplished necessity to hide such a twentieth-century object as the radar scanner—it was draped with old canvas so that it had the appear-ance of an eccentrically placed staysail—but only the eagle eye of the Designer, Colin Shaw, could detect such minute anach-ronisms as a modern galvanised eye-bolt. It was replaced with a brass one. The decks were suddenly cluttered with fibre-glass cannons, a fake wooden deck-pump, a large ship's wheel and other period features while below, the saloon became a combina-tion of dressing-room, canteen, prop department and, above all, waiting-room.

The prime function of a costume extra is waiting. You wait for the art director, the sound men, the lighting men and camera men and a host of other technicians to set up a scene. You are called. The director explains what you have to do. You wait while he explains to the actors what they have to do and you wait while director and actors discuss the matter. You rehearse the scene. You wait again as further changes arising from the rehearsal are discussed. A couple more rehearsals and the director is ready to shoot. You wait for the sun to come out. It remains firmly hidden behind growing banks of cloud. You wait while the lighting man makes the necessary adjustments. Just as the director is about to shout 'Action', the sun comes out. You wait for further lighting changes. By this time you are beginning to forget what you have to do. In a mild panic you wait for the

'Action' signal and had you have to wait a few minutes more because the art director has spotted some minute flaw which you would never have noticed but which the camera will assuredly pick up. Finally, you hear the almost imperceptible whirr of the camera, the clapper-boy does his stuff, the director cries 'Action' and you are on at last. Thirty seconds later, the scene is complete. Complete but not satisfactory. It is done again and again, the actors repeating the same lines of dialogue over and over until the words lose all meaning and you wonder how they can continue saying them with any conviction. At last, the director is satisfied that the scene is perfect and you are released . . . for another long wait while the next scene is set up.

You suddenly realise you are shivering from standing about in your inadequate costume in the cold air of Tierra del Fuego. If you have had no previous experience of filming—luckily I had— you will by this time consider the entire business a monstrous and bewildering waste of time. If you have not read the script you will not even know what story it is you are helping to tell. The scenes in which you participate are all out of sequence. You can have only the faintest notions about the relationships which are supposed to exist between the various characters or the motives behind their speeches and actions.

In order to make sense, therefore, of the scenes we filmed on the *Beagle* in Tierra del Fuego, it is necessary at this point to recount briefly the story of Captain Fitzroy, Charles Darwin, Rev. Mathews and three Yaghan Indians called Jemmy Button, York Minster and Fuegia Basket.

The story begins during the first visit the *Beagle* paid to Tierra del Fuego between 1825 and 1830. It was in the course of this pioneer surveying expedition, commanded by Captain Philip Parker King, that the Beagle Channel, an alternative route from Atlantic to Pacific south of the Magellan Straits, was discovered and that Robert Fitzroy was given command of the *Beagle*. Her original Captain, Pringle Stokes, unutterably depressed by the bleak and dismal channels of the extreme south and the thought that he would have to return to them for the second expedition, shot himself.

Not long after Fitzroy took over command a party of Indians stole one of the *Beagle*'s whale-boats. Fitzroy immediately took four hostages to ensure the return of the boat and, when the Indians refused to hand it back, decided to take his native prisoners to England.

Fitzroy's official reason for this grand-seigneurial action was to establish in Tierra del Fuego a nucleus of English-speaking natives, roughly trained in the arts of civilisation, who would be able to assist any British sailors subsequently wrecked on those distant and hitherto inhospitable shores. His true motives stemmed from his religious zeal. His four natives were to be turned into Christians ; they were to help in establishing the first Christian Mission in Tierra del Fuego and spread the Light of Christ in that benighted land.

Today one might regard such a concept as both presumptuous and, with the benefit of hindsight, absurd—doomed to failure from the outset. It is not for us to judge but rather to wonder at Fitzroy's faith especially as he, of all men, must have appreciated that Tierra del Fuego was the epitome of the stony ground of the parable — almost literally so.

The four Fuegans were duly shipped to England in the *Beagle*. One of them, Boat Memory, died almost immediately, probably of smallpox. Though Fitzroy had no means of knowing it, Boat Memory's fate presaged that of the vast majority of his people who towards the end of the nineteenth century were decimated by a succession of epidemics, mainly measles, unwittingly imported by white missionaries. Jemmy Button, Fuegia Basket and York Minster were placed under the care of Rev. William Wilson of Walthamstow, who was directed, in Fitzroy's own words, 'to teach them English and the plainer truths of Christianity, as the first object'.

The Fuegans became minor celebrities. Fitzroy introduced them into his own grand social circles where they were no doubt regarded as amusing curiosities. He even presented them at Court. King William IV asked them a great many pertinent questions about their native country and Queen Adelaide gave Fuegia Basket a bonnet, a ring and money to buy new clothes. Jemmy Button made a particularly good impression. He was respectful and friendly and very dapper in his tail coat and breeches. The story, which many people still believe, that he derived his quaint name from the fact that Fitzroy had bought him from his father in exchange for a brass button must have made him particularly interesting to the genteel ladies of London society. Later research into the real manners and customs of the Yaghans shows that the Indians had a highly developed sense of parental duty and that such a barbarous bargain would have been extremely unlikely. It also, incidentally, refutes the belief, widely held in the nineteenth century and even later, that the Yaghans were cannibals who ate their grandmothers.

The three Fuegans sailed with the *Beagle* when she left Devonport in 1831 and, during the voyage south, their religious instruction was continued by a young man called Richard Mathews who was the agent appointed by the Church Missionary Society to convert the Yaghans. The Indians were popular with both the officers and the crew. The only incident which marred this happy relationship was when York Minster, who had fallen in love with Fuegia Basket, attacked some drunken sailors who were flirting with her.

In January 1833, the *Beagle* anchored in Goeree Roads, a haven between Navarin and Lennox islands and Fitzroy, Darwin, Mathews and the Fuegans set off in whale-boats. They went west down the Beagle Channel, through the Murray Narrows and found a sheltered cove on the west side of Navarin called Wulaia. It was a pretty spot with a little meadow dotted with wildflowers and the soil was fertile and workable. The boats were unloaded and the extraordinary selection of goods, including chamber pots and table linen, provided by the Church Missionary Society and presumably considered by them essential to the founding of a new mission, were taken ashore. Darwin looked on scornfully. He considered the C.M.S.'s provisions absurd and irresponsible. Hundreds of Yaghans observed the scene with wonder, fear and ill-concealed greed.

A vegetable garden was dug, seeds planted and three huts built, one for Mathews, one for Jemmy, one for York and Fuegia who were by now married. Several of Jemmy's brothers and sisters were on hand and Darwin noted that they treated Jemmy with suspicion and that Jemmy seemed to have forgotten much of his native language. After a few days Fitzroy left Mathews and the Fuegans to fend for themselves. The great experiment had begun.

Fitzroy, however, was anxious about Mathews's safety. He had more faith in the natives than Darwin, but had experienced enough of their rapacity—the begging croon of 'Yammerschooner, yammerschooner' orchestrated every contact between the white men and the Indians—to suspect Mathews might run into trouble. He turned back to Wulaia, his apprehension increasing as he passed native canoes whose occupants were dressed up in clothes which he recognised as the former property of the Church Missionary Society. At Wulaia he found Mathews alive but in a state bordering on hysteria.

The minute Fitzroy and his party had gone the natives had begun to plague the wretched missionary, demanding to be given clothes, food and gifts. When Mathews refused to part with these things, they had stoned him, manhandled him and finally looted the encampment. York Minster had sided with his own people. Jemmy had remained loyal and had been beaten up for his pains. Mathews begged to be taken home to England and Fitzroy had no alternative but to accede to his wish. What was left of the Church Missionary Society's goods and chattels was divided between the three Fuegans and they were left to carry the torch of civilisation by themselves. Fitzroy promised to return.

Fifteen months later, he did. He found the little cove completely deserted. Towards evening a few native canoes appeared. In one of them was a particularly savage-looking Yaghan with a tangled mop of hair and naked except for a wisp of hide round his loins. He paddled up close to the *Beagle* and surprised the crowd of sailors and officers leaning over the rail by throwing a proper naval salute. To his horror Fitzroy realised that this wild barbarian was Jemmy Button. The bright, cheerful boy who had taken such a pride in his English suit and his button boots, who had appeared to respond so encouragingly to civilised ways had, in a few months, reverted to a savage state.

Jemmy came on board. He seemed to be ashamed of his nakedness and his filthy condition. Fitzroy invited him to dinner and perhaps drew some comfort from the fact that his erstwhile protégé was still able to handle a knife and fork correctly. Jemmy brought gifts; a bow, arrows and a spear for Fitzroy, hides for his best friends among the crew. He introduced Fitzroy to his young wife and told him that York Minster had built a huge canoe, had loaded it with all his, Jemmy's, goods and had gone away with Fuegia to another part of the country. He said that he was happy and did not want to return to England.

The next day, the *Beagle* left Wulaia. As she headed out into the channel, the crew noticed that Jemmy had built a great fire on the beach. The thin plume of smoke was a signal of farewell, final and absolute. Fitzroy's attempt to bring civilisation and Christianity to Tierra del Fuego had been an unmitigated disaster.

This was the story which we had come to Tierra del Fuego to film. The parts of the Fuegans — Jemmy, York, Fuegia and Jemmy's wife, were taken by members of the Punta Arenas

amateur dramatic society who, although not full-blooded Indians
—there is only one such left, an old gentleman in Puerto Williams
and his claim is considered dubious—looked convincingly savage,
especially when plastered with make-up and festooned with
scraps of fur. The girl who played Jemmy's wife was particularly
charming, and although only thirteen, displayed a remarkable
fortitude in the trying circumstances soon to be related.

The scenes at Wulaia cove which demanded scores of extras
had been shot on a location near Punta Arenas. It was obviously
impractical to transport hundreds of people to the middle of
nowhere and impossible to recruit local personnel since the
centre of Tierra del Fuego is entirely uninhabited. Our business
was with the scenes involving the *Beagle* herself and my own
memories concern two scenes in particular: one in which York
Minster rescues Fuegia Basket from the drunken sailors, the
other in which Jemmy, once more a savage, visits the *Beagle* for
the last time. In the former I made my début as a television
star, actually speaking, or at least mumbling, instead of merely
moving about in the background in costume; in the latter I
added some genuine lustre to my reputation as a life-saver.

I was selected, along with Dave the Rave, Nigel, Christian
and Mike the Rigger, to perform the rôle of an intoxicated and
lecherous nineteenth-century sailor. I must insist that in my
own case this was an example of serious miscasting, the equivalent of asking W. C. Fields to play Dr. Barnardo or Errol Flynn
to portray St. Francis of Assisi. Mike the Rigger, by contrast, was
born word perfect in his part.

I am certain that my performance would have been much
better if I had been allowed a liquid lunch. Five or six gins and
a couple of bottles of wine would have added a great deal of
depth and realism to my interpretation of the rôle. As it was, by
the wise decree of the BBC, no alcohol was served at lunch
during the filming and as a result my acting was stilted to a
degree. Not that I had much to do.

The sequence of action was as follows. Fuegia and the sailors
are in a huddle just under the fore-deck. Liquor—in reality, cold
tea—is circulating and one Grassy Green (played by Mr. Michael
Freeman) is being encouraged by his companions to kiss Fuegia,
or, in the immortal words of the hastily improvised script, 'give
'er one'. Fuegia is laughing and flirting and Grassy is beginning
to give of his best when suddenly the Fuegan girl looks up to see
York Minster rushing down the deck. She screams. York flings

himself at Grassy, dots him one, is attacked by the nearest sailor (myself) and a general scuffle ensues. The fight ceases as suddenly as it began when Lieutenant Wickham appears on the scene. The sailors, shamefaced and terrified, scramble to their feet. York Minster gibbers that they have attempted to rape Fuegia, who is led away weeping. Wickham then questions Green, who stutters out the standard defence of the experienced serviceman— 'Only a bit of fun, sir. No harm meant,'— upon which Wickham castigates the men for defiling the holy feast of Christmas—the whole outrage is the result of Yuletide jollities—like John Knox declaiming against the monstrous regiment of women. Chastened, hangdog, the erring sailors slink below.

I confess I found it difficult to slur my speech and sway about while as sober as an Aberdonian churchwarden. I found it even more difficult to produce the sort of ooo aar accent required without sounding like a poor parody of Long John Silver. But my problems were as nothing compared with those of the girl playing Fuegia. My colleagues, notably Mike, Dave and Nigel, portrayed brutal lust so convincingly that she became almost paralysed with fear, persuaded that she was indeed about to be the victim of their horrid passions. She was so frightened of us that her supposedly terrified gasp on spying the avenging York came out as a sigh of relief. Martyn Friend, the director, displayed amazing patience, reassuring Fuegia while encouraging us to be less wooden.

The first time we rehearsed the fight sequence, we did it with such gusto that the actor playing York Minster began to display the same panic symptoms as Fuegia. He had to be helped to his feet, dusted down, mollified and reassured with handshakes all round before he was able to continue.

It was Rigger Mike who stole the show. Under the basilisk eye of Wickham (David Ashton) he completely forgot his lines and began to stutter and gasp in genuine confusion, thus achieving a minor miracle of cinema vérité. In fact, it all seemed so real that when Wickham turned on us and denounced us as drunken brutes I was suddenly transported twenty years back in time. I was a quivering little schoolboy being publicly upbraided by my formidable headmaster for eating chocolate in chapel. When Wickham ordered us below, I crept away with a genuine shudder.

In the scene where Jemmy Button visits the *Beagle* for the last time, I do not appear on the screen at all. I volunteered to man the safety boat with Robin or, in other words, Robin informed me that he and I would man the safety boat. The 'safety boat' which sounds so grand was in fact just one of the rubber dinghies powered by an outboard. It was necessary because the scene involved Jemmy Button and his child-wife paddling about in the dug-out canoe which the BBC had had specially constructed. Neither of the actors could swim or had ever been in a small boat in their lives.

We began filming this sequence towards evening. It was cold, there was a fresh breeze blowing and the two actors were to all intents and purposes stark naked. The authentic strips of guanaco fur provided by the costume department preserved their modesty but afforded nil protection against the weather. As they climbed gingerly down into the canoe they were both shivering with cold and terror.

There were problems from the outset. The strong breeze was blowing the canoe away from the side of the *Beagle*. Since, for reasons of authenticity, there was no painter attached to the canoe, it had to be held against the hull by force. Robin positioned the rubber boat behind the canoe. He held the rubber boat tight against the side of the ship while I lay flat over the bow, gripped the stern of the canoe and pushed against the force of the wind. The camera angle was adjusted so that my arms were just out of frame and Jemmy Button began his clambering aboard act.

It sounds simple enough but in fact it was a particularly ticklish shot owing to that factor known in the film-making business as continuity. As films are made up of short sequences shot in an order which is based on practicality not chronology, it is not until they reach the cutting-room that they are spliced together in their proper order. The scenes of Jemmy's reception by the sailors on the *Beagle*, his meeting with Fitzroy and his farewell had been filmed earlier on in the day. It was vital that the shots of his climbing out of the canoe and then back into it, should tie in exactly with the material previously filmed.

It was a further example of 'hurry up and wait'. Waiting is all very well when you can loll about the deck smoking and chatting but it is a very different matter when you are stretched out over the bow of a rubber boat, fighting the wind. However, it was done at last and we could proceed to the next stage which was to tow the canoe away from the ship and give Jemmy Button his first lesson in the art of paddling. At this point another problem arose. In the centre of the canoe we had built a genuine Fuegan fire of dry twigs and driftwood laid on a bed of sand and shingle. The wind now began to fan the flames which leaped and crackled and threatened to catch the actors' fur costumes. I doused the fire with seawater, just enough to keep the flames down but not so much as would put the fire out. The canoe rocked alarmingly, Jemmy's wife let out a little wail of fear and I thought—before the day is over someone is going to fall in.

It took quite a time to instruct Jemmy in the technique of wielding a paddle. He seemed unable to grasp the basic principle of reversing the position of his hands as he moved the paddle from one side of the canoe to the other. Eventually we considered him expert enough to attempt the first sequence— paddling towards the *Beagle*. We manoeuvred him into position, checked with Martyn Friend on board the *Beagle* via two-way radio, revved up the outboard and roared away.

The canoe, with Jemmy paddling away like a demon, advanced slowly towards the *Beagle* then began to veer away and, gathering speed, headed out in the general direction of Cape Horn.

We whizzed off in pursuit, circled the canoe and went alongside—a feat which sounds easy enough but demands an experienced hand on the outboard which, needless to say, was Robin's not mine.

We found the fire blazing away and Mrs. Button almost in tears. After dousings, words of comfort and encouragement in pidgin Spanish and further instructions to Jemmy on how to *steer* a canoe, we again abandoned them.

This time, the canoe executed two concentric circles and came within an inch of capsizing. I thought again—in the next *ten minutes* someone is going to fall in.

Jemmy Button was undeterred by the failure of the first two attempts and assured us that this time it would be all right. He set off, hefting his heavy, clumsy paddle with some brio and heading unerringly towards the *Beagle*. Robin and I heaved sighs of relief.

Now all we had to do was to stand by as the camera took the final shot of the canoe moving away from the ship and then we could relax.

All went well. In the fading light the canoe, with its wispy column of smoke, slipped through the waves and I thought to myself—this will be one of the most moving moments of the film. Robin and I sped after the canoe, collected it and towed it back to the *Beagle*. Jemmy and his wife were smiling through their chattering teeth, happy that their ordeal was over. We brought the canoe alongside the *Beagle,* positioning it just under the steps and suggested that Jemmy climb out first.

This was our dreadful error. What we should have done was to transfer the two actors to the rubber boat which was stable and provided with painters and then helped them aboard the *Beagle*. As it was, Jemmy stood up in the canoe and chivalrously invited Mrs. Jemmy to go first. We said, No, no, you go first. He said, No, no, let the girl go first. The girl stood up, half sat down again, stood up again. The wind blew, the canoe rocked, the girl screamed, Jemmy made a wild grab for the side of the *Beagle,* the canoe capsized and our two non-swimmers were in the water.

It is extraordinary how, in a crisis, one can think quite complicated thoughts while at the same time acting swiftly. As I leaped from the rubber boat to the canoe and from the canoe into the sea and hauled Mrs. Button unceremoniously out of the water, across the canoe and into the rubber boat, the following reflections passed through my mind: (a) I told you so. (b) A man who panics in the sea can drown in half a minute. (c) If anyone does panic, should I use the approved method and knock him out? (d) Watch out for that bloody fire in the bottom of the canoe.

In the same instant that thought (d) occurred to me I put my rubber-booted foot straight into the glowing embers. Between us, Robin and I managed to manhandle Jemmy into the rubber boat and I found myself marooned in the canoe. Red hot stones were now scattered all over the bottom and I hopped about, cursing.

By this time, both the boats had drifted several yards away from the *Beagle*. We wrapped Jemmy and his wife in blankets— they were both beginning to recover and to laugh somewhat forcedly—and Robin declared he would take them back to the *Beagle*. I could follow in the canoe

The first thing I did was to douse the bottom. The hot stones and embers hissed and steamed. Then I picked up the paddle, sat down in the stern and dug powerfully into the sea. Nothing happened. Mildly surprised, I gave another, even more powerful thrust. The canoe moved forward a sluggish inch in the wrong direction. My admiration for Jemmy Button began to rise. I realised that the wretched canoe was the most impractical vessel since the Owl and the Pussycat's sieve. It was just a hollowed out tree trunk. It had no sort of keel and rolled and tipped in the water like a log. The paddle seemed to weigh about half a ton and was about as much use as a means of propelling the craft as a caber.

I began to wonder how Jemmy had managed to paddle to the *Beagle*. Did the dash of Indian blood in his veins give him some kind of innate mastery? My own efforts were achieving nothing more than an ever lengthening distance between myself and the *Beagle*. I strove manfully and began to make some small progress. I calculated that at my present speed I should reach the ship soon after midnight and felt the beginnings of a major blame-transference coming on. Luckily, I was spared any further agony as Robin whizzed out in the rubber boat to rescue me.

'What on earth are you doing?' he demanded testily.

'Just having a nice little paddle.'

'This is hardly the time for messing about in boats and you look as if you're making a right mess of it anyway.'

'Not at all. It demands a certain technique, of course. It's not easy. But I'm beginning to master the art. Most interesting. You'd think the Yaghans would have devised something more practical.'

'Perhaps you'd like to get back under your own steam?'

'No, no. Tow away. I can continue my experiments some other time.'

I never set foot in that canoe again and the future seems brighter for the thought that I will never have to.

On 27th December, just before midnight the *Beagle* slipped out of Angelito and passed up the Angostini and Keats channels back towards Punta Arenas. We were due to moor alongside the *Argonauta* in the harbour by noon the following day so that the whole crew could be present at a grand cocktail party in honour of the Chilean navy.

The next few days at Punta Arenas were, for almost everyone but me, concerned with filming the final scenes for which the actors were required out in the Magellan Straits and escorting admirals over the *Beagle*. I was busy with another project, namely the ship's pantomime which was due to be performed on the night of the 29th.

The percipient reader will have noted mysterious references to the pantomime elsewhere in this chronicle. The idea of concocting a traditional Christmas entertainment for our own crew and that of the BBC had been Rigger Mike's and our original thought had been to score a theatrical 'first' by performing it in the *Beagle* off Cape Furious, in south-west Tierra del Fuego. This delightful plan was abandoned because the actors and some of the film crew were flying back to England on 1st December and were anxious to see the show. It seems that professional thespians have a morbid passion for amateur theatricals.

The *Beagle* pantomime was based loosely—and loose is an apt description of the action and dialogue of the play—on the Cinderella story. In fact it was a satire on the internal politics of the *Beagle* in which Robin and Mark were portrayed as the Ugly Sisters. If I were to reproduce the script of the pantomime, even in an Appendix, this book would quite rightly be banned in four continents and available for purchase only in the sort of back-street shops where men in dark glasses furtively finger improbably illustrated magazines full of sado-masochism and misprints. Suffice it to say that Dick appeared throughout dressed in his rubber diving-gear and that for Cinderella's glass slipper was substituted a pair of black and scarlet knickers.

The production demanded the acquisition of a large quantity of female clothing and this led to a sociologically interesting discovery about Punta Arenas. There are no old-clothes shops. In an English provincial town I would have had no difficulty in dressing the cast for a few pounds from junk and charity shops. I discovered only one such shop in Punta Arenas and the few dresses they had for sale were grand ball-gowns of the late thirties and extremely expensive. It would appear that second-hand shops are the product of affluent societies where the balance of wealth is reasonably even. In countries where there is an extreme divide between rich and poor, the haves are not interested in buying hand-me-down goods and the have-nots hang onto their possessions because they cannot afford to replace them.

There was no alternative therefore but to buy new stuff. With Blond Geoff, who had been roped in as props and lighting man, I trailed round the drapery stores looking for bargains in the brassière, petticoat and night-dress line. After the first few attempts to explain to wondering shop assistants, in Spanish, that we wanted these things for a play, we gave up. It was far less exhausting to let speculation flourish. No doubt, as a result, British seamen have a reputation among the gossips of Punta Arenas as transvestites.

We had been rehearsing the pantomime, off and on, ever since leaving Mar del Plata and had made very little progress. I cannot think of a more inconvenient place to organise amateur theatricals than a ship at sea. Privacy is the first essential for such an enterprise not only because it is vital to the success of the show that none of the potential audience should have any inkling of the plot but also because amateurs tend to freeze up if they think any of their friends might be watching them making fools of themselves. Privacy was unobtainable in the *Beagle*. We tried the open-air approach, declaring the fore part of the main deck a no-go area and declaiming our lines into the breeze as the coast of Patagonia slipped by on the starboard side. But curious crew members kept inventing excuses to fiddle about on the fore-deck or tinker with anchor winch and, when chased away, became abusive. We tried sealing off the aft cabin and found that the engines suddenly and mysteriously required all manner of checks and adjustments. It was also difficult to concentrate on enunciation and delivery with the two Gardners pounding away a few feet from our improvised stage.

The cast, which consisted of Dick, Jay, Nigel, Manchester, Alf and Ravey Dave with Mike and myself as co-producers, was difficult to assemble. Watches and other duties were always getting in the way. To cap it all, Dick, who had a starring rôle as the Good Fairy, went down with Punta Arenas Tummy—a disease akin to dysentary and believed to emanate from the tap water — and I had to take on his part and write in a non-speaking character for him to play.

In a word, it was chaos. I had two days in which to organise the costumes and make props. My headquarters was the small private theatre rented by the BBC to house the costume department. This was in a basement and subject to frequent power-cuts. Blond Geoff and I had recourse to looting. We raided the local super-market for cardboard boxes to turn into props. We dismantled the spot-lights in the theatre and transported them, in secret, to the *Beagle*. The BBC costume department donated bolts of cotton dress-material and Alf was seconded from sail-making duties and abandoned the stormsail he was finishing in favour of frocks. We had time for only one full rehearsal with the whole cast which took place in the theatre at one in the morning with everybody exhausted from a full day's filming. Meanwhile Punta Arenas Tummy claimed another star, Ravey Dave, playing Cinders.

On The Night, the *Beagle* did not return from filming until after eight o'clock and we had under an hour in which to clear up the saloon, organise seating, remove the stairs, put on our costumes and make-up and fix the lights—which instantly fused. Our dressing-room was the centre cabin. This is about the size of an average bathroom. Most of the space is taken up with bunks. The remaining area was filled with nine people, a large cardboard boat, huge heaps of clothes and other clobber cleared from the saloon, Dick's diving-gear complete with oxygen cylinders and a bottle of rum which proved to be the most valuable item of all.

Our stage was a small area in the centre of the saloon which was ringed by sixty or seventy tipsy people who began a slow hand-clap as the stolen lights refused to function.

In spite of all the panic and confusion, when the lights were eventually coaxed into flickering life and the performance got under way, the play was a success. The only one who forgot his lines was the author. Jay and Nigel's slapstick scene, an orgy of shaving foam and dye-sprays, was a triumph. The attempted rape of little Cinders by the handsome Prince Charcoal (Manchester Geoff, smoking an outsize cigarette) was a milestone in the development of Realism in the theatre. Dick's antics with the diving-gear were worthy of Ionesco.

There is a treatise to be written on the psychology of amateur play-acting and I would not have described our own efforts if there had not been a serious purpose underlying the whole insane performance. The pantomime, which turned into a riotous party, finally closed the breach between the BBC and the *Beagle* which the dispute had caused. The wounds were healed with the most effective salve of all, laughter. The pantomime did more. It relieved many of our own internal tensions by bringing them out into the open, turning them upside down and making of them a preposterous farce.

I learned two things that night ; that satire should never be destructive and could be constructive, and that audiences respond to what the author considers his funniest lines with a polite titter and howl with laughter at the lines he was tempted to cut as being dull.

It may appear to be a commonplace remark but it is nonetheless true that however farcical an author may attempt to make a play, life produces the most extreme comedies.

As I have said, the pantomime turned into a party which raged

on into the small hours. The next morning found almost everyone on board the *Beagle* curled in his bunk nursing a hangover
and the ship herself in an unprecedented state of chaos. The
saloon looked like an opium den after a police raid—overturned
benches, empty bottles and beer cans, hundreds of cigarette
butts, heaps of clothes and broken glass everywhere. Above
decks it was even worse. Some wag had hoisted little Cinders'
knickers up the mizzen mast. Not a yard was square or a rope
properly coiled. The decks were a waste of BBC trunks, props,
upended cannons, more bottles and cans, intimate articles of
clothing, pools of spilled wine and general wreckage.

I tottered up on deck at about half past eight feeling that I
should have been buried at sea a week ago. The sunshine was
dazzling and the pure, clean light only served to emphasise the
disreputable and squalid state of the *Beagle*. I proceeded towards
the saloon, blinking. I glanced to my left and blinked even
harder. On the quay, standing stiffly in little formal groups, the
gold braid on their uniforms scintillating in the sun, were what
seemed like the entire top brass of the Chilean navy. In reality
there were only about twenty or thirty officers, most of them
admirals at least, and all of them resplendent in medals and
decorations.

I looked at them. They looked at me, silently, bleakly. I was
dressed in a pair of disintegrating jeans and a sweater full of
holes. I gave them a brief nod and a sickly smile and dived
down into the saloon.

I found Robin in the lavatories, enthroned. He looked three
times as fragile as I felt.

'Er, Robin,' I said, 'there seem to be an awful lot of officers
standing on the dock. Are we expecting someone?'

'I don't know. That chap from the naval base was here last
night, going on about another bloody admiral. In the middle of
the bloody pantomime. I don't know.'

'Well, er, don't you think we, I mean, you should do something
about it?'

'They seem to think this is the bloody Cutty Sark. I've got
enough to do without having to show a lot of admirals over the
ship.'

'I quite agree, but even so . . . I mean there must be twenty or
thirty officers out there.'

An evil grin spread over Robin's ashen features.

'They're in for a shock when they see the saloon,' he said.

'I'd better go and shake Mark.'

'Do what you like.'

'And what about the crew?'

'I told them they could all have a lie-in this morning and I'm not going back on that for all the admirals in Chile. I'm going to have a lie-in myself.'

'But for God's sake, you've got to put in an appearance. You're the Captain.'

'And as such, entitled to perform certain duties *in peace*.'

I went back on deck. There was some movement now among the officers, the sort of restive, impatient movement observable in a herd of cows shortly before milking-time. I saw that two of them were about to climb on board and fled to the aft cabin.

I found Mark groggy but conscious. I explained the situation to him while hastily changing out of my jeans and sweater into more respectable clothes.

'You'd better go and hold the fort while I get dressed,' Mark said.

I went back up on deck and hung about by the saloon hatch. After a moment, two officers emerged from the saloon. Their faces wore the stunned expression of Catholic prelates who, on entering the Vatican for an audience with the Pope, find His Holiness dancing the cachucha. They began talking to me urgently in Spanish. I gathered this much ; that someone very important was due to arrive at any moment and where was the captain and was there any possibility of clearing up the saloon? I affected total incomprehension. They looked helplessly, hopelessly at each other and then, suddenly, towards the dock.

An enormous black limousine was slowly approaching the groups of officers, who immediately stiffened to attention. The great car sighed to a halt right opposite the *Beagle* and amid smartly snapped salutes and heel clickings a very small man in a dark blue greatcoat stepped out. His face was the colour of old grey parchment, he had a thin, wispy moustache and in his eyes was an expression of profound sadness and resignation. Various officers stepped forward and were presented to him. There were further salutes and some mumbled conversation.

The little man moved slowly towards the narrow plank which, lashed to the shrouds and projecting onto the dock, formed the only means of access to the *Beagle*. It was low tide and the plank was tilted at a forty-five degree angle. The two officers already on board stepped forward swiftly to help the little man negotiate this perilous tight-rope. I realised that the little man must be someone Very Important Indeed.

I looked frantically along the deck. There was no sign of Mark. And where was Robin? Still sitting on the throne? Snoring in his bunk? It was appalling.

The little man reached the deck of the *Beagle* safely and stood aside for a moment as various other officers, some of whom I recognised, began to walk the plank. It was clear that in a few seconds I would be expected to step forward and offer our guest a formal welcome aboard the *Beagle*. He would assume, of course, that I was the captain and God knew what international incident would result when he discovered that I was merely a writer.

One of the officers looked at me expectantly. I gulped and, deciding to speak nothing but English and stick to it, was about to move forward when Mark came striding down the deck. He was immaculately turned out and though not, of course, in uniform had that indefinable air of formal elegance that smacks of State Occasions. Thank God for the British Navy, or, more accurately, the British Naval Reserve.

As Mark arrived, Robin simultaneously emerged from the saloon. He was dressed in his one and only suit, a much-creased light blue tropical number and while his appearance would have caused some raised eyebrows at a Royal Garden Party, in the circumstances he looked reasonably respectable. One would not have thought that he'd slept in the suit for more than a fortnight or that he'd spent more than half his adult life living under hedgerows.

The situation was saved. Robin and Mark behaved in a courtly, welcoming manner and the little man essayed the ghost of a smile. I was led up to shake his hand. It may have been my imagination but I thought the smile faded rather rapidly when he was informed of my profession.

The tour of the ship began and I suddenly knew I could not face it.

'I think I'll just nip off and buy some stuff for breakfast.' I whispered to Robin.

'Skiver!' he hissed back.

I knew that it was my duty to remain on board and record for posterity the little man's reaction to the saloon but there were too many officers, too much sunshine and my head was splitting.

I walked down the quay, out through the harbour gates and into the streets. I went to the bakery and bought some eggs in the little general store. I began to notice curious things. At every street corner there was a man standing motionless. Each man wore a bulky overcoat and scuffed shoes, the universal uniform of the plain-clothes policeman. At intervals down the street police cars were parked. In the cars, uniformed officers were speaking quietly into radio mikes.

I walked back towards the docks with my carrier bags. At the gates, the sentry searched them, a thing I had never seen him do before. I began to have a clue to the identity of our mysterious little visitor. There was a major security blanket over the whole harbour area of Punta Arenas. Could it be . . . ? Surely not. The local admiral would have warned us in advance. Maybe he had and it had gone in one of Robin's ears and out of the other. Maybe they had kept it secret for security reasons . . .

Thus speculating I strolled down the quay towards the *Beagle*. The limousine was still there. The little man was standing beside it. Suddenly he snapped his fingers and one of the officers stepped forward with an attaché case. The little man opened the case and took out a camera. It was a very small, very battered, very ancient camera like a box brownie. He put it to his eye and pointed the lens at the *Beagle*'s mainmast. The yards were all askew and the sails, hastily furled the previous night by tired men, looked like a lot of dirty laundry hung out to dry. Click.

The little man pointed the camera towards the poop deck and mizzen mast where Cinders' knickers were fluttering in the breeze. Click.

The little man pointed the camera towards the bow where the most seemly item on view was somebody's vest draped over the edge of the fore-deck. Click.

The little man replaced his camera in the attaché case. There was a flurry of salutes. He climbed into the limousine and the door was shut behind him. The car moved forward, executed a U turn and, accompanied by four motor-cycle outriders, accelerated smoothly towards the harbour gates.

I scrambled back on board the *Beagle* and tackled Robin.

'Who *was* that?' I asked.

'Charming chap. Absolutely mad about old sailing ships. Did you see him taking photos with that extraordinary old camera?'

'But what was his name?'

'I don't know. I didn't quite catch it. Began with an **M.**

Moreno or Merino or something?'

'Exactly. He's one of the three men who rule this country. The junta.'

8

THE BEAGLE CHANNEL

1 - 7 December

A FEW hours after the visit of the tyrant of Chile, at four
o'clock in the afternoon of December 1st, we left Punta
Arenas. This was not because we expected any reprisals from the
admiral. My brief encounter with this formidable ruler had left
me with a rather favourable view of his character. No man who
loves old ships can be entirely bad and any man who reaches
the pinnacle of power and, presumably, wealth and clings to an
old box brownie camera must have sound values. The sad,
haunted look in his eyes gave me the impression that though he
was presumably a party to the crimes committed by the junta —
torture, imprisonment without trial, suppression of the Left and
so on — he was not a monster, rather a sensitive man, probably
a brilliant administrator, forced to condone the horrors out of a
sense of duty and patriotism.

We left Punta Arenas under sail and, in convoy with the
Argonauta, steered west along the Straits. Our mission for the
next five days was to go south towards the Beagle Channel and
find spectacular locations in which the *Beagle* could be filmed,
under full sail, against the unique scenery of Tierra del Fuego.

I am ashamed to say that soon after leaving Punta Arenas I
retired to my bunk, prostrate with Punta Arenas Tummy. I did
not surface again until eight o'clock the following morning when
I was due to go on watch. I have remarked before on the healing
properties of Fuegan scenery and its capacity to cure spiritual
ills. I will now go on record and say that it is not a bad medicine
for physical ailments. The symptoms of Punta Arenas Tummy,
apart from the obvious ones, are a permanent headache, dull
muscular pains and a feeling of helpless lassitude. I was suffering
from all these at eight o'clock and could not look at breakfast.
By half-past eight I had completely forgotten that I was ill and
at half-past one ate a hearty lunch.

We were sailing through the Canal Gabriel, approaching the
point where it narrows to a hair-raising 300 yards. All around

us rose high mountains. The lower slopes were coated with a dense, dripping maze of evergreen forest. Above the tree-line, huge crags were seamed with the silver of plunging streams and rivers and above the rocks was the snow, its dazzling whiteness lending an air of unreality to the endless peaks and crests of the mountains. There were glaciers too, glowing blue-grey in the distance and, on all sides, this bleak, wild, inexpressibly grand picture was mirrored in the waters of the channel.

This is what makes Tierra del Fuego unique ; the combination of eternal snows and the sea. In Tierra del Fuego, the sharp narrow spine of the Andes which, further north, divides southern Chile and Argentina like a wall, splits and spreads, the great valleys running from east to west. The range ceases to be regular, it becomes fragmented, a confusion of lakes and valleys, plateaux and gorges through which the sea flows, creating thousands of tortuous channels and islets. And because the latitudes are so southerly, the snows never melt. In winter they smother the forests down to the edge of the sea, in summer they retreat a few hundred feet. It is as if the Alps or the Pyrenees have been suddenly immersed in innumerable tons of water.

It is an empty land. For thousands of square miles there is nothing. South and west of Ushuaia and Puerto Williams there is virtually no human habitation of any kind. It is the end of the world. Beyond it there is nothing but Antarctica.

Darwin's view of Tierra del Fuego was that death, rather than life, seemed to be the prevailing spirit. He was comparing the Fuegan forests with the lush tropical jungles of Brazil and by contrast, they are almost untenanted. The guanaco, a member of the camel family, is the only indigenous quadruped south of the Magellan Straits. There are a few members of the rodent order including the coypu, which the Indians considered a delicacy. Otters live in the rivers and the sea but there are very few reptiles, only a few lizards and small frogs on the main island. Tierra del Fuego is rich only in bird-life, with over a hundred varieties, nearly all of which are migratory. On a still, dry day a Fuegan forest is silent.

Such barrenness depressed Darwin; it had little, indeed, to offer a naturalist. But Darwin lived in an age when huge areas of the world were undeveloped and untamed, where the spirit of man was still expansionist, where virgin country cried out to be settled and cultivated. In the late twentieth century, with our vast cities devouring and modern agricultural systems despoiling the land and our teeming populations — unimaginable to a Victorian — demanding that the process of destruction should continue, it is Tierra del Fuego which suggests life and the Brazilian jungles, torn up to make six-lane highways, bull-dozed to make room for new towns and new industries, that suggest the death-process. In a world which is over-inhabited, a land without people seems to be a precious place.

No man appreciated the value of unspoilt country more than Darwin. For most of his life he lived at Down House in Kent. It was sixteen miles from London and seemed so remote from the metropolis that he feared he would turn into a 'Kentish hog' — the complete country bumpkin. Down House is now part of suburbia, surrounded by the sprawls of Bromley and Croydon, though the Green Belt policy preserves some of the views and walks Darwin knew. In the face of the M2, the M20, the rapidly expanding Medway towns and the general disfigurement of North Kent, Darwin would have fled. Observing Greater London or even larger urban areas like New York, San Francisco, Tokyo and Sao Paulo, he might have recalled, with longing, the empti-ness of Tierra del Fuego.

For my own part, as one brought up in an urban environment and in an English countryside being rapidly destroyed by hous-ing development and intensive farming, Tierra del Fuego was a revelation. I accept that the needs of modern societies and ex-panding populations will and possibly must override the desire of conservationists and ecologists to preserve something of the world in its natural state. My hope, which has scant chance of being fulfilled, is that somehow a balance will be found and that we will agree to halt the process by which we devour everything before the moment comes when there is nothing left to devour but ourselves. There seems to be no limit to human ingenuity. It is quite within our capabilities to build nuclear-heated cities in Tierra del Fuego and it is possible that if enough oil is dis-covered down there we will do so. In the meantime, storm and ice and snow protect its solitude ; its green waters remain clean and clear and rich; its forests remain silent, empty and serene.

We had come to Tierra del Fuego to sail — and sail we did. In the afternoon we turned back down the Canal Gabriel on a south-easterly course and set both topsails, the fore t'gallant, three jibs, the main staysail and the mizzen. The wind gusted to force six or seven and we flew along.

It was an exhilarating experience. The *Beagle* which, from

some angles, might be considered something of a tub, became a vessel of grace and speed. Her sails assumed those beautiful curves which only the winds can create. She seemed to skim the water like a sea-bird, dipping and gliding. And all the time she was moving against a backdrop of mountains and glaciers, under the constantly changing Fuegan skies which, in the space of one hour, can display all the variabilities of four English seasons from blazing sunshine to purple storm through every combination of cloud, haze, shower and rain.

In the evening we anchored in Morris Bay.

There now began an undeclared war of attrition between Robin and the captain of the *Argonauta* whose battle-ground was the chart. The basic plan was for the *Beagle* and the *Argonauta* to proceed in convoy, going south towards the Beagle Channel. When the filming was finished the two ships would separate, the *Argonauta* to steam back to Punta Arenas, the *Beagle* to go where she would.

The problem was that to the captain of the *Argonauta* the Beagle Channel represented storms, reefs, narrows and shipwrecks. To Robin and to everyone in the *Beagle*, it represented our ultimate destination, the climax, in a sense, to our voyage. It seemed to us essential that *Beagle II* should sail in the channel named after her predecessor. Apart from a few undistinguished rocks in Patagonia, the channel discovered by Fitzroy is the only major natural feature named after the *Beagle*. We wanted to go there desperately. The captain of the *Argonauta* was equally desperate to avoid so notoriously dangerous a place. It looked like deadlock until Robin decided to do a little fact-finding.

The Beagle Channel links the Atlantic and the Pacific oceans, starting, in the east, at Picton Island and continuing west to Gordon Island where it splits into two arms, the north-west and the south-west. From that point, most charts do not show it as the Beagle Channel but as the Brecknock. However the Brecknock Channel is in fact the western end of the Beagle Channel which officially ends only in the open Pacific beyond Desolation Bay.

Robin's plan, therefore, was to appear to capitulate on the Beagle Channel issue and promote a compromise scheme of going to the *Brecknock*. The Beagle Channel, he would agree was far too dangerous but the Brecknock . . . The *Argonauta* captain, blissfully unaware that Brecknock = Beagle, readily agreed.

Morris Bay was in many ways similar to Angullo and I had a chance of going ashore to explore. The shallow water along the beach abounded in mussels. We collected hundreds for a monster *moules marinières*. Near the beach I discovered what must have been an old Indian camp. There was a circular pile of empty mussel shells enclosing a small area in which a few sticks, jutting out of the ground and now soft and spongy with lichen, showed that many years ago some Yaghans or Alacaloofs had built a wigwam.

I climbed up the steep hill, away from the beach, through a belt of thorny bushes which may have been the type of berberis whose berries, called by the Yaghans *umushamaim*, are edible. I could see no fruit however and, not for the first time, bemoaned the fact that I was so ignorant about natural history. *Umushamaim* are probably quite disgusting but I would have liked to have found some and tasted them. Another staple food of the Indians, clams, I knew only too well. On the *Argonauta* where, during filming, we ate our main meals since we could not operate the galley on the *Beagle*, the cook served these tasteless lumps of rubber daily.

I wandered for a time in a stretch of forest, collecting samples of the innumerable varieties of moss which cover the trunks of the trees, clothe the rocks in soft, green fur and form strange little pyramids and outcrops of their own. It was not until the end of the day that I had a chance to explore a Fuegan forest in real depth. After hours of filming, we sailed down a narrow channel called the Seno Magellanes, at the end of which, glowing blue in the fading light, was the most beautiful glacier we had yet seen.

We anchored at the end of the channel in a cul-de-sac formed by sheer cliffs on two sides and, opposite the entrance, a wide, shingle beach behind which was thick forest. Looming over the forest, so close we thought it must be only a short walk, was the glacier.

There is no such thing as a short walk in a Fuegan forest. Every yard is a struggle with clinging brambles, slippery moss, fallen branches which crack under your weight and almost impenetrable tangles of crazily twisted, half-uprooted trees. Moreover, it is vital to tread warily. The ground appears to be solid, in fact it is as treacherous as quicksand.

The forest has been growing, untouched by man, for thousands of years. Each winter the heavy snows settle on the trees. Rotten

with age and moss and lichen, the trees are crushed and fall,
forming a bed of broken limbs and branches, a heaped pile, like
an unlit bonfire. Through this bed, which may be as much as
twenty or thirty feet deep, new trees grow. Moss and ferns mask
the skeletons of the dead trees and give the ground an appearance of solidity. This is an illusion. Everywhere there are gaps
and holes and if you are unfortunate enough to fall into one,
you might find yourself entombed under many feet of rotting
vegetation, probably with a broken leg. For this reason it is
unsafe to explore the forests alone.

It was extraordinary that one or two of the *Beagle*'s crew did
not end up in a Fuegan forest pit on the evening when we
fought our way through to the glacier. A kind of fever gripped
everyone, a fever to get to the glacier before dark.

There was a shallow, pelting stream running between the
forest and the cliffs out into the channel and we knew that this
must be the outlet from the glacial lagoon. All we had to do,
then, was to follow the stream, skirting the edge of the forest.
This was possible depending on how soaked you were prepared
to get or how much you relished the thought of being swept
away by the powerful current and playing water-polo with the
little icebergs constantly swirling through the rocks and rapids.
Personally, I chose to hack my way through the forest using the
noise from the stream as a directional guide — the forest itself
was a labyrinth. Not so, Mark. He had been unable to visit the
glacier near Angelito owing to film-extra duties ; he was absolutely determined not to miss out on this one. Currents, icebergs,
slippery rocks, overhanging branches, he cared nothing for such
hazards. His was not a brisk stride or even a dogged trot — he
ran. His face was the grim mask of a man ruthlessly set on
seeing a glacier.

I plodded steadily through the forest then down to an open
space where the stream divided in grey-blue mud-flats and was
easily fordable. I paused to examine the mud which was made
up of incredibly fine particles and would make the fortune of
any porcelain manufacturer. I chose the right-hand branch of
the stream.

Two minutes later I rounded a bend and there was the glacier.
It lay in a circus of desolate grey rock and shale like an enormous sapphire. The lagoon at its base was packed with icebergs
which were so tightly jammed together it seemed possible to walk
out over them right up to the face of the glacier itself.

Several of my companions were in fact attempting this feat.
I could see Manchester Geoff, intrepid as ever, leaping from
block to block ; coming towards me, his nineteenth-century naval
officer's uniform drenched and dripping, was Mark, who had
evidently tried to follow Manchester and had fallen into the
lagoon for his pains.

I was not in the mood for acrobatics. I preferred to sit on a
rock and contemplate the scene. It was awesome enough. The
glacier did not have the majestic height of the one near Angelito
but paradoxically this made it all the more impressive. One
could really think of it as a frozen river ; it was accessible, intimate. One could reach out and touch its blue glass surface, one
could dip one's hand into the lagoon and feel the chill, the bitter
chill of the Ice Age transported, through centuries of the glacier's
slow movement, into the still water.

Six or seven wild duck flew over the lagoon in an arrow
formation. The light was fading fast from the sky though the
glacier still radiated its soft, blue luminence. It was time to go.
We began to make tracks back towards the ford. Suddenly there
was a noise like a thousand thunderclaps. We looked back
towards the glacier. There had been a huge fall. Vast chunks
of blue ice were shunting into the white ice. The whole lagoon
seemed to be boiling with ice. When we arrived at the ford, we
found the level of the stream six or seven inches higher. In a
few minutes the pressure from the ice-fall had turned the stream
into a torrent. We crossed it with difficulty.

I re-entered the forest and began to battle my way back towards the beach. I tripped over a concealed root, rolled and
slithered down a sodden moss-bank, landing with a squelch in
the bottom of a little dell. I scrambled to my feet but did not
move on for some minutes. The last rays of the sun were filtering
through a gap in the dense foliage, lighting up the interior of
the dell. I found that I was standing in a cavern of green, a
kaleidoscope of green. Every subtle nuance of the colour was
represented: the pale, crusty, yellowish tinge of ancient lichen,
the fresh translucent hue of budding fern-shoots, the almost
black colour of the strands of dripping moss which hung from
the branches like stalactites. The only way I can think of describing the effect of all these thousands of delicate dots and
intricate patterns of green is to say that it was like a vast
pointilliste painting. But I doubt if the brush even of a Seurat
could have captured the infinite variations on the theme of green

encapsulated in that little Fuegan dell.

It was extraordinary and wonderful.

The next day, Sunday 4th December, the *Beagle* entered the channel which bears her name.

We had left the Seno Magellanes at 0200 hours. Between 1030 and 1100 we passed into the Pacific Ocean, encountering a typical long swell, and by 1715 were sailing down Brecknock towards the west arm of Edwards Bay. Nearly one hundred and fifty years after Robert Fitzroy had discovered this channel, a three masted barquantine called the *Beagle* was scudding through its green, choppy waters with — for the record — her fore and main topsails and inner jib set.

It was my luck that I had the day off that particular Sunday and could spend the time wallowing in history. The names of some of the small islands we passed — Isla Fitz Roy, Isla King, Isla Basket, Isla Button — confirmed, as if it needed confirmation, that we were in genuine *Beagle* territory at last. Each name was rich in associations with the past, the past which we were recreating for the BBC camera on the *Argonauta*.

Isla Button was particularly evocative not only because Jemmy Button was so bound up in the history of the voyage of the *Beagle* but because he continued to play a rôle in the later history of Tierra del Fuego, forming a link between Fitzroy's pioneering attempt to convert the Yaghans and the first, catastrophic ventures of the Patagonian Missionary Society.

Until I began to read in detail about the history of Tierra del Fuego I assumed that the Patagonian Missionary Society was an amusing myth, like the List of Huntingdonshire Cabmen, and was surprised to find that it had actually existed. It was founded by an ex-naval captain called Allen Gardiner who, after the death of his wife, dedicated himself to spreading the Word among the heathen. The remotest and most heathenish heathen he could think of were the natives of Tierra del Fuego.

In 1850, after an initial attempt to contact Jemmy Button had failed, he and seven companions were landed at Banner Cove. Though they had adequate supplies for six months they almost immediately discovered that the most important items, their reserves of ammunition, had been left behind on the support vessel which would not return for six months. This was a disaster. They had no means of hunting for the food they would need and no means of defence against the swarms of Indians who now began to plague them, steal from them and generally harass them in true

Yaghan style. The party was forced to quit Banner Cove and
seek shelter in Spaniard Harbour, a place so desolate and wind-
swept that even the natives kept away from it. There, the first
agents of the Patagonian Missionary Society starved to death.
Allen Gardiner was the last to die, on September 5th 1851 and
in his final testament, an extraordinary document found by his
body months later, he not only exhorted his friends in England
to carry on the work of the Lord in Tierra del Fuego but
detailed practical suggestions as to how this work should be
accomplished.

This was that the Society should establish a settlement in the
Falkland Islands where Yaghans, temporarily transported from
the hostile environment of Tierra del Fuego, could be taught in
peace and security and then taken back to their native country
to spread the Word.

For a man dying of exposure and starvation to produce such a
practical scheme was amazing. Gardiner's unquenchable faith
inspired the Rev. George Despard, the Honorary Secretary of the
Society, to put the plan into action. A settlement was founded
on Keppel Island in the Falklands and in early 1855 the Society's
schooner, the *Allen Gardiner*, commanded by a tough old salt
called Captain Snow, anchored in Wulaia Cove.

It was a repetition of the scene Fitzroy had witnessed over
twenty years before. Five or six canoes came out to meet the ship
and standing in the bow of the first was Jemmy Button. All that
remained of his years in the *Beagle*, his visit to England, his
audience with the King, was a smattering of English and a faint
modesty about being seen naked by Captain Snow's wife. He
demanded a pair of breeches and braces to hold them up.

Jemmy refused point blank to return to Keppel Island with
Snow and was unable to persuade any of his compatriots. In the
light of this initial failure, Rev. Despard decided to take over
the project personally. With one of his adopted sons, Thomas
Bridges, he went out to Tierra del Fuego and, under his leader-
ship, some progress was made. A few Yaghan families were
settled on Keppel Island and Thomas Bridges began to learn
their language. In 1859 it was decided to set up a permanent
mission at Wulaia.

The new captain of the *Allen Gardiner*, Mr. Fell, and a young
missionary called Garland Philips, were entrusted with this task.
When they arrived at Wulaia there was the usual trouble over
pilfering and the standard cacophony of begging—led by Jemmy

Button. However, the white men persevered, constructed a small hut and on 6th November, the whole crew of the schooner, with the exception of the cook, Alfred Cole, with over a hundred natives, attended the first church service ever held in Tierra del Fuego. It began with a hymn and ended, a few minutes later, in a massacre.

Without warning the Indians attacked the white men with spears, stones and clubs. Garland Philips managed to escape from the scene of carnage in the little, makeshift church, and ran down to the beach. Jemmy Button's brother, known as Tommy, struck him down and left him, unconscious, to drown in the shallows.

The ringleader of the massacre was undoubtedly Jemmy Button and nobody has ever been able to offer a satisfactory explanation of why this once cheerful and friendly boy, who had never received anything but kindness from white men, should have turned into a bloody murderer.

The sole survivor of the bloodshed was Alfred Cole. When the natives paddled out to the *Allen Gardiner* to loot it, he escaped in a dinghy and took to the woods. For weeks he lived a life of semi-starvation subsisting on limpets, mussels and berries and then he was captured. For some reason the natives spared his life but they pulled out his beard, moustache and eyebrows and stripped him naked.

In this condition he was rescued three months later by a vessel sent out from Keppel Island. The artful Jemmy, frightened of reprisals, went back to Keppel Island to give his version of the story. It naturally absolved Jemmy of all blame. According to him it had been the fierce, almost legendary, Ona tribe who had been responsible for the killings. Nobody believed Jemmy but nobody was prepared to take action against him.

Rev. Despard now despaired of ever establishing the Christian religion among the Yaghans. He left for England. But Thomas Bridges remained. He believed that the secret of converting the Indians lay in learning their language — and he proved it. Between 1863 and 1866 he helped Rev. Whait Stirling establish firm contacts between Keppel Island and Wulaia. Jemmy Button was still alive and his attitude was now one of absolute co-operation. In 1866 Rev. Stirling took four Yaghan boys to England. One of them was Jemmy Button's son, Threeboy.

The mission was moved from Wulaia to a new site in the Beagle Channel called Ushuaia in 1869. Jemmy remained at

The author in costume
and, below, with Socky
in Chiloé, deadlocked

Bureaucracy and disaster
in Chile:

A typical document, with
stamps and official signatures
almost outnumbering the crew

A Chilean warship aground
off Tierra del Fuego

Wulaia and passes out of history. It is likely that such a skilled
opportunist lived to a ripe old age.

So much for Jemmy Button. What happened to Fitzroy's other
two protégés, Fuegia Basket and York Minster? Curiously enough
there is a record of their fate and it is owing to the remarkable
Thomas Bridges that we know about it.

Bridges was the founding father of Ushuaia, until recently the
world's southernmost town and still a flourishing community.
In 1887 he gave up missionary work and carved a farm out of
the Fuegan wilderness. It was called Harberton and, with other
estancias, is still in the possession of his descendants. He also
wrote the first and only dictionary of the Yaghan language which
contained over thirty thousand words. The history of the Bridges
family is the history of Tierra del Fuego.

A few years after Bridges' Mission had been started at Ushuaia,
a party of Yaghans called Alisimoonoala paid a visit. They came
from the Brecknock Peninsula — precisely where *Beagle II* was
completing her filming over a hundred years later — and among
them was Fuegia Basket. She had forgotten almost all her English but remembered Captain Fitzroy and the *Beagle* and Queen
Adelaide. She told Bridges that York Minster was dead. He had
killed a man and had himself been murdered in revenge. Fuegia
had a new husband, a youth of eighteen.

Ten years later, in 1883, Bridges was visiting the western part
of Tierra del Fuego, the Brecknock Channel and London Island,
and decided to call on Fuegia. She was well over sixty and dying.
He tried to console her by reviving her memories of the Christian
religion, the certainty of God's forgiveness and the after-life but
the concepts were meaningless to her. She had long since forgotten the precepts taught to her by Rev. Wilson all those years
ago in Walthamstow. Fuegia Basket, like Jemmy Button and
York Minster, died a pagan.

It was a curious feeling, sailing among the islands and channels
where Fuegia had lived for so many years in a ship which she
would probably have recognised as the *Beagle*.

On our last day of filming, in Desolation Bay, we passed and
re-passed Basket Island. It was grey, drizzling weather and the
island looked bleak and dour. For the first time I felt depressed
about the emptiness of the land. The thought of Fuegia Basket's
death reminded me of the fate of her people, wiped out by the
viruses imported by the white men, the remnants hunted down
and shot by the panners and diggers of the brief Fuegan gold-

rush of the late 1890's. I was reminded too of the extermination of the Yaghans' great enemies, the Ona, who lived in the forests north of Ushuaia and who were systematically butchered by men like the notorious McInch who, in the early years of this century, were establishing vast sheep ranches on the main island of Tierra del Fuego.

The history of Tierra del Fuego is as strange and savage as its landscapes.

By the afternoon of the 5th December, the filming schedule was complete. The final sequences were rough weather shots. The whole crew was dressed in extraordinary costumes, apparently copies of early nineteenth-century sou-westers, which appeared to be made out of cotton and tar. As the *Beagle* dipped and rolled in the Pacific swell, we hopped about the rigging simulating panic. We were all tired. The strain of playing extras and simultaneously running the ship was beginning to tell. Punta Arenas Tummy was still claiming victims and there was a frayed, faintly mutinous atmosphere in the ship.

Before we finally parted from our BBC friends, there was a ritual to be observed. This was a systematic search of the *Beagle*, Gestapo-style, by Reg and Michael, who were in charge of the wardrobe department.

It was a long-established custom that all the members of the *Beagle*'s crew would attempt to hang on to the choicer items of their costumes. It was equally established that Reg and Michael would try to thwart them. As a result they were familiar with every nook and cranny of the ship. They burrowed away like professional customs men, unearthing a wealth of contraband. The growing pile of stolen hats, shirts, jackets and trousers on the deck proved that, in the thieving line, the crew of the *Beagle* was streets ahead of the Yaghan Indians.

This is the moment to pause and consider the outstanding talent and professionalism of the BBC film crew. As I have said before there is no more difficult a task than to film a costume drama. With all the resources of a well-found studio, with constant access to craftsmen, experts and special technicians, it presents enormous problems. Switch the enterprise to the extreme south of Chile, substitute for a studio an ex-Rhine riverboat and you would think it impossible to maintain the standards of precision and authenticity for which the BBC are world-famous. The men and women selected to make *The Voyage of Charles Darwin* simply achieved the impossible and they were able to do so because each one was the very best in his particular speciality.

The men responsible for co-ordinating their efforts were no less remarkable. Martyn Friend, the director, is one of the nicest people one could ever hope to meet. If film directors can be divided between dictators and diplomatists, Martyn was the diplomatist *par excellence* — and there were many times when he needed to be! I will not embarrass my old shipmate Ned Kelly, naturalist and co-producer, with fulsome compliments. He would not like it. It would not be decent. I will only say that it is a measure of his selfless generosity that he once gave me a bottle of pure malt whisky, thereby saving my life. The supremo of the whole enterprise was, of course, Chris Ralling. The ultimate responsibility for the filming, with all the complexities of administration and organisation and all the potential for disaster, was his. Men who are prepared to shoulder such burdens are rare. I am certainly not one of them.

At half-past two in the afternoon of the 5th December the *Beagle* and the *Argonauta* parted for the last time. The *Argonauta* set a course for Punta Arenas, and the *Beagle* . . . Well, where were we to go?

It was a matter of some debate. There was a strong movement in favour of continuing down the Beagle Channel and rounding Cape Horn which was only a few hundred miles away. In theory this was an exciting idea. There is undeniably a certain magic about Cape Horn. But certain factors militated against it. The first was that we were not insured for rounding the Horn. The second was that everybody on board was exhausted and in no condition to encounter a storm. Our luck so far had been so phenomenal, it would seem like tempting fate to go further south. Finally, Christmas was approaching. Robin and I were flying home but the rest of the crew would be celebrating on board and none of them wanted to be stuck in the middle of nowhere. The nearest centre of civilisation suitable for the sort of revels people had in mind was one of the large Chilean ports to the north and the general consensus was in favour of Valparaiso, some 1600 miles away. It the ship were to get there by Christmas, we could not afford any delays. We still had some formidable obstacles to surmount. We had to make our way out of the Magellan Straits into the Pacific, historically as dangerous a venture as rounding the Horn itself. We had to negotiate the serpentine channels of Archipelagic Chile. We had to cross the notorious Gulf of Penas and we were bound to encounter contrary winds.

These were the arguments of logic and common sense. The counter argument was to hell with the insurance company, to hell with Christmas, to hell with storms, let's go to Cape Horn.

I have never been able to work out which view I favoured but in the event we turned north, not south.

It is probably as well that we did so because during that first day after the filming, hardly a soul stirred on the *Beagle* apart from the watches. By tacit consent it was an unofficial and much-needed day off. The weather was deteriorating, with heavy rain and the wind and sea rising. At about four in the afternoon we were passing through the sinisterly named Paso Tortuoso and at six all hands were called to lash and secure the decks which were still cluttered with BBC props.

On the 7th I was on the dreaded midnight to four watch. We were now back in the Magellan Strait. There was a strong head wind howling down the channel and we were making a bare 1 knot in the face of it. It was a pitch black night with driving rain and all we really needed to complete our misery was to collide with another ship. At 2.30 in the morning we nearly did. We spotted a light directly ahead of us and, after ten or fifteen minutes identified it as that of a ship. In the prescribed manner we altered course slightly in order to pass her, port side to port side. All was proceeding according to the rules when the other ship suddenly and unaccountably veered to port. As once before, I found myself frantically spinning the wheel, putting on full starboard helm and cursing fluently while Mark, cool as ever, said: 'Most extraordinary. Can't think what the chap's playing at.'

It was a near-run thing. We were making very little way and the *Beagle* seemed to take an age to pay off to starboard while the other ship seemed determined to ram us. It passed us with a few yards to spare and was swallowed up by the night.

All night the wind increased until the ship was virtually stationary. We decided to run for shelter and wait for it either to diminish or veer to a favourable quarter. At eight o'clock we put into a small bay called Puerto Augusto on the north-west coast of Desolation Island.

This was my last chance to explore a Fuegan island and I have described elsewhere how I scaled the cliff by a waterfall and looked down at the *Beagle* riding at anchor in the bay and felt that I had stepped through a gap in time.

This curious experience, however, did not occupy more than a few minutes of the two or three hours I spent rambling about the island.

My companion initially was Robin and by the time we had explored the big lake which lay directly behind the head of the waterfall, had examined the soil near a placid stream, overhung with beech trees, which might have been somewhere in Wales or Scotland, we had worked out a complete scheme for a self-sufficient farm on Desolation Island.

We selected a spectacular site for a house on a ledge of flat rock half-way up the cliff, near the waterfall, with a magnificent view down the channel out into the Strait. Below the house was an acre or so of dry, level ground, suitable for growing vegetables. The forests rising behind the lake would support a considerable herd of reindeer and in the bay itself there was a narrow lagoon, protected by a thin spit of land which would form a natural harbour for our small boats. By the time Robin had to return to the *Beagle* our scheme was worked out to the last detail.

I now teamed up with Jason and we decided to climb the nearest hill. As we mounted higher and higher we discovered small lakes at every level, diminishing in size, until, at the summit, a flat table two or three hundred yards round, we found a perfectly circular pool, three or four feet deep, out of which a tiny stream ran to the very edge of the precipice then plunged vertically down, six or seven hundred feet into the forest below.

Earlier we had come across traces of previous visitors to the island. On a ledge or rock were some stones laid out in a pattern that appeared to spell the word MORIPUE. It was evident that the winds had shifted some of the smaller stones over the years and we did not waste much time puzzling over the possible significance of moripue but instead yielded to the overwhelming temptation similarly to record our own visit. We gathered the largest stones we could find and so placed them that they formed the following:

BEAGLE
77

I hope that, if the winter gales of Desolation Island obliterate the date, the name Beagle will remain to excite future explorers.

We decided to make our way back down from the top of the hill via a steep gulley which was choked with trees. It was the same wild tangle and with the same vivid profusion of greens, as the forest at the Seno Magellanes, but vertical rather than horizontal. At times we seemed to be descending a ladder of rotting tree-trunks and twisted boughs. We saw several species of birds. They were evidently so unused to the presence of human beings that they showed no fear of us, merely observing our slithering progress with an ironical tweet or two.

As we sat on the beach, waiting to be collected by the rubber boat, we saw an otter pop his head out of the green, glistening water, then disappear, leaving a trail of bubbles on the surface. I decided that Desolation Island was wrongly named. It was a perfect example of all that I found exhilarating about Tierra del Fuego — it's peace, its sombre beauty, its invulnerability to the despoiling hand of man.

And, strange to relate, it was while thus pondering, that I suddenly realised I wanted to go home.

I was once in a small city in France which contained a large cathedral. It was July, the heat was intense, my car had broken down and my wallet had been stolen. I had spent a nightmare morning arguing with garage mechanics, bank officials and policemen. I had lost both my temper and my capacity to speak comprehensible French. I had a pain in my head and about two francs in my pocket. On an impulse I turned into the cathedral. It was empty and silent, deliciously dim and cool after the white glare of the streets outside. I sat down in a pew and looked up at the slender, graceful columns and arches, at the soft, jewelled light glowing in the great rose window. From some distant vestry or lady-chapel I heard the sound of a medieval chant, a simple cadence uncluttered with harmonies and descants and I had a sudden feeling of revulsion against the hectic tawdriness of the modern world and a longing for a life of simplicity and quiet contemplation.

The singing ceased, a gaggle of youths, released from choir-practice, clattered down the aisle, chewing gum. I walked out of the cathedral. I went to the bank. Telexes had been clacking efficiently between France and England. I fingered a wad of crisp banknotes. I went out into the main square where in the simple, contemplative days they had burned heretics and proceeded to the garage. The car was repaired, its engine running sweetly again, ready to take me to Spain or Italy or anywhere I wanted to go. I was free.

The ten minutes I had spent in that cathedral had been an

interlude. For better or for worse I was a child of the twentieth
century and there was nothing I could, or particularly wanted,
to do about it.

Sitting on the rocks by the still waters of Desolation Island,
with the great cliffs towering over me like the nave of a cathedral
built out of living rock, I realised that my time in Tierra del
Fuego was also an interlude. Tierra del Fuego was a place for
reflection and refreshment, a place to which I wanted to return
some day and explore more deeply but not a place of which I
could ever be part.

I would never build that house by the waterfall or plant vegetables in the lush little acre by the beach.

I recalled an experiment Adler carried out with rats. He
constructed two cages linked by a corridor. In the first cage
there was overcrowding, sex, violence and cannibalism. In the
second cage there was space, food and water. One day he opened
the corridor between the two cages, expecting the rats to migrate
permanently to the paradise of cage two. They didn't. They
went to cage two only to feed, drink, rest a while, then they
scurried back to cage one, where the action was. They liked it.

I do not see myself precisely as an Adlerian rat but there is a
sense in which Tierra del Fuego can be compared with Adler's
second cage. Maybe one day I will have the sense to go and
live in it.

Part Three

GOING NORTH

South-Western Coast of Chile

0   50   100 Nautical miles

SOUTH

PACIFIC

OCEAN

Puerto Montt

Ancud

Isla Chiloé

Chonos Archipelago

Bahia Anna Pink

Golfo de Peñas
Wager Is.

Wellington Is.

Angostura Inglesa

Queen Adelaide Archipelago

Strait of Magellan

Isla Desolación

Isla Santa Inez

Canal Cockburn
Beagle Channel

Punta Arenas

Cordillera de los Andes

Cordillera Darwin

C   H   I   L   E

40°S

45°S

50°S

55°S

78°W   75°W   72°W

9

TIERRA DEL FUEGO—CHILOÉ

8-13 December

WE left Desolation Island at three o'clock in the afternoon. Prior to weighing anchor Robin had gone out into the Straits in the rubber boat to see what the wind and waves were doing and, as was his invariable policy in ventures likely to be particularly uncomfortable, he insisted that I accompany him.

From the shelter of the channel the waves in the Strait appeared to be much less steep than they had been in the morning and the wind had definitely abated.

'Better just nip out and make sure,' said Robin, gunning the outboard.

We sped out into the Straits and immediately the waves took on the appearance of moving mountains. Robin steered across and round them expertly.

'What if you made a mistake and went straight into one?' I enquired.

'We'd sink.'

'Oh.'

I noticed that the bow of the boat, normally taut and rigid, was flopping about.

'Is this thing leaking?' I asked.

'Yes.'

'Badly?'

'Oh no.'

'The bow seems to be flapping about like a burst balloon.'

'Well sit on it then.'

'But I'll get wet.'

'You'll get even wetter if you don't.'

So I sat on it, comforting myself with the thought that I was at least getting a fish-eye view of the Magellan Straits.

The *Beagle* finally quitted the Straits at 9.40 that evening, turning north into the Canal Smyth.

There was a new face on board. This was the pilot provided by the Chilean admiralty to take us up through the maze of channels and islands extending for seven hundred miles from Desolation Island to the island of Chiloé.

We called the pilot Rocky, an in-joke too convoluted to explain. Rocky was in his mid-forties. He had a neat moustache and smartly trimmed black hair. His appearance was dapper.

When he arrived at the dock in Punta Arenas and saw the *Beagle*, all of ninety feet long, he could not believe his eyes. He was almost tearful as he explained to Robin that his special expertise was piloting the largest vessels currently afloat. Indeed he was one of two Chilean pilots specially trained in Holland to guide super-tankers through the deadly narrows of the southern archipelago. When he was shown the accommodation below decks he nearly fainted.

'But where am I going to *sleep?*' he cried.

'Oh, don't worry, we'll clear out Alf's old bunk in the centre cabin.'

(Alf's leave of absence from the Navy had terminated in Punta Arenas. He had flown back with the BBC, leaving a void in the life of the ship.)

Rocky was used to luxuriously appointed commercial ships in which the pilot was provided with his own cabin and bathroom and dined, in style, with the officers. We discovered that he had not brought with him so much as an anorak, let alone the wet-weather gear which was vital to one's comfort on the *Beagle*.

Needless to say, whilst we had been in convoy with the *Argonauta*, Rocky hardly set foot on the *Beagle*. But now he had no alternative. He was doomed to Alf's old bunk and a seat at the communal table in the saloon. We rummaged around and found him an old horse-hair mattress (yes, the very one I had long ago discarded), a couple of blankets, some sea-boots which were far too small and some oil-skins that were far too large. He received these gifts with bulging eyes.

My heart bled for him, especially one morning, very early, when I found him standing alone in the centre of the saloon looking as if someone had just bashed him on the head with a belaying pin.

'What's the matter?' I asked him. He spoke English fairly fluently but with a very pronounced accent.

'This ship,' he stuttered. 'Never in my life have I known such a ship. Dreadful. Dreadful.'

I saw his point but was slightly nettled by his attitude.

'It's not exactly a luxury liner,' I said, 'but it's not that bad.'

'Terrible, terrible,' said Rocky. 'I do not expect much on such a ship but now I cannot even brush my teeth.'

I suddenly realised what had happened. I tried, and failed, to keep a straight face.

At sea, in order to conserve our fresh water supplies, we filled the tanks serving the showers and the taps in the lavatories and galley, with sea-water. Rocky, unaware of this, had pottered into the lavatory to brush his teeth and had got a mouthful of salt.

'Sea-water! In the taps!' he cried. 'Incredible.'

If Rocky found our living conditions primitive, he was terrified by our apparent lack of seamanship. His job, which he shared, on a rota system, with Robin and Mark, was navigation. When on duty he would give the helmsman course alterations. He was used to the electronic gadgetry of ultra-modern ships where the courses are worked out on a computer and fed to an automatic pilot. The *Beagle* had no such refinements. In any kind of sea it was difficult to keep her to within five degrees either side of her course. Rocky did not understand this.

'What are you steering?' he would ask the helmsman.

'340,' would come the reply.

There would be a pause while Rocky pored over his chart, then he would say.

'Hmm, go to 299.'

The helmsman would look helplessly at his fellow watch-members and mutter:

'Is he mad?'

In the *Beagle* some helmsmen were better than others and others were, quite frankly, pretty casual.

When there was a particularly sloppy man on the helm Rocky would go through agonies. He would stand on the quarterdeck watching the bowsprit swinging wildly from side to side, wringing his hands.

Once, I tried to reassure him.

'Don't worry,' I said, 'she's a difficult ship to steer, but we've come all the way from England without hitting anything.'

'You are all crazy,' exploded Rocky. 'You do not know how to steer a ship.'

'Well, never mind. If we do hit a reef we can always string the culprit up from the yard-arm. That's one of the handy things about a yard-arm.'

This pleasantry goaded Rocky to further fury.

'You don't understand. We hit the rocks and the admiral takes my papers and tears them up. I am finished, ruined.'

He made tearing-up gestures with his hands.

'Don't worry,' I said soothingly, 'we'd always find a job for you on the *Beagle*.'

He stared at me unbelievingly for a moment then managed to smile.

'You English. Your humour is very dark.'

'Black.'

'Yes, black.'

The bowsprit swung round through thirty or forty degrees Rocky shuddered.

'Never have I had such a pilotage,' he muttered.

After a few days on board, during which we managed to keep off the rocks, Rocky began to unbend a little. He was teased unmercifully and he began to enjoy it. It was clear that he still regarded us all as maniacs, but comparatively harmless ones. Once, in a mellow mood, after I had bought him several large whiskies, he said:

'Seriously, you have come all this way from England. How is it possible?'

'You may well ask,' I replied.

In every decent tale of travel and adventure there comes a dramatic moment when, through some unforeseen disaster, the food runs out. There is a shipwreck or a landslide or an avalanche and the protagonists are forced to live off the land or the sea and there follow pages of the most gruesome descriptions of people sucking the fluid from fish-spines, devouring the raw flesh of jungle-rats and chewing bark. It is inadvisable to read such passages after a heavy dinner.

We did not run out of food in the *Beagle*, we ran out of tobacco which, for some of us, was very much worse.

We had been relying on the stores in the *Argonauta* to replenish our own supplies of cigarettes and were horrified to discover, on the last day of filming, that the *Argonaut*'s supply officer had miscalculated and there was none to be had.

The main sufferer was, of course, Manchester Geoff. After three or four days without cigarettes, he became positively ill. Suzanne diagnosed nicotine withdrawal symptoms. I was luckier than some because, as well as cigarettes, I smoke a pipe and I had plenty of tobacco. Even so, I shall never forget the feeling of savage joy I experienced when, searching through the debris in my bunk for the twentieth time, I discovered a crumpled, half-empty packet of the cheapest Brazilian cigarettes. The sense of power I felt as I decided who should share this priceless hoard with me was disgusting.

It was Ravey Dave who unearthed a box of clay pipes, the property of the BBC props department. Soon the most hardened cigarette addicts were puffing away at these early Victorian items and if I had had an ounce of commercial get-up-and-go I would have made a fortune selling pipe-tobacco.

One evening, drawing contentedly at my trusty old briar, I suggested to Manchester that this was a golden opportunity for him to give up smoking once and for all. He was slumped on a banquette in the saloon, hollow-eyed and shaking.

If I am not allowed to print the text of the pantomime, then I cannot print his reply.

The real horror of the Great Tobacco Crisis was that between Desolation Island and the port of Ancud on Chiloé, there is absolutely nothing. There is one small port, called Puerto Natales, but that was several hundred miles off our course. We could not possibly make such a detour in order to buy a few thousand fags.

I rather regretted this. I should have liked to visit Puerto Natales because I think it must be the place where, towards the end of the nineteenth century, my sea-faring great-grandfather killed the ship's cook.

He did not physically kill the cook, of course, he merely instructed the sawbones to sign a death certificate which he then countersigned. The reason was as follows.

He was the master and owner of a trading ship whose home port was Belfast. On every voyage he made sure that there was a good stock of Irish linen which commanded a very high price in remote places and was subject to even higher duty. He had pre-sold a large quantity of linen to some Chilean merchants but the customs officials had been tipped off and had demanded an extortionate tax.

My great-grandfather decided therefore that the time was ripe for the cook, who was extremely fat, officially to expire. The ship's carpenter made a suitably vast coffin which was carried ashore and interred, with impressive rites, in the local cemetery. During the service, the Chilean merchants slipped my great-grandfather a large wad of money and, the same night, when his ship was well out to sea, returned to the grave-yard and dug up the coffin—which, of course, was packed with Irish linen.

Apart from the Great Tobacco Crisis, the first few days sailing north through the archipelago were calm and uneventful. We saw only one other vessel, a Chilean warship heading our way. We contacted her by radio—the radio had been cured of Victor's Disease by naval technicians in Punta Arenas—and the captain agreed to keep an eye on us.

Initially the scenery was very much like that of Tierra del Fuego but as we went north snow gave way to forest, the mountains became less jagged and more rounded. It grew perceptibly warmer. We were visited several times by schools of dolphins and one morning I saw a remarkable sight—an albatross playing a game of Blind Man's Bluff with some baby seals.

Southern Chile appeared to be almost emptier than Tierra del Fuego. The huge southern archipelago is virtually uninhabited. Only three per cent. of Chile's total population live south of Chiloé. It caused quite a stir, therefore, when, one morning we saw a plume of smoke rising from the woods on the starboard side of the channel—the Canal Concepción.

Partly because smoke is a recognised international signal of distress, mostly out of curiosity, we altered course towards the smoke. We hove to a few yards from the shore — Rocky wringing his hands and muttering about shoals—and found not a party of marooned sailors, but a group of mussel-divers.

In Punta Arenas I had bought a pound of smoked mussels which were packed together on a loop of string but I had never got round to eating them. The rubbery, black blobs did not, in any case, look very appetising. But in this part of the world they are considered a delicacy and we now discovered how they were gathered and smoked.

The mussel-men seemed astonished to see a nineteenth-century British warship in their forgotten little cove but courteously, if a little nervously, allowed a few of us to go ashore and showed us round their camp.

It consisted of two makeshift huts constructed of corrugated iron and old packing cases. One hut was piled with mattresses and cushions and this was where the five men and three boys slept. The other hut was the smokery and was more flimsily built, with a slatted roof to allow the smoke to escape. On the floor were slow-burning wood fires above which the shelled mussels were strung.

Beyond the smokery was the shelling department, nothing but

an enormous pile of old shells, most of them well over six inches long. There were two boats and in one was an antiquated diving suit with a brass, glass-fronted helmet and next to it a hand-operated air pump. This was the primitive tackle with which the mussel-divers collected the giant shellfish which are found only in deep water. I asked one of the divers how much of the year they spent in these lonely channels and he told me not more than a month.

We suspected that the divers were camping there illegally as they would not allow us to photograph the site close to. I wondered how many mussels they needed to gather in a month to provide an income for the rest of the year. Judging by the huge pile of empty shells, it must be hundreds of thousands.

Towards noon the weather began to deteriorate. The sky became overcast and a fine drizzle began to fall. We were approaching the most dangerous narrows in the whole of southern Chile, the Angostura Inglés.

These narrows are just wide enough to admit a large tanker, with about six inches to spare either side, but their danger does not lie simply in their narrowness but in the vicious currents at either end and the tide-rips that can turn them into boiling whirlpools.

Long before we reached the Angostura Inglés, poor old Rocky had begun to die. He paced the deck in an agony of nerves, doubtless seeing visions of admirals tearing up his precious papers, his wife and children on the streets and himself a stoker, second class, on a tramp steamer.

As we rounded a bend in the channel in the approaches to the narrows, I thought Rocky really would die. The first sight that met our eyes was the Chilean warship which had been going to keep an avuncular eye on us, wrecked on the rocks.

She was hard aground and round her stove-in hull bobbed gaily-coloured life-rafts.

Rocky hurried up to me.

'You see,' he said, 'it is *very* dangerous. You tell your friend the captain he must not go through. It is not a joke.'

Even the irrepressible Robin had to admit that the spectacle of the doomed warship was not a good omen. But he was determined to press on. The tide was right, the wind was right, the current was right. There was no point in delay.

A moment later we had a further omen and we could not decide whether it was good or bad. Another Chilean naval vessel was coming towards us, through the Angostura, summoned, presumably, to aid the stricken warship. The name of this ship, painted in bold, black letters on the stern, was BEAGLE.

We motored towards the narrows, the ship gathering speed as the strong current gripped her.

Rocky stood on the quarter-deck, Robin stood by the wheel. At the wheel was the unflappable Haggis.

I thought a few words of reassurance to Rocky might not go amiss. His face was more than usually ashen.

'Don't worry,' I said. 'There's a very good man on the wheel.'

Rocky crossed himself.

'Very steady chap,' I went on. 'He was shot at in Argentina, you know, and didn't turn a hair.'

Rocky looked at me as if I was insane. I decided he was best left alone.

I went and stood by Robin. He did not seem unduly alarmed but when he spoke, it was softly and quietly, a sure sign of tension. He was gently relaying Rocky's instructions to Haggis whose concentration was wholly engaged on the compass dial.

We entered the narrows. The rugged shore looked dangerously close. The water seethed and swirled with currents and eddies. We seemed to be moving at a terrifying pace.

We came to the end of the first stretch. This was the critical point. We must go firmly to starboard to avoid the reefs on the port side but we must make allowances for the strong cross-current waiting to sweep us onto the rocks on the starboard side.

All went well. We surged past a little island on which stood a large statue of the Virgin Mary—a disturbing sight in the circumstances—and began to approach the second set of narrows.

I think Rocky must have been so relieved to have survived the first test that his expertise—which was second to none—momentarily deserted him. We were expecting a course change to starboard. Rocky announced a ten degree turn to port. Robin discreetly countermanded the order and we went to starboard. There was no reaction from Rocky.

Five minutes later we were through.

I went over to Rocky to congratulate him and offered to buy him a drink. He must have been feeling very shaken indeed because all he wanted was a cup of tea.

The next morning, at about six o'clock, the *Beagle* entered the Golfo de Penas, the very aptly named Gulf of Pain.

This is the only point in the route north through the archipelago where a ship is obliged to leave the shelter of the channels and venture into the open Pacific.

The Gulf of Pain has something in common with the equally notorious Bay of Biscay. Like Biscay it is shallow, with a broken, uneven bottom and the great ocean rollers pour in and are chopped up, their regular swelling rhythm turned into seething confusion. There is nothing between the Gulf of Pain and New Zealand, nothing, that is, except the Pacific. And behind it are the Andes with the winds shrieking down through the valleys to make the water in the Gulf churn and boil.

We had encountered much steeper seas on the voyage but never such confused seas. The waves converged on the ship from all angles and the *Beagle* rocked and plunged and reared and rolled and shuddered and reeled.

At times she was pitching so violently, her propellors came right out of the water and her bowsprit, all twenty feet of it, disappeared into the foaming waves.

The reader may imagine what effect all this had on my stomach. It was not as bad as that first night coming out of Salvador—by now I had some sort of sea legs—but it was pretty bad.

Suzanne was thrilled. She had several hundred doses of intravenous anti-nausea serum in her medical stores and so far she had not been able to discharge a single one into a single buttock. She was determined to make me her first victim. She cornered me in the aft cabin, brandishing a syringe. I pleaded that injections made me faint. I argued that with the ship moving so violently the tip of the needle would break off in a vein and, being pumped back to the heart, kill me. She was inexorable and, though I am reluctant to give her the credit in the circumstances, a dab hand with a syringe.

The injection had not the slightest effect. I decided to try more direct methods ; do something to take my mind off my stomach. I shinned up the fore-mast. This was certainly exciting enough to make me forget everything but clinging on to the shrouds but after a few minutes, the novelty wore off.

I tried the bowsprit where Roger and a few like-minded maniacs were enjoying being tipped in and out of the sea. I got very wet but still I could not control the nausea. I decided on shock tactics and attempted to eat a cheese sandwich. Readers with delicate stomachs have permission to skip the next couple of lines but those interested in the strange workings of the human body may be interested to learn that it is possible to ingest and regurgitate food simultaneously.

I was by no means the only one to suffer, though I was certainly the only one to do so openly. In rough seas a curious and not entirely attractive ethic emerges. However ill you may be feeling, you deny that you have even the slightest twinge of sea-sickness, as if there was something shameful and unmanly in it. You put on an exaggerated air of bravado and pretend you are revelling in the hideous motion of the ship. Crossing the Gulf of Pain I detected a great many forced smiles in ash green faces. For myself I saw no point in or indeed any possibility of denying that I was as sick as a dog and I rather enjoyed brief snatches of dialogue like this:

X. (finding me hanging over the rail, gasping): 'Pretty bad, eh?'

Self (shakily wiping my mouth): 'Can't you see I'm dying? Go away.'

X. (all concern): 'You might try sucking a pebble.'

Self (grimly): 'I haven't got a pebble. And anyway that's an old wives' tale. How are you feeling by the way?'

X. (swallowing hard and wiping a clammy brow): 'Oh, fine, fine. Nothing like a good hard blow.'

Self (clutching the rail as the ship lurches sickeningly): 'You never get sea-sick then?'

X. (the colour of detergent): 'Lord, no. Has no effect on me at all.'

Self (lying): 'Well, I think I could force down some lunch. Coming?'

X. (edging away): 'As a matter of fact I'm not very hungry. Still got a touch of P.A. tummy.'

Self: 'Try sucking a pebble.'

By mid-morning we had hoisted a few sails to help steady the ship, but our progress against the huge seas was slow. We were making between three and four knots. By late afternoon the seas began to settle into a regular swell and, although the ship's motion was still fairly extreme, I had conquered my sea-sickness. Perhaps Suzanne's injection had some effect after all.

At 6.50 the next morning we rounded the northern tip of Taytao Peninsula and sailed back into the sheltered channels of the Chonos Archipelago.

For the first time since leaving tropical waters a month and a half before, it was hot, hot enough to bask on deck and to make it desirable to cool drinks in buckets of sea-water. The sea itself was not even remotely warm.

We were now approaching a point where Chile is a mere 46 miles wide and where the great Cordillera, the mighty Andes, dominate the landscape in a way that makes you wonder if you are not seeing a mirage.

The mountains form a bastion between Chile and Argentina, a graceful edifice ; slender white peaks, as delicately pointed as icicles, and saucer-topped crests, once volcanoes. Winter and summer, the snow gleams and shimmers and the wonderful spectacle fills the horizon on the landward side as if it had been painted onto the sky.

Such was the magical backdrop to my last full day and night in the *Beagle*. There were other magical aspects. The day had begun with a spectacular sunrise over the Cordillera. It was the last time I would stand the early morning watch and the dawn was so beautiful, the pink-tinged peaks of the Andes seeming to swim in a sea of crimson cloud, I felt that nature was conspiring to make me regret that I was going home.

This feeling persisted as the day wore on, a day spent largely up the foremast where we were bending on our new course sail, Alf's masterpiece of fresh, white canvas. As I moved about on the yards, confidently, enjoying every moment of the ship and the steady, warm breeze, I reflected on the changes two or three months can bring about in a vertigo sufferer.

However, to counter my feelings of regret, was a delightful end-of-term sensation I had not experienced for years. I dug my battered suitcases out of the pile of tackle in the engine room and began to pack. In my imagination I was already home, already working out a list of people to telephone, dishes I would choose in my favourite restaurant, the route of a long walk with my dog.

In the evening we turned off the engines and set all our square sails and the feelings of regret returned. The canvas billowed against a brilliant night sky. The light of the moon turned the Cordillera into a milky dream-scape. The air was balmy and faintly scented with the spring flowers blowing on the nearby shores. It was perfection. I had to remind myself sharply that such a night was a rarity and that part of its romantic atmo-sphere was due to the fact that it was the *last* night.

At 6.40 the next morning we made our landfall at the port of Ancud on Chiloé island. A thick, white mist enveloped the ship.

We could hear a cock crowing somewhere on the invisible island.

Long before the sun began to disperse the mist an intrepid party of cigarette-addicts rowed ashore determined to knock up the nearest tobacconist. An hour or so later the mist cleared and there, before us, was . . . Devonshire.

Little round-shouldered hills, neat, green fields, hanging woods . . . A hundred and forty-three years ago Darwin had noted in his journal that the undulating, woody country of Chiloé reminded him of England. In his day the process of clearance and cultivation had barely begun. Now, large areas of the island, especially near towns, had been transformed into a landscape which vividly recalled the wilder regions of the West Country. It was like a homecoming indeed.

Robin and I had determined to leave the ship at Ancud because we were booked onto a flight from the capital, Santiago, on the 19th and we could not be sure that the *Beagle* would make Valparaiso in time. There was another reason which I will come to in due course.

Ancud was a pretty town whose steep streets were lined with clapboard buildings which time and weather had rendered pale grey and blue and pink. There was a crisp, Germanic atmosphere about the place, it was trim and orderly, but the cottage gardens with their narrow brick paths and riot of flowers reminded one of England.

There was one modern hotel in Ancud, called the Honsa, whose management was publicity-conscious. The hotel was built on a magnificent site above the town with a wonderful view of the bay and the *Beagle* riding at anchor. The management invited the whole crew to lunch and Robin and I decided to make the place our headquarters for the next four or five days. We had conceived a Scheme.

The *Beagle* was due to leave Ancud in the evening. I went aboard for the last time to collect my baggage.

It is necessary to record that a ceremony of presentation was performed on the deck—and acutely embarrassing it was too—during which I was handed a four foot long model of a barquantine, with masts two feet high, made entirely of woven reed. It was a miracle of craftsmanship and potentially one of the most conspicuous pieces of excess baggage ever to excite the greed of a rapacious airline. This was the parting gift of my shipmates, purchased by public subscription that afternoon in Ancud. As I stammered my thanks I wondered how in hell I was ever going to get the damned thing ten thousand miles back to England.

From the rocks below the hotel Robin and I watched the *Beagle* weigh anchor. It was a clear, cool evening. The sun was going down behind the hills, a great, glowing orange on a curtain of velvet. We saw the topsails run out and the mizzen hoisted and the ship moved slowly across the bay, her beautiful lines silhouetted against the purple sky.

Mark was her captain now. It was his responsibility to take her to Valparaiso, to the Galapagos for the final filming and then home to Charlestown.

We watched the *Beagle* until all we could see of her was the pin-point of light from the lamp on her mast-head twinkling in the dusk.

'Parting,' the poet Emily Dickinson once declared, 'is all we know of heaven, and all we need of hell.' Her gnomic verse exactly describes the strange mixture of feelings you experience in saying goodbye when you are at one and the same time looking back over experiences shared and happy associations formed and forward to the bright prospects of further adventures and, eventually, going home. I can think of no better way of describing my emotions as I took my leave of a ship and a crew I had grown to love.

Part Four

FOLLOWING IN DARWIN'S FOOTSTEPS

MAINLAND OF CHILE

CHILOÉ

Ancud

Castro

Chonchi

Cucao

Lake Huillinco

South Pacific Ocean

Miles
0   10   20

0   10   20   30   40   50 km

CHILOÉ

13-22 December

THE original *Beagle* made several visits to Chiloé. Fitzroy used
the island as a base for the arduous business of charting the
Chonos Archipelago, to the south. Indeed the route *Beagle II*
had taken through the channels north from Desolation Island
to Ancud had been discovered and mapped during the two
voyages of the *Beagle*.

Chiloé Island is the last outpost of civilisation as you travel
south and the first, as you travel north. The island is approximately 118 miles long and between 35 and 40 miles wide. The
principal towns are Ancud, in the north, which in Darwin's day
was called San Carlos, and Castro, formerly the capital, on the
east coast.

Darwin visited the island in January 1835. The near-by
volcano of Osorno was in eruption. Darwin watched the
spectacle through a glass. The red glow lit up the night,
throwing a long, bright reflection on the water. Later Darwin
learned that Aconcagua, a mountain 480 miles to the north, had
also been in action on the same night and, still more extraordinary, Coseguina, over 2500 miles north of Aconcagua. He
began to speculate on subterranean links between volcanoes.

On January 22nd, accompanied by Midshipman King, Darwin
set out on a journey across the island to the Pacific coast, to a
remote headland called Cucao. He went on horse-back. The first
oddity he notes is that the road from Ancud to Castro was made
out of huge logs of wood. The broader logs were laid length-
ways and the narrow ones, transversely. Such construction was
merely a succession of dangerous pitfalls for horses, especially in
winter when the wood was slippery with rain. But the Chilotan
horses had acquired, through long experience, a remarkable
nimbleness. They seemed to skip along, never putting a foot
wrong, and Darwin was able to observe the tall, impenetrable
forests through which the road zig-zagged.

He remarks on the friendly hail-fellow-well-met character of the people. A woman and two boys attached themselves to his little party and Darwin records that Chiloé was one of the rare places in South America where it was safe to travel without fire-arms.

On the first night they camped in the forest, sleeping on the bare ground under a magnificent night-sky. The next day they arrived at Castro which Darwin describes as pretty and quiet. They were entertained by the governor, Don Pedro, who offered to accompany them to Cucao. They rode south to Chonchi and then struck west, across the island, to Cucao Lake, which is now called Huillinco. The lake is twelve miles long and at its western end flows into the Pacific. There was a road of sorts to Cucao (today it does not exist) but it was so rough, Darwin decided to hire a periagua. This primitive craft was crewed by Indians whose appearance was squat and simian. 'I doubt if six uglier little men ever got into a boat together,' says Darwin. His astonishment was increased when a large cow was taken on board. It is a measure of his extraordinary passion for detail that he describes the method by which the Indians introduced a quart, so to speak, into a pint pot.

'They brought the cow alongside the boat, which was heeled towards her ; then placing two oars under her belly, with their ends resting on the gunwale, by the aid of these levers they fairly tumbled the poor beast, heels over head, into the bottom of the boat, and then lashed her down with ropes.'

There were thirty or forty Indian families living at Cucao in those days and Darwin was mildly shocked by the craven and servile attitude they displayed towards their Spanish masters whom, he could see, they hated. There was only one building there, an 'uninhabited hovel' used by the local priest on his rare visits to this isolated end of his parish.

Darwin made an excursion along the wide, flat beach towards Punta Huantamo. For weeks the weather had been fine, sunny and calm, yet the roar of the surf was deafening. Darwin states that, after a heavy gale, the noise of the Pacific rollers breaking on this shore could be heard at Castro. He also observed a curious plant, called Bromelia, which bears an artichoke-like fruit which the natives turn into a kind of milky cider. He ponders on the fact that, with the exception of the Indians of Tierra del Fuego and the Australian aborigines, there were no primitive peoples in the world who had not discovered the delightful secret of brewing alcohol.

Darwin's summing up of Chiloé was that in winter it was a place of gloom and unceasing rain but that in summer it had an almost English charm, enhanced by the 'simplicity and humble politeness' of the people.

Robin and I had decided to re-enact, as faithfully as possible, Darwin's modest journey from Ancud to Cucao. I have described, earlier on, the sense of frustration everybody in the *Beagle* felt from time to time in being unable to follow in Darwin's footsteps to the extent they wanted.

For myself, ever since leaving London, my main reading had been Darwin's *Journal of Researches,* the wonderfully rich and lucid account he wrote of the voyage of the *Beagle.* I felt that I had come to know Darwin, almost as a friend, through the limpid prose and quiet humour of his writings. Every day, as some small incident or sight reminded me of something in the *Journal* I compared my own feelings and reactions with those of Charles Darwin. My own abysmal ignorance of science and natural history served to increase my admiration for the depth and scope of his knowledge. In one sense—and in only one sense!—Darwin's experience had been similar to mine. Like me, he had been a landlubber going to sea for the first time. He too had suffered the agonies of sea-sickness and had been bewildered by the mysteries of tacks and clews and bunts. For him too it was a first venture into remote places. The difference was, of course, that Darwin's curiosity and zest for discovery was backed by one of the finest scientific minds whereas my own was hampered by a lack of any scientific training. How often, as I observed some strange effect of light or some odd-looking bird or insect, did I envy Darwin his knowledge. How often, as, under the pressure of the film schedule, the *Beagle* sailed past places where Darwin had spent days observing nature, the seeds of his epoch-making theory slowly germinating in his mind, did I long to stop, to tread where he had trod, to see the things that he had seen. I could imagine him, tall, bronzed, bushily bearded, striding through the pampas with his note-books, his geological hammers, his sample-cases and bottles of preserving fluid, ceaselessly observing, noting, thinking. He was tireless and fearless. Wherever he went his frankness, cheerfulness and simple goodness of heart won him friends. I could picture him climbing up through the valleys of the Andes towards the snow-line, at one moment puzzling over the mysteries of the earth's formation, at the next considering whether there was anything in the old

Indian cure for the breathlessness that afflicts travellers in those
rarefied zones, namely the chewing of an onion.

Now, on Chiloé, for the first time in months, I had a little
time ; four or five days in which to do as Darwin had done.

Robin was as keen as I was and had, indeed, furnished himself
with a large album in which he proposed to press wild-flowers.
He intended to carry out his own botanical survey of the flora
of Chiloé.

We were determined to have no truck with half measures.
Darwin had made his journey on horse-back, so would we.

I confess I put in a mild word of protest. I agree with Oscar
Wilde that horses are dangerous at both ends and uncomfortable
in the middle, But Robin would have none of it.

We proceeded to a small square in the lower part of Ancud
where we had seen a number of horses and carts for hire. These
rickety equipages were not the kind of thing you find in Central
Park, New York or in south-west Ireland, twee little carriages
designed for tourists. They were the main means of carrying
freight round the town and to outlying villages.

We approached an enormously fat individual who looked like
a cross between Rabelais and a Sicilian bandit.

It was some minutes before we could make him understand
that we required not a horse and cart but horses for riding.
When he finally got the message he laughed so long and so
loudly I thought he would burst a lung. By this time a small
crowd of owners and dealers had gathered. Signor Rabelais
elaborated the joke for their delectation. He told us that it
would be quite impossible to hire horses for riding. Horses, he
explained, were very valuable. We began to canvass among the
other owners but they backed up Rabelais. It was clear that we
would have to compromise. We decided that, in the circumstances, the shade of Charles Darwin would not object to a horse
and cart.

We re-opened negotiations with Rabelais. When we explained
that we might require a horse and cart for two or three days, he
was astonished.

'But where do you intend going, signor?' he asked Robin, who
was handling the deal.

'To Cucao,' Robin replied.

We understood Rabelais to say that he could not possibly
take us to Cucao. We replied that we had no intention of taking
him anywhere. We would drive the vehicle ourselves. This

provoked a fresh outburst of mirth. Rabelais obviously thought we were mad. It was the psychological moment to produce a few crisp banknotes. In any country poor madmen are a menace, but well-heeled lunatics are a gift from the gods. Rabelais saw a chance of fleecing us.

Poor deluded soul! He thought he was dealing with an ignorant and eccentric foreigner. In fact, of course, he was dealing with Robin Cecil-Wright, the greatest haggler of modern times, the only man I know who, on descending into the Underworld via the Styx, would demand a discount for cash from Charon.

Ten minutes late, a dazed Rabelais had agreed to hire us, for a reasonable sum, an ancient cart which was flat and open-ended, had wooden sides full of splinters, a rusty chassis and two of the baldest rubber tyres in South America. Attached to the cart by a cat's-cradle of peeling leather harness was a horse called Soqueto, which means little sock. Robin and I called this animal Socky. He was the stubbornest, laziest, cunningest, most gluttonous, wilful and work-shy beast of burden I have ever encountered. And we grew to love him dearly.

Our arrival back at the Honsa hotel in this disreputable vehicle flabbergasted the management. So bewildered were they that they immediately agreed to store our luggage and lend us two blankets. The blankets and a pocket-knife were the only equipment we possessed when we set out to re-trace Darwin's route.

All the time we were in the town, Socky behaved with reasonable decorum. The only fault I could find in his behaviour was a passion for going in the wrong direction down one-way streets. But the minute we started to head out into the country, he began to play up.

Our route lay along the main road and, in the outskirts of the town, there were a great many turnings-off, to left and right. To Socky each side-street appeared to be more attractive than the way ahead and every few minutes he would attempt to dart off at a tangent. We shouted and hauled on the reins and sweated and cursed and flicked the whip in a vain attempt to make him trot. This he would not do. It was obvious that he was, at heart, a metropolitan creature. The prospect of country lanes and lush meadows appalled him. It was all we could do to make him walk—which he did with an air of injured innocence.

Eventually we left the town behind us and Socky, now resigned to the inevitable, consented to speed up. Our troubles, however, were by no means over. The animal seemed to have no conception of the rule of the road. We naturally attempted to drive on the right. Socky was determined to trot along the left-hand verge. We zig-zagged from right to left as monstrous lorries thundered by, hooting and flashing their lights.

It was the lorries that decided us to turn off the main road and take to the country. We had no map. We had tried to buy one in Ancud and had learned, to our amazement, that no such documents existed. All we had was a rough sketch-map, part of the bumph handed out to guests at the Honsa. However, the little lane we took seemed to be going in the right direction. The main road had in any case offered nothing of a Darwinian nature—the logs of wood had long since been replaced by tarmac, without, it must be said, any marked lessening of general bumpiness.

Away from the main road, we entered a stretch of countryside which seemed to be straight out of Cobbett's *Rural Rides* and which, except that the primeval forest had by now totally retreated against the advance of field and orchard, can have changed little since Darwin's day. The 'road' was an unmade track which meandered between hedgerows which, innocent of pesticides and weed-killers, were a pageant of wild-flowers. We met one or two carts similar to ours, mostly drawn by oxen, and one or two locals on horses, tough, brown wiry men who were shy but friendly. The horse is still almost the sole form of transport—we never saw a car.

The countryside was hilly, which was splendid for us because it afforded endless views of the intimate little valleys, patched with woods and tiny farms and with glistening peaks of the Andes always in the background to remind us that this was not Dorset but Chile ; but it was hell for poor old Socky who laboured up the step hills, grunting, sweating and panting. At the top of a particularly perpendicular climb we would allow Socky ten minutes rest while Robin busily picked flowers for his album and I mused on Darwinian subjects.

With all the novelty of going to sea for the first time, with the unfamiliar heat and technicolour extremes of the Brazilian jungle, the wonderful savage emptiness of Tierra del Fuego, I had forgotten the pleasures of unspoilt, cultivated countryside, the more modest beauties of a simple, pastoral setting. It

a

b

c

a Gauchos in Chiloé; *b* Kelp gatherers in Patagonia; and *c* Mussel fishers in the Chilean archipelago

a

b

a St. Paul's Rocks

b Kelp harvest, Isla Tova

c Larval rock, Galapagos Islands

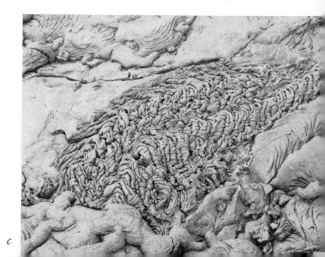

c

reminded me that the hand of man need not always be destructive, that when gently and decently applied it could create little
masterpieces. We passed one farm which would have had Gray
or Goldsmith reaching for their rhyming couplets. The old
clapboard house with its absolute lack of adornment had an
eighteenth-century elegance, its pleasing proportions based on
function rather than ostentation. Round the house huddled a
group of crazy, thatched farm buildings, stables, chicken houses,
sheds. In front of it was a pond with a family of ducks. On one
side were meadows, through which trickled a stream and where
cows were munching the rich grass. On the other was a garden
full of roses and behind the garden were woods. A woman was
working in the garden with a very young girl. The old woman,
who spoke a kind of dialect we found incomprehensible, picked
a rose and gave it to the child who shyly presented it to us.

Charming—except that bloody Socky chose that moment to
play one of his tricks and attempted to back into the pond.

In the early evening we began to look for a suitable place to
bivouac, Darwin style. We knew exactly what we wanted. A
meadow with plenty of grass for Socky, a tinkling brook and a
view of the Andes.

It is extraordinary how, when you are searching for the
perfect camp-site, you suddenly become highly critical of even
the most beautiful country. The trouble is that you have a clear
mental picture of what you are looking for and nothing quite
conforms to it. After an hour or so of heated little arguments
('What's wrong with it? There's a perfectly good river.' 'It's
downstream from that farm.' 'Look at the grass in that field.
Socky'll have a feast.' 'Too near the road and anyway it's a bog')
we decided to turn down a track leading to a farm. And there
we found our perfect spot. The farmer's wife showed us a
meadow well out of sight of the buildings where Socky could
graze to his heart's content. There was a lively little stream and
plenty of dead wood for a fire. We bought eggs and milk fresh
from the cow (ueech!) and with the bread and cheese we had
brought from Ancud and a borrowed frying pan were able to
make the best supper I had eaten for many a day.

Towards dusk the farmer came in from the fields and sat for
a time with us round the fire. He was a short, dark man who
spoke surprisingly cultivated Spanish in explosive bursts. The
most frequently used expression in Spanish is the word 'Claro'
which means literally 'That's clear' and, by extension, 'Under-

stood', 'Agreed', 'I see' &c. One of the more amusing games one can play in Spanish-speaking countries is to count the Claros. I once heard a man use this word over thirty times in the space of five minutes. The quality of Claros is as interesting as the quantity. Our hospitable farmer friend said it in a unique manner, very curtly, crisply and emphatically. He did to Claro what a Regimental Sergeant Major does to 'Yes, sir'. The RSM barks 'Saah!', our farmer barked 'Claah!'

We released Socky from his harness and led him down to the stream to drink which, to prove the adage, he refused to do. We rolled ourselves in our blankets and lay by the embers of the fire looking up at the night sky where flocks of wild parakeets were wheeling and shrieking.

Just before dawn it began to rain.

We sheltered under the cart and as soon at it was light enough re-kindled the fire. I experienced a mild blame-transference in favour of Darwin.

After a breakfast of fried eggs we attempted to re-hitch Socky to the cart. We had been very careful to memorise the complicated sequence of loopings, bucklings and threadings this task required and had naturally forgotten most of it. Socky looked outraged and kicked testily as we heaved and fumbled. Trial and error eventually won the day and we were able to proceed. We had asked the farmer if the road led anywhere. He assured us that it did. We climbed higher and higher and both the weather and the road-surface began to deteriorate alarmingly. I was convinced that the road would end in some half-forgotten farm-yard but everyone we met reassured us that it led somewhere whose name was incomprehensible. Eventually we reached the summit of a long, steep hill, where the road turned into a mud-bath. There was a farm, little better than a collection of shacks, and beyond it a brand new barbed wire fence and tall, strongly-built gates which seemed to be protecting a large and very private estate of some kind.

We knocked on the door of the farm and two ancient women, patently nervous, appeared. We asked them about the road. After five minutes of sign language—their patois was difficult to follow—we realised that, in the minds of the locals, the road did indeed lead somewhere, to some unpronounceable farm. In our terms, it was a cul-de-sac. We asked the women for some hot coffee and they invited us in. It was an incredibly poor place. The main room contained nothing but a rough table and a few chairs. The only modern object was a wood-burning stove and the plank walls were bare except for a crucifix. But the old women had no need of pictures. Their cracked and dusty windows looked out onto the Cordillera. The house was built on one of the highest points in the island and the panorama of mountains was breathtaking. They would not let us pay for the coffee but were happy to accept a few pesos 'for the view'.

We asked them about the barbed-wire fence and the gates. They became slightly uneasy, wary. It was a big estancia, they said. It belonged to a German. We pricked up our ears at this. South America is, of course, a classic hideaway for ex-Nazis and we had been told that Chiloé Island was a favourite retreat for such exiles. It is extremely remote but at the same time has a distinctly European atmosphere.

We pressed the old women. How long had the German gentleman been here? We discovered he had arrived in 1946. We looked at each other with a wild surmise. Had we stumbled on Martin Bormann? We asked the old ladies whether it would be possible to visit the German. They looked thoroughly alarmed. No, no, they said, nobody ever went to the estancia There were dogs.

We said goodbye to the old women, who blessed us piously, and began to retrace our steps back towards the main road. It began to rain in sheets and we were soon soaked to the skin.

'At this rate,' I said to Robin, 'we won't get to Cucao before next Christmas.'

'There's something in that.'

'I mean Socky's all very well but he's not exactly a prancing thoroughbred.'

'No.'

'The important thing is to get to Cucao.'

'Quite.'

'We've done our horsey bit. Honour is satisfied. Darwin would understand.'

'What would he have done?'

'He would have gone back to Ancud, had a hot bath, put on dry clothes and hired a car.'

'Right,' said Robin. 'That's exactly what we'll do.'

The naiveté of it! We really thought we would be able to hire a car. We very soon found out that this was impossible. Undeterred, we chartered a taxi.

We returned Socky to his owner. Senor Rabelais seemed

amazed—and relieved—to see us back so soon. Robin tentatively
suggested that he might like to refund a proportion of our
money. Rabelais laughed heartily and, with an expansive
gesture, indicated that we were out of our minds. Even Robin
did not have the gall to press the point. It was undoubtedly my
imagination but I thought I saw a glint of satisfaction in Socky's
eye at our discomfiture.

Very early the next morning, we set off. Towards Castro,
which is 80 or 90 kilometres south of Ancud, the countryside is
flat and dull. Castro itself is no longer quiet or pretty. The
main feature of the place is an extraordinary church, of an
elaborate design, made entirely out of corrugated iron painted
green. There is also a branch of the Honsa hotel group. We
decided to press on to Chonchi, still further south, in the hope
of finding a modest hotel or boarding house which we could
make our base. We had discovered that taxis cost about a
hundred pounds a mile and had decided to explore the possi-
bilities of buses.

Chonchi is a very strange place indeed. With its clapboard
buildings, empty streets and raised wooden sidewalks, it is
exactly like a wild west town where the women and children
have taken cover prior to a shoot-out. There is no hotel of any
description. The best we could find was a transport café-cum-
bordello of which we did not think Darwin would have
approved. We decided to make the Honsa in Castro our base
and duly returned there. Having deposited our meagre luggage
we boarded a bus bound for Chonchi and Huillinco, the village
at the eastern end of Darwin's lake. The bus was crammed with
enormously fat people. I have often noticed that thin people
almost never travel on buses. One is invariably crushed between
vast women whose obesity is exceeded only by the profusion of
parcels they are carrying.

Between Chonchi and Huillinco, the countryside was more
recognisably Darwinian. In the distance we could even see dark
patches of virgin forest.

We arrived at Huillinco at lunchtime. There was a dingy sort
of bar-restaurant where we had a drink and something to eat
and made enquiries about boats. The sun had reappeared at
last and we realised it would be impossible to get back to Castro
that night. The buses were few and far between, taxis prohibi-
tively expensive. We decided we would spend the night at
Cucao, as Darwin had done, and wondered if the priest's rude

hut was still standing.

After much jabbering and patient negotiation we were introduced to a man who owned a boat. He was in many ways
similar to Socky's Rabelaisian master but with a great deal more
of the Sicilian bandit about him.

The bandit agreed to take us the twelve miles down the lake
to Cucao and to return for us at noon the following day.

His boat was powered with a spluttering outboard and did
not, alas, contain a cow. Only a bright, talkative man who said
he was the local schoolmaster.

We cast off and began to putter off down the lake. The schoolmaster seemed to know a little about Darwin but was amazed to
learn that the great man had visited Huillinco and Cucao. The
bandit produced a bottle and a drinking-horn. He poured a
measure of milky, potent alcohol and, to my delight, I realised
that this was the very brew, made from Bromelia, of which
Darwin wrote. It had a tangy, slightly bitter taste, somewhat
like grapefruit juice, and a kick like Socky's hind leg.

To complete the Darwinian picture, the scenery on either side
of the lake now began to change from cultivated fields to virgin
forest. The slight feelings of guilt I had felt about abandoning
Socky for taxis and buses now evaporated. We were now really
following in Darwin's footsteps, or at least in the wake of his
periagua.

As we approached Cucao, we could see that the land on the
left hand side of the lake had been cleared but that, to the right,
the forest was untouched, exactly as it had been in Darwin's day.

Cucao today consists of perhaps twenty or thirty wooden
houses and shacks strung along a deep, rutted lane, which seems
more like the bed of a dried-up stream. It is Brig-a-doon. You
feel you have stepped out of the present. Everything about the
place suggests the past. There are no cars. There is no electricity
or running water. There is not a shop or an inn. We did not
see a single television aerial. The only building of any size was
a ruined church, made of clapboard and once very handsome.
Bullocks and oxen wandered about freely and in the flat fields
by the river there were flocks of brown-wool sheep.

We found a house near the beach belonging to a widow who
was prepared to let us a room and feed us. Her garden was full
of enormous bones, fossils and other thrillingly Darwinian things.
We asked where she found them and she told us in the cliffs
along the beach.

We walked down to the beach. It was exactly as Darwin described it. A wide expanse of sand and shingle onto which the huge Pacific rollers were breaking with such violence that the air was filled with a permanent haze of fine salt spray. We walked along the beach towards the headland. A man on a sprightly horse passed us and gave us a salute. We came to the fossil-bearing cliff which was composed of a soft, red rock like packed, dried mud. We began to climb about on the cliff-face, looking for samples. Thirty feet above us, we could see five or six round stones, like eggs, protruding from the vertical surface of the cliff. Somehow we knew that these would contain rare and valuable fossils. Robin was determined to capture them. I was not so eager as I had already found several similarly round stones lying about in the gorse and coarse grass and could not wait to crack them open. Robin began to climb. It was a reckless and somewhat foolhardy thing to do. The cliff-face was completely unstable. Sizeable chunks kept dropping off. But Robin succeeded —doesn't he always?—and hacked away at the stones with my knife. Climbing up a cliff is, of course, a great deal easier than climbing down. Clutching his precious fossil-stones Robin began to descend. Half-way down, he halted, spread-eagled on a shaky-looking ledge and declared that he was terrified. I scrambled up to help him.

'This is mad,' he panted. 'A broken leg for a few old fossils.'

'Think of Darwin,' I said encouragingly.

'Shut up and hold on tight. I'm going to step down on your shoulders.'

'What?'

'Get on with it.'

After much slithering and mutual insult we regained the beach in safety. Robin had four or five large stones.

He selected a couple of heavy rocks and cracked open the first one between them. It contained nothing but compacted mud.

I avoided his eye.

He cracked open the second one. Nothing.

The third stone shattered into small fragments.

The last stone proved difficult to split. As Robin hammered away at it, a look of furious concentration on his face, I couldn't resist saying:

'I'm sure it will contain some priceless rarity.'

'It had better,' growled Robin.

Eventually the stone cracked. It contained nothing at all.

Gravely, I produced my own humble find.

'Try this one,' I said.

'Where did you get it?' Robin asked suspiciously, wiping his brow.

'I just sort of picked it up.'

'I see.'

Wollop, crack — the stone split . . . and inside was a perfectly fossilised prehistoric fly.

Robin glared at me, speechless for a moment. Then:

'You mean to tell me you just picked it up off the ground?'

'Yes. It looks like a fly.'

'And I risked my life climbing all over that bloody cliff . . . '

'It might be a million years old. Still, it's only a fly.'

'Not very interesting.'

'Oh no.'

'Shall I throw it into the sea?'

'I wouldn't do that. I'd quite like to keep it. Darwin and all that.'

We did keep it and we kept several other odd items we found on the beach, in particular some bones which we hoped were megatherium but which, I fear, were only part of the spinal column of a whale.

Our landlady turned out to be a mild lunatic. She owned two or three hundred acres of land under which she firmly believed there was not only a fortune in gold but quantities of oil and diamonds as well. She produced a dog-eared geological map of the farm and told us we could buy the whole place for sixty thousand pounds.

This good lady looked after an ancient father, a ninety year old retired sea captain who spoke a little English. I asked him about the gold.

'It is very important for my daughter to believe in it,' he said. 'If she did not she would go mad.'

Which put an end to that conversation.

The bed with which I was provided was soft and damp. It was like sleeping in blancmange. I read a few pages of Darwin by the light of a single candle. Outside the Pacific was roaring and thundering and I slept like the dead.

We were up very early next morning — it was another bright, sunny day — in order to explore the primeval forest before the Bandit came to collect us at noon.

By the riverside we found an old man who had one of the

cushiest jobs in South America. He was the municipal ferryman. It was his task to row members of the public back and forth across thirty feet of water about three times a fortnight. He was intensely proud of the fact that he was a public servant with a Town Hall salary rather than a commercial operator.

He was horrified when we suggested he might like to hire us his boat. He explained that he was an official, that the boat belonged to the regional authority. However his cousin . . .

His cousin's boat was a periagua-like craft with two massively heavy oars and Robin's strictures on my handling of these became explosive. This suited my book extremely well. While he heaved away I could look around me and savour each sweet Darwinian moment.

We ran the boat up on to a little strip of pebble beach and, to our delight, found a rough path which wound up and into the very heart of the forest. Without this path we would not have been able to penetrate more than a few yards. The forest was like a wall. The bases of the trees were matted with cane and bamboo. In contrast to a Fuegan forest, this one was full of sound ; the zing and drone of insects, the exotic cries of birds and, in the background, the roar of the Pacific.

While Robin busied himself with gathering and pressing flowers, I sat on the stump of a tree and tried to believe that Darwin had not thought it worth recording in his journal that he had rowed across the lake in a small boat and found a path through the forest and sat on a tree-stump and listened to the soft wind, the dull crash-crash of the ocean, the songs of the birds.

There was a profound peace in that age-old forest. I felt closer to Darwin, to Fitzroy, to the *Beagle* than I had ever felt before. Pacing the decks of *Beagle II*, exploring the mountains and glaciers of Tierra del Fuego, I had always found that present realities obscured my sense of the past. Now, I felt that at last I had recaptured something of what had been before, that this strange forest with its luxuriant ferns, its intricate patterns of leaf and branch and flower, was the furthest point I would reach on my voyage, not perhaps in terms of miles but in terms of its remoteness, its fastness, its power to conjure up ghosts.

If it was a moment to think about Darwin and the voyage of the *Beagle* it was also a moment to think about myself and wonder if all the experiences of the past three months, novel and bizarre, alarming and exhilarating, had changed me. Most people set out on voyages because they are looking for some thing. Either they want to 'find themselves' or they want to 'escape'. What they seek in the four corners of the world, they can find only inside themselves and they can find it as well in Teddington as in Tierra del Fuego. The greatest journey a man can make is within his own head. He may travel to the ends of the earth and fail to find the spiritual peace he is looking for. It is possible that on his travels he will encounter the sort of experiences that change people, love-affairs, suffering, but it is more likely that his ultimate destination will remain a chimera and that his journey will be nomadic.

Sitting on that tree-trunk I concluded that I was, in all essentials, the same person who had set out from Salvador three months before and I wondered if the same could be said for Charles Darwin. Was it a different Darwin who landed at Falmouth on 2nd October 1836 after five years in the *Beagle*? There is much evidence to suggest that it was. Although he was still a young man when the voyage of the *Beagle* ended, he never set foot outside England again. Within a few years he had changed from a strapping young man full of vigour and health into a permanent invalid, prematurely valetudinarian, able to work only a few hours in the day, relying absolutely on the care and patient love of his wife and family. Why?

One theory is that, during the voyage of the *Beagle*, he contracted a rare and crippling disease as the result of being bitten by a Chagas beetle. Another theory is that permanent illness was Darwin's defence against the powerful and domineering influence of his father, that his sickness was largely psychosomatic. Certainly towards the end of his life, when he was one of the most famous men in the world, his health took a remarkable turn for the better.

Whatever the reason, illness did not effect his capacity for work and in that work I find an interesting clue to his character. With the theory of evolution bubbling in his mind, with the mass of data he had collected during the voyage of the *Beagle* waiting to be sifted, he devoted eight years of his precious time to a monumental scientific treatise on, of all things, the barnacle. I am sure that the reason he did so was a desire to prove himself, to establish himself as a serious, professional scientist capable of producing a tome. When he first joined the *Beagle* Darwin was worried by the fact that people might consider him an amateur. In terms of professional qualifications, he *was* an amateur. Five years later, he still felt the need to prove himself. The voyage had not changed him as a man though it had provided him with the means to bring about a revolution in scientific thought.

It was time to go. Robin and I walked back through the forest, climbed into our cumbersome little boat and cast off. I took up the heavy oars, then paused.

'You know,' I said to Robin, 'this is the point where our journey back to England really begins. In an old rowing boat, on a lake by the Pacific, in an island off Chile. In three days we'll be in London.'

'It'll be a miracle if we are. Getting back to Ancud is going to be a major operation.'

'I expect we'll battle through somehow.'

'All right,' Robin said, 'let's go home.'

POSTSCRIPT

And there, I suppose, I should leave it.

But if I must have a Prelude, I don't see why I should not be allowed the indulgence of a Postscript.

The prospect that lay before Robin and me that sunny morning on Lake Huillinco was one of incessant travel by virtually every means devised by man — rowing boats, horses and carts, every kind of motor vehicle from taxis and private cars to lorries and coaches, ferryboats, aeroplanes, trains and — almost — a hovercraft.

We thought the journey might present a few problems but had we known the appalling saga of double-crossing, chaos, pressure and confusion we were in for we would undoubtedly have become naturalised Chilotans on the spot and put in for the job of municipal ferrymen.

The Bandit did not arrive at noon as arranged. His boat did, but its unknown skipper affected to know nothing about us. Blessing our foresight in not having paid the Bandit in advance, we bribed this man to take us to Huillinco. Half-way back across the lake we passed the Bandit and discovered that our own boatman was his brother. The two of them were hand in glove. We were victims of the old one-two method by which these fraternal Fagins extorted double payment from innocent travellers. But if we could get out of Huillinco before the Bandit caught up with us . . .

We did — by the skin of our teeth, begging a ride in a large, shiny Mercedes. This was the property of an old German who appeared to be on a rent-collecting spree. The minute he realised we were English he shut up like a clam and decanted us at the nearest town — Chonchi. Sure, by now, that we had discovered *another* Martin Bormann, we proceeded to the bus station. No buses. We paid a lorry driver to take us to Castro. At the hotel they were very understanding and did not charge us for our unused room. We decided we would have to sleep at Ancud that night to be in time to catch the ferry to the mainland and a bus to Puerto Montt, the nearest airfield, in the morning.

Another taxi, another fortune.

At Puerto Montt airport, the airline officials licked their lips when they saw our pile of luggage, weighing my great model boat with particular relish. Another fortune was paid out. We staggered on to the plane carrying four pieces of 'hand-luggage' each.

In Santiago airport we struck a major problem. My original ticket had been a return from Rio to London on airline A. In Mar del Plata Robin had tried to buy an identical ticket and had been persuaded to buy one on airline B. Airline B assured him that they would accept my A ticket and that everything had been booked. Thus both Robin and I bought tickets from Santiago to Rio on airline B.

At Santiago airline B denied they had ever heard of me and implied that my A ticket wasn't worth the paper it was written on. Scenes, arguments, inter-telexing and phoning. I was permitted to proceed as far as Rio.

We arrived in Rio at midnight for a one-hour stop-over and were met in the transit lounge by seven or eight officials, all carrying clip-boards. Airline B's senior man informed me that I could not continue on the flight to London. He was adamant. The main prop of our argument was that it had been his own people in Argentina who had arranged the thing in the first place and that it was the duty of the airline to get me to London. Robin threatened massive lawsuits and disturbed the officials by taking down notes of everything they said. We had reached deadlock when suddenly the senior man capitulated and said he would accept my A ticket. Warm handshakes all round. The official, who, once the battle was over, turned out to be charming, told us that one of the reasons why he was reluctant to take my ticket was that airline A had just had one of its three jumbo jets impounded by the Brazilian government.

Utterly drained, Robin and I staggered on to the plane which was bound for Dakar, Paris and London. The only plus factor was that, in all the confusion, nobody had bothered about our mounds of excess baggage.

We arrived in Paris in the early evening, at France's prestige new airport, Charles de Gaulle. We found a state of anarchy. Europe was fog- and strike-bound. Six hundred hysterical travellers were besieging the airline B desk where one girl was tearfully trying to cope. She was very nice about it all. She said there was no possibility of a flight to London for 24 hours. We

could have a lovely day in Paris courtesy of airline B We
explained that we did not want a lovely day in Paris, that we
had just had several hundred lovely days in South America. All
we wanted to do was to *go home.*

Experienced air-travellers will know what I mean when I say
that airports are run on systems which rely on Grade A, perfect
conditions to function at all. The merest hiccup — a blizzard
in New York, a strike in Helsinki, a revolution in Nicaragua —
and the whole structure topples into ruins.

Charles de Gaulle airport was ancient chaos. It was so bad
that the passport control and customs officials had given up. I
passed in and out of the customs area five or six times and all
I got was a Gallic shrug of hopelessness from the man on duty.

Robin and I decided to abandon the air and take to the rails.
First we had to find our luggage. Thousands of trunks and cases
and parcels were being spewed out of the carrousels at random.
Nobody knew which pile belonged to which flight number. This
was where my model boat proved invaluable. I had wrapped it
in bright red paper and it was easy to identify. I retrieved my
baggage and Robin was waiting for his when it was suddenly
announced that the baggage-handlers were on strike.

While Robin set about bribing someone to extricate his things,
I opened negotiations with the S.N.C.F. The young man was
polite, helpful and pessimistic. The last boat-train was fully
booked, absolutely packed. There was no chance of getting on it.

Right, I thought, a hired car up to the channel ports and on
to the late ferry.

Six hire-car companies in turn informed me that there was not
a vehicle available in Paris.

'Everybody is seeking to leave Paris, m'sieur. It is Christmas,
you see.'

Back to the S.N.C.F.

'A car, m'sieur, but certainly. We have a limousine. To Boulogne? Nine hundred francs.'

'Done.'

I went off to telephone England with the good news. When I
got back I found that the S.N.C.F. chauffeur was refusing to
drive that night. Too much fog.

Eventually Hertz produced a car for us. I went back to the
S.N.C.F. man to double-check the time of the Hovercraft he
had sworn left Boulogne at 4 a.m.

'Boulogne?' he said, greatly astonished. 'You mean Calais.'

'But you said Boulogne.'

'No, no — Calais. It is Calais.'

We drove up the autoroute through swirling fog. Since I did not have my driving licence with me, Robin took the wheel. He had not driven a car for six months and had not driven on the Continent for several years. The fog seemed to be full of murderous lorries ; we abandoned the autoroute and tried to pick our way across country, peering at semi-legible signposts, arguing about the rule of the road and reflecting apprehensively that neither of us had ever heard of a 4 a.m. hovercraft.

We arrived at the Hoverport at three in the morning to find it completely deserted. Not a cat stirred or a light showed. The place was dead. Robin groaned.

'Perhaps he meant the ferry,' I suggested.

We drove to the port. It was a maze of tramlines and signposts that sent you round in circles.

We found the ferry on the point of leaving. We scrambled aboard.

On the ferry we met a kind Englishman who agreed to drive Robin to London and to deposit me at my destination in Kent.

At six in the morning I said goodbye to Robin. His ultimate destination was Cornwall.

'I'll get the nine o'clock from Paddington,' he said, 'and sleep all the way down.'

'Our troubles seem to be over.'

'Don't ever say that. It's tempting fate.'

It was, too.

Somewhere between Reading and Plymouth Robin's train broke down.

There is not much more to say. Coming home after a long absence is always strange and disconcerting. You are back among familiar faces and places but part of you is still somewhere out on the blue Atlantic or among the eternal snows of Tierra del Fuego.

I did not get back to my own home until after Christmas. For several days I felt like an alien among my own furniture and pictures and books. I was back but for some reason I did not feel back.

Then one evening, about half past six, there was a ring on the bell. I opened the door and there was a large, middle-aged man holding a briefcase.

'Mr. Goldsmith? Mr. J. Goldsmith?'

'Yes.'

'I am . . .'

'There's no need to tell me who you are. I know. Come in. What is it this time?'

'Well, it's a matter of X pounds due to Y and Co. and outstanding for over four months.'

'I've been away, you see. For three months. South America.'

'I see. Even so . . .'

'Don't worry. I'll give you a cheque now.'

The bailiff's face brightened.

'Oh, well, that's all right then,' he said. 'Sorry if I've spoiled your homecoming.'

'On the contrary,' I said, 'until you arrived I didn't feel I was really home at all.'

Much of this book was written in an hotel bedroom overlooking the little harbour of Charlestown, home port of the *Beagle*.

It is a very small harbour indeed and large ships have to manoeuvre most delicately to enter without smashing into the walls. I can now observe such movements with professional interest. When somebody shouts: 'Take a spring off the stern,' I know that he is not suggesting a suicide attempt.

Very soon, now, the *Beagle* will be sailing back into Charlestown. I have had some news of her since leaving her at Ancud. Christmas in Valparaiso was a riotous success. Somewhere in Ecuador Jason was arrested and cast into gaol. The filming in the Galapagos Islands went smoothly. There was, inevitably, more engine trouble in Miami. Also inevitably, the ship ran aground in the Royal Yacht Club in Bermuda.

From time to time I have heard from the BBC. Studio and English location filming has been going on since Christmas and, though nobody is committing himself, it is clear that *The Voyage of Charles Darwin* is going to be a spectacular programme.

Under Mark's expert command, the *Beagle* will make it back across the Atlantic without mishap. The trade winds will be with her. The long voyage will soon be over and then . . . well, what?

There is a fanatical glint in Robin's eye these days which presages a new Scheme. His conversation contains intriguing references to the Caribbean. Who can say what is brewing in his fertile mind? What is certain is that before too long the *Beagle* will set out on another voyage and I have a feeling, which is partly one of eager anticipation, partly one of foreboding, that I have not seen the last of the t'gallant yard.

Charlestown - Highgate.
January - April 1978.

INDEX